Human Rights in Global Age

HUMAN RIGHTS IN GLOBAL AGE

B Kumar

MD PUBLICATIONS PVT LTD
NEW DELHI
www.mdppl.com

Published by :

MD Publications Pvt Ltd
"MD House", 11, Darya Ganj,
New Delhi - 110 002
Phone : +91-11- 45355555
E-mail : contact@mdppl.com
Website: www.mdppl.com

ISBN : 978-81-7533-327-7

Published and Printed by Mr. Pranav Gupta on behalf of **MD Publications Pvt Ltd** at Repro India Limited.

Preface

Human rights refer to the basic rights and freedoms to which all humans are entitled. Examples of rights and freedoms which have come to be commonly thought of as human rights include civil and political rights, such as the right to life and liberty, freedom of expression, and equality before the law; and economic, social and cultural rights, including the right to participate in culture, the right to food, the right to work, and the right to education.

Human rights are international norms that help to protect all people everywhere from severe political, legal, and social abuses. Examples of human rights are the right to freedom of religion, the right to a fair trial when charged with a crime, the right not to be tortured, and the right to engage in political activity. These rights exist in morality and in law at the national and international levels.

They are addressed primarily to governments, requiring compliance and enforcement. The main sources of the contemporary conception of human rights are the Universal Declaration of Human Rights (United Nations, 1948b) and the many human rights documents and treaties that followed in international organizations such as the United Nations, the Council of Europe, the Organization of American States, and the African Union.

The philosophy of human rights addresses questions about the existence, content, nature, universality, justification, and legal status of human rights. The strong claims made on behalf of human rights (for example, that they are universal, or that they exist independently of legal enactment as justified moral norms) frequently provoke skeptical doubts and countering philosophical defences.

The Universal Declaration of Human Rights (1948) sets out a list of over two dozen specific human rights that countries should respect and protect. These specific rights can be divided into six or more families: security rights that protect people against crimes such as murder, massacre, torture, and rape; due process rights that protect against abuses of the legal system such as imprisonment without trial, secret trials, and excessive punishments; liberty rights that protect freedoms in areas such as belief, expression, association, assembly, and movement; political rights that protect the liberty to participate in politics through actions such as communicating, assembling, protesting, voting, and serving in public office; equality rights that guarantee equal citizenship, equality before the law, and nondiscrimination; and social rights that require provision of education to all children and protections against severe poverty and starvation.

I am very grateful to Mr. Pranav Gupta, Director of MD Publications Pvt Ltd, New Delhi, for his kind cooperation and support for this book.

B Kumar

Contents

1

Origin and Nature of Human Rights

'The term human rights indicate both their nature and their source: they are the rights that one has simply because one is human. They are held by all human beings, irrespective of any rights or duties individuals may (or may not) have as citizens, members of families, workers or parts of any public or private organisation or association. They are universal rights. If all human beings have them simply because they are human, human rights are held equally by all. And because being human cannot be renounced, lost or forfeited, human rights are inalienable. Even the cruelest torturer and the most debased victim are still human beings. In practice, not all people enjoy all their human rights, let alone enjoy them equally. Nonetheless, all human beings have the same human rights and hold them equally and inalienably.'

What does this mean? It might suggest, first of all, that the definition of the human being can be provided by a scientific or behaviourist statement of the human's basic 'needs'. However, the requirements of humanity are perhaps difficult to state and to agree upon, even if they are approached in a strictly empirical manner. Perhaps there cannot even be a scientific statement of basic human nature, because human nature depends on qualities that are not suitable for scientific measurement; faith or morality, for instance. No doubt, though, the social sciences can provide a definition of humanity, and hence grounding for a theory of human rights: indeed, anthropology sets out to achieve this end. However, there is also a problem with this approach. Societies have not always been organised around notions of human dignity.

Historical and cross-cultural examples show that societies have organised themselves around a class or grouping of 'inferiors' who are deprived of the privileges enjoyed by others. Can we turn from anthropology and the social sciences to other disciplines to resolve this problem? There are, of course, philosophical accounts of human rights. These come from a variety of perspectives, and provide different theoretical foundations for human rights. Their very diversity would militate against any over-arching or detailed consensus, but would perhaps stress that the nature of the human being is related to language, the ability to reason and rational action. There would, of course, also be theological or religiously oriented accounts of humanity, which would consider its fundamental value to be of divine origin. You do not have to look hard to see that theological accounts also compel little overall agreement, even within the great faith traditions of the world.

We could suggest, then, that although a universal definition of the human is elusive, there is a tendency, in different areas of study, to continue to try and posit a universal value. To some extent, we can avoid these difficulties, because - at least as far as the law is concerned - the universality of human rights is founded on the UDHR. This does not resolve the debate, but it does at least allow us to see that the debate around human rights is of continuing importance for a culture of human rights. We will examine the way that this has been linked to arguments about cultural relativism and universalism, although we will also suggest that this debate itself is somewhat limited.

Human rights that belong to an individual or group of individuals as a consequence of being human, they refer to a wide continuum of values or capabilities thought to enhance human agency and declared to be universal in character, in some sense equally claimed for all human beings. It is a common observation that human beings everywhere demand the realization of diverse values or capabilities to ensure their individual and collective well-being. It also is a common observation that this demand is often painfully frustrated by social as well as natural forces, resulting in exploitation, oppression, persecution, and other forms of deprivation. Deeply rooted in these twin observations are the beginnings of what today are called "human rights" and the national and international legal processes that are associated with them.

COMMONLY ACCEPTED POSTULATES

Despite this lack of consensus, a number of widely accepted (and interrelated) postulates can assist in the task of defining human rights. Five in particular stand out, though not even these are without controversy. First, regardless of their ultimate origin or justification, human rights are understood to represent both individual and group demands for political power, wealth, enlightenment, and other cherished values or capabilities, the most fundamental of which is respect and its constituent elements of reciprocal tolerance and mutual forbearance in the pursuit of all other such values or capabilities.

Consequently, human rights imply both claims against persons and institutions impeding the realization of these values or capabilities and standards for judging the legitimacy of laws and traditions. At bottom, human rights qualify state sovereignty and power, sometimes expanding the latter even while circumscribing the former (as in the case of certain economic and social rights). Second, human rights are commonly assumed to refer, in some vague sense, to "fundamental," as distinct from "nonessential," claims or "goods." In fact, some theorists go so far as to limit human rights to a single core right or two—for example, the right to life or the right to equal freedom of opportunity. The tendency is to emphasize "basic needs" and to rule out "mere wants."

Third, reflecting varying environmental circumstances, differing worldviews, and inescapable interdependencies within and between different value or capability systems, human rights refer to a wide continuum of claims, ranging from the most justiciable to the most aspirational. Human rights partake of both the legal and the moral orders, sometimes indistinguishably. They are expressive of both the "is" and the "ought" in human affairs. Fourth, most assertions of human rights—though arguably not all—are qualified by the limitation that the rights of individuals or groups in particular instances are restricted as much as is necessary to secure the comparable rights of others and the aggregate common interest.

Given this limitation, which connects rights to duties, human rights are sometimes designated prima facie rights, so that ordinarily it makes little or no sense to think or talk of them in absolutist terms. Finally, if a right is determined to be a human right, it is understood to be quintessentially general or universal in character, in some sense equally possessed by all human beings everywhere, including in certain instances even the unborn. In stark contrast to the divine right of kings and other such conceptions of privilege, human rights extend in theory to every person on Earth, without discriminations irrelevant to merit or need, simply for being human. In several critical respects, however, all these postulates raise more questions than they answer. Granted that human rights qualify state power; do they also qualify private power?

If so, when and how? What does it mean to say that a right is fundamental, and according to what standards of importance or urgency is it so judged? What is the value of embracing non justiciable rights as part of the jurisprudence of human rights? Does it harbor more than rhetorical significance? If so, how? When and according to what criteria does the right of one person or group of people give way to the right of another? What happens when individual and group rights collide? How are universal human rights determined? Are they a function of culture or ideology, or are they determined according to some transnational consensus of merit or value? If the latter is the consensus regional or global?

How exactly would such a consensus be ascertained, and

how would it be reconciled with the right of nations and peoples to self-determination? Is the existence of universal human rights incompatible with the notion of national sovereignty? Should supranational norms, institutions, and procedures have the power to nullify local, regional, and national laws on capital punishment, corporal punishment of children, "honour killing," veil wearing, female genital cutting, male circumcision, the claimed right to bear arms, and other practices? How would such a situation comport with Western conceptions of democracy and representative government? In other words, though accurate, the five foregoing postulates are fraught with questions about the content and legitimate scope of human rights and about the priorities, if any, that exist among them. Like the issue of the origin and justification of human rights, all five are controversial.

THREE "GENERATIONS" OF RIGHTS

Like all normative traditions, the human rights tradition is a product of its time. Therefore, to understand better the debate over the content and legitimate scope of human rights and the priorities claimed among them, it is useful to note the dominant schools of thought and action that have informed the human rights tradition since the beginning of modern times. Particularly helpful in this regard is the notion of three "generations" of human rights advanced by the French jurist Karel Vasak. Inspired by the three themes of the French Revolution, they are: the first generation of civil and political rights (*liberté*); the second generation of economic, social, and cultural rights (*égalité*); and the third generation of solidarity rights (*fraternité*).

Vasak's model is, of course, a simplified expression of an extremely complex historical record, and it is not intended to suggest a linear process in which each generation gives birth to the next and then dies away. Nor is it to imply that one generation is more important than another. The three generations are understood to be cumulative, overlapping, and, it is important to note, interdependent and interpenetrating.

LIBERTÉ: CIVIL AND POLITICAL RIGHTS

The first generation of civil and political rights derives primarily from the 17th- and 18th-century reformist theories noted above (i.e., those associated with the English, American, and French revolutions). Infused with the political philosophy of liberal individualism and the related economic and social doctrine of laissez-faire, the first generation conceives of human rights more in negative terms ("freedoms from") than positive ones ("rights to"); it favours the abstention over the intervention of government in the quest for human dignity.

Belonging to this first generation, thus, are rights such as those set forth in Articles 2–21 of the Universal Declaration of Human Rights, including freedom from gender, racial, and equivalent forms of discrimination; the right to life, liberty, and security of the person; freedom from slavery or involuntary servitude; freedom from torture and from cruel, inhuman, or degrading treatment or punishment; freedom from arbitrary arrest, detention, or exile; the right to a fair and public trial; freedom from interference in privacy and correspondence; freedom of movement and residence; the right to asylum from persecution; freedom of thought, conscience, and religion; freedom of opinion and expression; freedom of peaceful assembly and association; and the right to participate in government, directly or through free elections.

Also included are the right to own property and the right not to be deprived of it arbitrarily—rights that were fundamental to the interests fought for in the American and French revolutions and to the rise of capitalism. Yet it would be wrong to assert that these and other first-generation rights correspond completely to the idea of "negative" as opposed to "positive" rights. The right to security of the person, to a fair and public trial, to asylum from persecution, and to free elections, for example, manifestly cannot be assured without some affirmative government action.

What is constant in this first-generation conception is the notion of liberty, a shield that safeguards the individual—alone and in association with others—against the abuse of political authority. This is the core value. Featured in the constitution of almost every country in the world and dominating the majority of international declarations and covenants adopted since World War II, this essentially Western liberal conception of human rights is sometimes romanticized as a triumph of the individualism of Thomas Hobbes and John Locke over Hegelian statism.

ÉGALITÉ: ECONOMIC, SOCIAL, AND CULTURAL RIGHTS

The second generation of economic, social, and cultural rights originated primarily in the socialist tradition, which was foreshadowed among adherents of the Saint-Simonian movement of early 19th-century France and variously promoted by revolutionary struggles and welfare movements that have taken place since. In large part, it is a response to the abuses of capitalist development and its underlying and essentially uncritical conception of individual liberty, which tolerated, and even legitimized, the exploitation of working classes and colonial peoples. Historically, it is a counterpoint to the first generation of civil and political rights, conceiving of human rights more in positive terms ("rights to") than in negative ones ("freedoms from") and requiring more the intervention than the abstention of the state for the purpose of assuring the equitable production and distribution of the values or capabilities involved.

Illustrative are some of the rights set forth in Articles 22–27 of the Universal Declaration of Human Rights, such as the right to social security; the right to work and to protection against unemployment; the right to rest and leisure, including periodic holidays with pay; the right to a standard of living adequate for the health and well-being of self and family; the right to education; and the right to the protection of one's scientific, literary, and artistic production. But in the same way that all the rights embraced by the first generation of civil and political rights cannot properly be designated "negative rights," so all the rights embraced by the second generation of economic, social, and cultural rights cannot properly be labeled "positive rights." For example, the right to free choice of employment, the right to form and to join trade unions, and the right to participate freely in the cultural life of the community (Articles 23 and 27) do not inherently require affirmative state action to ensure their enjoyment.

Nevertheless, most of the second-generation rights do necessitate state intervention because they subsume demands more for material than for intangible goods according to some criterion of distributive justice. Second-generation rights are, fundamentally, claims to social equality. However, partly because of the comparatively late arrival of socialist-communist and compatible "Third World" influence in international affairs, the internationalization of these rights has been relatively slow in coming, and with free-market capitalism in ascendancy under the banner of globalization at the turn of the 21st century, it is not likely that these rights will come of age any time soon.

On the other hand, as the social inequities created by unregulated national and transnational capitalism become more and more evident over time and are not accounted for by explanations based on gender or race, it is probable that the demand for second-generation rights will grow and mature, and in some instances even lead to violence. This tendency is apparent already in the evolving European Union and in wider efforts to regulate intergovernmental financial institutions and transnational corporations to protect the public interest.

FRATERNITÉ: SOLIDARITY RIGHTS

Finally, the third generation of solidarity rights, while drawing upon and reconceptualizing the demands associated with the first two generations of rights, is best understood as a product of both the rise and the decline of the nation-state in the last half of the 20th century. Foreshadowed in Article 28 of the Universal Declaration of Human Rights, which proclaims that "everyone is entitled to a social and international order in which the rights set forth in this declaration can be fully realized," this generation appears so far to embrace six claimed rights. Three of these rights reflect the emergence of Third

World nationalism and its "revolution of rising expectations" (i.e., its demand for a global redistribution of power, wealth, and other important values or capabilities): the right to political, economic, social, and cultural self-determination; the right to economic and social development; and the right to participate in and benefit from "the common heritage of mankind" (shared Earth and space resources, scientific, technical, and other information and progress, and cultural traditions, sites, and monuments).

The other three third-generation rights—the right to peace, the right to a healthy and sustainable environment, and the right to humanitarian disaster relief—suggest the impotence or inefficiency of the nation-state in certain critical respects. All six of these rights tend to be posed as collective rights, requiring the concerted efforts of all social forces, to a substantial degree on a planetary scale. However, each of them also manifests an individual dimension. For example, while it may be said to be the collective right of all countries and peoples (especially developing countries and nonself-governing peoples) to secure a "new international economic order" that would eliminate obstacles to their economic and social development, so also may it be said to be the individual right of every person to benefit from a developmental policy that is based on the satisfaction of material and nonmaterial human needs.

It is important to note too that the majority of these solidarity rights are more aspirational than justiciable in character and that their status as international human rights norms remains ambiguous. Thus, at various stages of modern history, the content of human rights has been broadly defined not with any expectation that the rights associated with one generation would or should become outdated upon the ascendancy of another, but expansively or supplementary. The history of the content of human rights reflects evolving perceptions of which values or capabilities stand, at different times, most in need of responsible attention and, simultaneously, humankind's recurring demands for continuity and stability.

LIBERTÉ VERSUS ÉGALITÉ

The fact that the content of human rights has been broadly defined should not be taken to imply that the three generations of rights are equally acceptable to everyone. Nor should it suggest that they or their separate elements have been greeted with equal urgency. The debate about the nature and content of human rights reflects, after all, a struggle for power and for favoured conceptions of the "good society." First-generation proponents, for example, are inclined to exclude second- and third-generation rights from their definition of human rights altogether or, at best, to regard them as "derivative." In part this is because of the complexities involved in putting these rights into operation.

The suggestion that first-generation rights are more feasible because they stress the absence over the presence of government is somehow transformed into a prerequisite of a comprehensive definition of human rights, such that aspirational claims to entitlement are deemed not to be rights at all. The most compelling explanation, however, has more to do with ideology or politics. Persuaded that egalitarian claims against the rich, particularly where collectively espoused, are unworkable without a severe decline in liberty and equality, first-generation proponents, inspired by the natural law and laissez-faire traditions, are partial to the view that human rights are inherently independent of organized society and are individualistic.

Conversely, second- and third-generation defenders often look upon first-generation rights, at least as commonly practiced, as insufficiently attentive to material—especially "basic"—human needs and, indeed, as instruments in service to unjust social orders, hence constituting a "bourgeois illusion." Accordingly, if they do not place first-generation rights outside their definition of human rights, they tend to assign such rights a low status and to treat them as long-term goals that will come to pass only after the imperatives of economic and social development have been met, to be realized gradually and fully achieved only sometime vaguely in the future. This liberty-equity and individualist-collectivist debate was especially evident during the period of the Cold War, reflecting the extreme tensions that then existed between Liberal and Marxist conceptions of sovereign public order.

Although Western social democrats during this period, particularly in Scandinavia, occupied a position midway between the two sides, pursuing both liberty and equity—in many respects successfully—it remains true that the different conceptions of rights contain the potential for challenging the legitimacy and supremacy not only of one another, but, more importantly, of the sociopolitical systems with which they are most intimately associated.

THE RELEVANCE OF CUSTOM AND TRADITION

With the end of the Cold War, however, the debate took on a more North-South character and was supplemented by a cultural-relativist critique that eschews the universality of human rights doctrines, principles, and rules on the grounds that they were Western in origin and therefore of limited relevance in non-Western settings. The viewpoint underlying this assertion—that the scope of human rights in any given society is fundamentally determined by local, national, or regional customs and traditions—may seem problematic, especially when one considers that the idea of human rights and many of its precepts are found in all the great philosophical and religious traditions. Nevertheless, the historical development of human rights demonstrates that it cannot be wholly mistaken.

Nor is it surprising that it should emerge soon after the end of the Cold War. First prominently expressed at an Asian meeting preparatory to the second UN World Conference on Human Rights convened in Vienna in June 1993, it reflects the end of a bipolar system of alliances that had discouraged independent foreign policies and minimized cultural and political differences in favour of undivided Cold War loyalties. Against the backdrop of increasing human rights interventionism on the part of the UN and by regional organizations and deputized coalitions of states (as in Bosnia and Herzegovina, Somalia, Liberia, Rwanda, Haiti, and Serbia and Kosovo, for example), the viewpoint serves also as a functional equivalent of the doctrine of respect for national sovereignty and territorial integrity, which had been declining in influence not only in the human rights context but also in the contexts of national security, economics, and the environment. As a consequence, there remains sharp disagreement about the legitimate scope of human rights and about the priorities that are claimed among them.

INHERENT RISKS IN THE DEBATE

On final analysis, however, this legitimacy-priority debate can be dangerously misleading. Although useful for pointing out how notions of liberty and individualism have been used to rationalize the abuses of capitalism and Western expansionism and how notions of equality, collectivism, and culture have been alibis for authoritarian governance, in the end it risks obscuring at least three essential truths that must be taken into account if the contemporary worldwide human rights movement is to be objectively understood.

First, one-sided characterizations of legitimacy and priority are very likely, at least over the long term, to undermine the political credibility of their proponents and the defensibility of the rights they regard as preeminently important. In an increasingly interdependent global community, any human rights orientation that does not support the widest possible shaping and sharing of values or capabilities among all human beings is likely to provoke widespread skepticism. The last half of the 20th century is replete with examples. Second, such characterizations do not accurately reflect reality.

In the real world, virtually all societies, whether individualistic or collectivist in essential character, consent to, and even promote, a mixture of all basic values or capabilities. President Franklin Delano Roosevelt's Four Freedoms (freedom of speech and expression, freedom of worship, freedom from want, and freedom from fear) is an early case in point. A more recent demonstration is found in the Declaration and Programme of Action of the Vienna conference mentioned above, adopted by representatives of 171 states. It proclaims that, "while the significance of national and regional particularities and various historical, cultural and religious backgrounds must be borne in mind, it is the duty of States, regardless of their political, economic and cultural systems, to promote and protect all human rights and fundamental freedoms."

Finally, none of the international human rights instruments currently in force or proposed says anything about the legitimacy or priority of the rights it addresses, save possibly in the case of rights that by international covenant are stipulated to be "non derogable" and therefore, arguably, more fundamental than others (e.g., freedom from arbitrary or unlawful deprivation of life, freedom from torture and from inhuman or degrading treatment and punishment, freedom from slavery, and freedom from imprisonment for debt). To be sure, some disagreements about legitimacy and priority can derive from differences of definition (e.g., what is "torture" or "inhuman treatment" to one may not be so to another, as in the case of punishment by caning or by death).

Similarly, disagreements also can arise when treating the problem of implementation. For instance, some insist first on certain civil and political guarantees, whereas others defer initially to conditions of material well-being. Such disagreements, however, reflect differences in political agendas and have little if any conceptual utility. As confirmed by numerous resolutions of the UN General Assembly and reaffirmed in the Vienna Declaration and Programme of Action, there is a growing consensus that all human rights form an indivisible whole and that the protection of human rights is not and should not be a matter of purely national jurisdiction. The extent to which the international community actually protects the human rights it prescribes, on the other hand, is a different matter.

DEVELOPMENTS BEFORE WORLD WAR II

Ever since ancient times, but especially since the emergence of the modern state system, the Age of Discovery, and the accompanying spread of industrialization and European culture throughout the world, there has developed, for economic and other reasons, a unique set of customs and conventions regarding the humane treatment of foreigners. This evolving International Law of State Responsibility for Injuries to Aliens, as these customs and conventions came to be called, represents the beginning of active concern—however much they served the interests of colonial expansion—for human rights on the international plane. The founding fathers of international law—particularly Francisco de Vitoria, Grotius, and Emmerich de Vattel—were quick to observe that all persons, outlander as well as other, were entitled to certain natural rights, and they emphasized, consequently, the importance of according aliens fair treatment.

With the exception of occasional treaties to secure the protection of Christian denominations, it was not until the start of the 19th century, however, that active international concern for the rights of nationals began to make itself felt. Then, in the century and a half before World War II, several noteworthy efforts to encourage respect for nationals by international means began to shape what today is called the International Law of Human Rights (which for historical but no theoretically convincing reasons was treated separately from the International Law of State Responsibility for Injuries to Aliens).

Throughout the 19th and early 20th centuries, numerous military operations and diplomatic representations, not all of them with the purest of motives but performed nonetheless in the name of "humanitarian intervention" (a customary international law doctrine), undertook to protect oppressed and persecuted minorities in the Ottoman Empire, Syria, Crete, various Balkan countries, Romania, and Russia. Paralleling these actions, first at the Congress of Vienna (1814–15) and later between the two World Wars, a series of treaties and international declarations sought the protection of certain racial, religious, and linguistic minorities in central and Eastern Europe and the Middle East. During the same period, the movement to combat and suppress slavery and the slave trade found expression in treaties sooner or later involving the major commercial powers, beginning with the Treaty of Paris (1814) and culminating in the International Slavery Convention (1926).

In addition, beginning in the late 19th century and continuing well beyond World War II, the community of nations, inspired largely by persons associated with what is now the International Committee of the Red Cross, concluded a series of multilateral declarations and agreements designed to temper the conduct of hostilities, protect the victims of war, and otherwise elaborate the humanitarian law of war (now commonly referred to as International Humanitarian Law). At about the same time, first with two multilateral labour conventions concluded in 1906 and subsequently at the initiative of the International Labour Organisation (ILO; established in 1919), a reformist-minded international community embarked upon a variety of collaborative measures directed at the promotion of human rights.

These measures addressed not only concerns traditionally associated with labour law and labour relations (e.g., industrial health and safety, hours of work, and annual paid holidays), but also—mainly after World War II—such core human rights concerns as forced labour, discrimination in employment and occupation, freedom of association for collective bargaining, and equal pay for equal work. Finally, during the interwar period, the covenant establishing the League of Nations (1919)—though not formally recognizing "the rights of Man" and failing to lay down a principle of racial nondiscrimination as requested by Japan (owing mainly to the resistance of Great Britain and the United States)—nevertheless committed its members to several human rights goals: fair and humane working conditions, the execution of agreements regarding trafficking in women and children, the prevention and control of disease in matters of international concern, and the just treatment of indigenous colonial peoples.

Also, the victorious powers—that as "mandatories" were entrusted by the League with the tutelage of colonies formerly governed by Germany and Turkey—accepted responsibility for the well-being and development of the inhabitants of those territories as "a sacred trust of civilization." This arrangement was later carried over into the trusteeship system of the United Nations. As important as these efforts were, however, it was not until after the war—and the Nazi atrocities accompanying it—that active concern for human rights truly came of age internationally. In the proceedings of the International Military Tribunal at Nürnberg in 1945–46 (the Nürnberg trials), German high officials were tried not only for "crimes against peace" and "war crimes" but also for "crimes against humanity" committed against civilian populations, even if the crimes were in accordance with the laws of the country in which they were perpetrated. Although the tribunal, whose establishment and rulings subsequently were endorsed by the UN General Assembly, applied a cautious approach to allegations of crimes against humanity, it nonetheless made the treatment by a state of its own citizens the subject of international criminal process.

The ad hoc international criminal tribunals established in 1993–94 for the prosecution of serious violations of International Humanitarian Law in the former Yugoslavia and in Rwanda were its first heirs on the international plane. Both courts were empowered to impose sentences of life imprisonment (though not the death penalty), and both focused their efforts, with some success, on political leaders who had authorized human rights abuses. Most conspicuous was the arrest and detention in June 2001 of former Yugoslav president Slobodan Miloševiæ by the International Criminal Tribunal for Yugoslavia, representing the first time a former head of state has been placed in the physical custody of an international judicial authority. The tribunal charged him with war crimes and crimes against humanity allegedly committed by Serbian forces in Kosovo in 1999 and subsequently with the crime of genocide allegedly committed by Serbian forces during the war in Bosnia and Herzegovina in 1992–95.

Also heir to the Nürnberg tribunal is the International Criminal Court, authorized by the adoption by 160 countries of the Rome Statute of the International Criminal Court in July 1998. The statute creates a permanent international criminal court whose jurisdiction includes crimes against humanity, crimes of genocide, war crimes, and crimes of "aggression" (pending the adoption of an acceptable definition of that term). However, the creation of the court, which depends on the ratification of the statute by at least 60 signatory states, was resisted by some countries, notably the United States, on the ground that it would unduly infringe upon their national sovereignty. The long-term future of the court is therefore uncertain.

HUMAN RIGHTS IN THE UNITED NATIONS

The Charter of the United Nations (1945) begins by reaffirming a "faith in fundamental human rights, in the dignity and worth of the human person, in the equal rights of men and women and of nations large and small." It states that the purposes of the UN are, among other things: to develop friendly relations among nations based on respect for the principle of equal rights and self-determination of peoples...and to achieve international co-operation...in promoting and encouraging respect for human rights and for fundamental freedoms for all without distinction as to race, sex, language, or religion.

In addition, in two key articles all members "pledge themselves to take joint and separate action in co-operation with the Organization" for the achievement of these and related purposes. It must be noted, however, that a proposal to ensure the protection as well as the promotion of human rights was explicitly rejected at the Charter-drafting San Francisco conference establishing the UN. Also, the Charter expressly provides that nothing in it "shall authorize the United Nations to intervene in matters which are essentially within the domestic jurisdiction of any state," except upon a Security Council finding of a "threat to the peace, breach of the peace, or act of aggression." Furthermore, though typical of major constitutive instruments, the Charter is conspicuously given to generality and vagueness in its human rights clauses, among others.

Thus, not surprisingly, the reconciliation of the Charter's human rights provisions with the history of its drafting and its "domestic jurisdiction" clause has given rise to legal and political controversy. Some authorities have argued that, in becoming parties to the Charter, states accept no more than a nebulous promotional obligation toward human rights and that, in any event, the UN has no standing to insist on human rights safeguards in member states. Others have insisted that the Charter's human rights provisions, being part of a legally binding treaty, clearly involve some element of legal obligation; that the "pledge" made by states upon becoming party to the Charter consequently represents more than a moral statement; and that the domestic jurisdiction clause does not apply because human rights no longer can be considered a matter "essentially within the domestic jurisdiction" of states. When all is said and done, however, it is clear from the actual practice of the UN that the problem of resolving these opposing contentions has proved less formidable than the statements of governments and the opinions of scholars would suggest.

Neither the Charter's drafting history nor its domestic jurisdiction clause—nor, indeed, its generality and vagueness in respect of human rights—has prevented the UN from investigating, discussing, and evaluating specific human rights situations. Nor have they prevented it from taking concrete action in relation to them—at least not in the case of "a consistent pattern of gross violations," as in the Security Council's imposition of a mandatory arms embargo against South Africa in 1977 and its authorization of the use of military force to end human rights abuses in Somalia and Haiti in the early 1990s. Of course, governments usually are protective of their sovereignty, or domestic jurisdiction. Also, the UN organs responsible for the promotion and protection of human rights suffer from most of the same disabilities that afflict the UN as a whole, in particular the absence of supranational authority, the presence of divisive power politics, and the imposition of crippling financial constraints by member states (most notably the United States). Hence, it cannot be expected that UN actions in defense of human rights will be, normally, either swift or categorically effective.

Indeed, many serious UN efforts at human rights implementation have been deliberately thwarted by the major powers. In 1999, for example, opposition by China and Russia prevented the Security Council from agreeing on forceful measures to end the persecution by Serbia of ethnic Albanians in the province of Kosovo, prompting the United States and other members of the North Atlantic Treaty Organization

(NATO) to take matters into their own hands through a massive bombing campaign against Serbian targets. Nevertheless, assuming some political will, the legal obstacles to UN enforcement of human rights are not insurmountable. Primary responsibility for the promotion and protection of human rights under the UN Charter rests in the General Assembly and, under its authority, in the Economic and Social Council (ECOSOC), the Human Rights Council (formerly the Commission on Human Rights), and the UN High Commissioner for Human Rights (UNHCHR).

The UN Commission on Human Rights, an intergovernmental subsidiary body of ECOSOC that met for the first time in 1947, served as the UN's central policy organ in the human rights field until 2006, when it was replaced by the Human Rights Council, a subsidiary body of the General Assembly. The UNHCHR, a post created by the General Assembly in 1993, is the official principally responsible for implementing and coordinating UN human rights programs and projects, including overall supervision of the UN's Geneva-based Centre for Human Rights, a bureau of the UN Secretariat.

THE UN COMMISSION ON HUMAN RIGHTS AND ITS INSTRUMENTS

For the first 20 years of its existence (1947–66), the UN Commission on Human Rights concentrated its efforts on setting human rights standards, believing it unauthorized to deal with human rights complaints. Together with other UN bodies such as the ILO, the United Nations Educational, Scientific and Cultural Organization (UNESCO), the UN Commission on the Status of Women, and the Commission on Crime Prevention and Criminal Justice, it drafted standards and prepared a number of international human rights instruments. Among the most important of these were the Universal Declaration of Human Rights, the International Covenant on Economic, Social and Cultural Rights (1966), and the International Covenant on Civil and Political Rights together with its Optional Protocols (1966; 1989).

Collectively known as the "International Bill of Human Rights," these three instruments served as touchstones for interpreting the human rights provisions of the UN charter. Also central in this regard were the International Convention on the Elimination of All Forms of Racial Discrimination (CERD; 1965), the Convention on the Elimination of All Forms of Discrimination against Women (CEDAW; 1979), the Convention against Torture and Other Cruel, Inhuman or Degrading Treatment or Punishment (1984), and the Convention on the Rights of the Child (1989), each of which elaborated on provisions of the International Bill of Human Rights.

Beginning in 1967 the commission was specifically authorized to deal with violations of human rights, and it subsequently set up elaborate mechanisms and procedures to investigate alleged human rights violations and otherwise monitors compliance by states with international human rights law. Thus, much of the work of the commission was investigatory, evaluative, and advisory in character. Each year it established a working group to consider and make recommendations concerning alleged "gross violations" of human rights, reports of which were referred to it by its Sub-Commission on Prevention of Discrimination and Protection of Minorities (on the basis of both "communications" from individuals and groups and investigations by the Sub-Commission or one of its working groups). Also, on an ad hoc basis, the commission appointed Special Rapporteurs, Special Representatives, Special Committees, and other envoys to examine human rights situations both country-oriented and thematic and report back to it on the basis of trustworthy evidence.

These fact-finding and implementation mechanisms and procedures were the focus of the commission's attention during the 1970s and '80s. In the 1990s the commission increasingly turned to economic, social, and cultural rights, including the right to development and the right to an adequate standard of living. Increased attention was paid also to the rights of minorities, indigenous peoples, women, and children. In the early 21st century the Commission on Human Rights was increasingly perceived as ineffective, in part because its membership included some countries with poor human rights records.

In 2006 the General Assembly replaced the commission with a Human Rights Council, whose smaller membership (47 instead of 53 states) would be elected to three-year terms by an absolute majority of the General Assembly by secret ballot rather than by a majority of ECOSOC members present and voting. The responsibilities of the new council included conducting a "universal periodic review" of the human rights records of every UN member state, including members of the council itself during their terms of membership. The council was also required to assume, and where possible improve upon, the special mechanisms and procedures created by the commission, including the Special Rapporteurs.

THE UN HIGH COMMISSIONER FOR HUMAN RIGHTS

Appointed by the secretary-general in a regular rotation of geographic regions and approved by the General Assembly, the UNHCHR serves a fixed term of four years with the possibility of renewal for an additional four-year term. The first high commissioner, José Ayala Lasso of Ecuador, took office in April 1994, and Mary Robinson, formerly president of Ireland, became the second high commissioner in September 1997. Among other duties, the high commissioner is charged by the General Assembly to promote and protect all civil, political, economic, social, and cultural rights; to provide advisory services and technical and financial assistance in the field of human rights to states that request them; to coordinate human rights promotion and protection activities throughout the UN system, including education and public-information programs; and otherwise to enhance international cooperation for the promotion and protection of human rights—all within the framework of the International Bill of Human Rights.

THE UNIVERSAL DECLARATION OF HUMAN RIGHTS

The catalog of rights set out in the Universal Declaration of Human Rights, which was adopted without dissent by the

General Assembly on December 10, 1948, is scarcely less than the sum of most of the important traditional political and civil rights of national constitutions and legal systems, including equality before the law; protection against arbitrary arrest; the right to a fair trial; freedom from ex-post facto criminal laws; the right to own property; freedom of thought, conscience, and religion; freedom of opinion and expression; and freedom of peaceful assembly and association.

Also enumerated are such economic, social, and cultural rights as the right to work, the right to form and join trade unions, the right to rest and leisure, the right to a standard of living adequate for health and well-being, and the right to education. The Universal Declaration, it should be noted, is not a treaty. It was meant to proclaim "a common standard of achievement for all peoples and all nations" rather than enforceable legal obligations. Nevertheless, the Universal Declaration has acquired a status juristically more important than originally intended, and it has been widely used, even by national courts, as a means of judging compliance with human rights obligations under the UN Charter.

THE INTERNATIONAL COVENANT ON CIVIL AND POLITICAL RIGHTS

The civil and political rights guaranteed by the International Covenant on Civil and Political Rights, which was opened for signature on December 19, 1966, and entered into force on March 23, 1976, incorporate almost all those rights proclaimed in the Universal Declaration, including the right to nondiscrimination but excluding the right to own property and the right to asylum. The covenant also designates several rights that are not listed in the Universal Declaration, among them the right of all peoples to self-determination and the right of ethnic, religious, and linguistic minorities to enjoy their own culture, to profess and practice their own religion, and to use their own language. To the extent that the Universal Declaration and the covenant overlap, however, the latter is understood to explicate and to help interpret the former.

In addition, the covenant calls for the establishment of a Human Rights Committee, comprising persons serving in their individual expert capacities, to study reports submitted by the state parties on measures they have adopted to give effect to the rights recognized in the covenant. For state parties that have expressly recognized the competence of the committee in this regard, the committee also may respond to allegations by one state party that another state party is not fulfilling its obligations under the covenant. If the committee is unable to resolve the problem, the matter is referred to an ad hoc conciliation commission, which eventually reports its findings on all questions of fact, plus its views on the possibilities of an amicable solution. State parties that become party to the covenant's first Optional Protocol further recognize the competence of the Human Rights Committee to consider and act upon communications from individuals claiming to be victims of covenant violations.

Other treaty-based organs within the UN system that are empowered to consider grievances from individuals in a quasi-judicial manner are the Committee on the Elimination of Racial Discrimination and the Committee on Torture, under the 1965 race discrimination and the 1984 torture conventions, respectively. Also noteworthy is the covenant's Second Optional Protocol, which is aimed at abolishing the death penalty worldwide. Adopted in 1989 and entered into force in 1991, it has been favourably received in most of the countries of Western Europe and many countries in the Americas, though not in the United States.

THE INTERNATIONAL COVENANT ON ECONOMIC, SOCIAL AND CULTURAL RIGHTS

Just as the International Covenant on Civil and Political Rights elaborates upon most of the civil and political rights enumerated in the Universal Declaration of Human Rights, so the International Covenant on Economic, Social and Cultural Rights elaborates upon most of the economic, social, and cultural rights set forth in the Universal Declaration: the right to work, the right to just and favourable conditions of work, trade union rights, the right to social security, rights relating to the protection of the family, the right to an adequate standard of living, the right to health, the right to education, and rights relating to culture and science.

Unlike its companion agreement, the International Covenant on Civil and Political Rights, however, generally this covenant, sometimes called a "promotional convention," is not intended for immediate implementation, the state parties having agreed only "to take steps" toward "achieving progressively the full realization of the rights recognized in the...Covenant," and then subject to "the maximum of their available resources."

One obligation, however, is subject to immediate application: the prohibition of discrimination in the enjoyment of the rights enumerated on grounds of race, colour, sex, language, religion, political or other opinion, national or social origin, property, and birth or other status. Also, the international supervisory measures that apply to the covenant oblige the state parties to report to the UN Economic and Social Council on the steps they have adopted and on the progress they have made in achieving the realization of the enumerated rights.

OTHER UN HUMAN RIGHTS CONVENTIONS AND DECLARATIONS

Numerous other human rights treaties drafted under UN auspices address a broad range of concerns, including the prevention and punishment of the crime of genocide; the humane treatment of military and civilian personnel in time of war; the status of refugees; the protection of stateless persons; the abolition of slavery, forced labour, and discrimination in employment and occupation; the suppression and punishment of the crime of apartheid; the elimination of discrimination in education; the promotion of the political rights of women; the protection of minorities and indigenous peoples; and the promotion of equality of opportunity and treatment among migrant workers. In addition to overseeing human rights treaties, the UN also adopts declarations, in the form of resolutions, aimed at promoting human rights.

Although technically not binding on member states in the sense of a treaty or a resolution of the Security Council, such declarations—particularly when they enunciate principles of great and solemn importance—may nevertheless create strong expectations about authority and control. Perhaps the best-known examples subsequent to the Universal Declaration are the Declaration on the Granting of Independence to Colonial Countries and Peoples (1960) and the Declaration on Principles of International Law concerning Friendly Relations and Cooperation among States in accordance with the Charter of the United Nations (1970), which affirms, among other things, "the duty of all states to refrain from organizing, instigating, assisting or participating in ... terrorist acts." Other declarations have addressed the rights of disabled persons; the elimination of all forms of intolerance and discrimination based on religion or belief; the right of peoples to peace; the right to development; the rights of persons belonging to national, ethnic, religious, and linguistic minorities; and the elimination of violence against women.

HUMAN RIGHTS AND THE HELSINKI PROCESS

After World War II, international concern for human rights was evident at the global level outside the UN as well as within it, most notably in the proceedings and aftermath of the Conference on Security and Co-operation in Europe (CSCE), convened in Helsinki, Finland, on July 3, 1973, and concluded there (after continuing deliberations in Geneva) on August 1, 1975. Attended by representatives of 35 governments—including the NATO countries, the Warsaw Pact nations, and 13 neutral and nonaligned European states—the conference had as its principal purpose a mutually satisfactory definition of peace and stability between East and West, previously made impossible by the Cold War. In particular, the Soviet Union wished to gain recognition of its western frontiers as established at the end of World War II (which ended without the conclusion of an omnibus peace treaty).

The West, with no realistic territorial claims of its own, sought concessions primarily on security requirements and human rights, largely in that order. The Final Act of the conference, also known as the Helsinki Accords, begins with a Declaration on Principles Guiding Relations between Participating States, in which the participating states solemnly declare "their determination to respect and put into practice," alongside other "guiding" principles, "respect for human rights and fundamental freedoms, including the freedom of thought, conscience, religion or belief" and "respect for the equal rights of peoples and their right to self-determination." It was hoped that this declaration, the importance of which is reflected in its having been signed by almost all of the principal governmental leaders of the day, would mark the beginning of a liberalization of authoritarian regimes.

From the earliest discussions, however, it was clear that the Helsinki Final Act was not intended as a legally binding instrument. The expression "determination to respect" and to "put into practice" were seen as moral commitments only, the Declaration of Principles was said not to prescribe international law, and nowhere did the participants provide for enforcement machinery. On the other hand, the Declaration of Principles, including its human rights principles, was always viewed as being at least consistent with international law, and in providing for periodic follow-up conferences, it made possible a unique negotiating process ("the Helsinki process") to review compliance with its terms, thus creating normative expectations concerning the conduct of the participating states. In these ways it proved to be an important force in the fall of the Iron Curtain and the transformation of Eastern Europe in 1989–90.

The Helsinki process, involving long-running "follow-up," "summit," and other meetings, served also to establish a mechanism for the evolution of the CSCE from a forum for discussion to an operational institution, beginning with the adoption of the Charter of Paris for a New Europe in 1990. In 1994 the CSCE was renamed the Organization for Security and Co-operation in Europe (OSCE), and its principal organs and bureaus now include an Office for Democratic Institutions and Human Rights (in Warsaw), a Conflict Prevention Centre (in Vienna), a High Commissioner on National Minorities (in The Hague), and a Court of Conciliation and Arbitration (in Geneva). These offices have been increasingly pressed into service to alleviate major deprivations of human rights, particularly those arising from ethnic conflicts.

In addition, the Vienna Human Dimension Mechanism and the Moscow Human Dimension Mechanism provide a preliminary formal means of raising and seeking to resolve disputes about violations of human rights commitments, including the possibility of on-site investigation by independent experts. All these mechanisms, however, bespeak an essentially interstate process; neither individuals nor nongovernmental organizations (NGOs) have access to them except indirectly as suppliers of information and conveyors of political pressure. They thus contrast markedly with the individual complaint procedures that are available within the UN and in regional human rights systems.

REGIONAL DEVELOPMENTS

Action for the international promotion and protection of human rights has proceeded at the regional level in Europe, the Americas, Africa, the Middle East, and, to a minor extent, Asia. Only the first three of these regions, however, have created enforcement mechanisms within the framework of a human rights charter.

EUROPEAN HUMAN RIGHTS SYSTEM

On November 4, 1950, the Council of Europe agreed to the European Convention for the Protection of Human Rights and Fundamental Freedoms, the substantive provisions of which are based on a draft of what is now the International Covenant on Civil and Political Rights. Together with its 11 additional protocols, this convention, which entered into force on September 3, 1953, represents the most advanced and successful international experiment in the field to date. Over the years, the enforcement mechanisms created by the convention have developed a considerable body of case law on questions regulated by the convention, which the state parties typically have honoured and respected. In some

European states the provisions of the convention are deemed to be part of domestic constitutional or statutory law. Where this is not the case, the state parties have taken other measures to make their domestic laws conform to their obligations under the convention.

Notwithstanding these successes, a significant streamlining of the European human rights regime took place on November 1, 1998, when Protocol No. 11 to the convention entered into force. Pursuant to the protocol, two of the enforcement mechanisms created by the convention—the European Commission of Human Rights and the European Court of Human Rights—were merged into a reconstituted court, which now is empowered to hear individual (as opposed to interstate) petitions or complaints without the prior approval of the local government. The decisions of the court are final and binding on the state parties to the convention. A companion instrument to the European Convention—similar to but preceding the International Covenant on Economic, Social and Cultural Rights—is the European Social Charter (1961) and its additional protocol (1988).

In contrast to the adjudicatory enforcement procedures of the European Convention, the charter's provisions are implemented through an elaborate system of control based on progress reports to the various committees and organs of the Council of Europe. In July 1996 the Revised Social Charter, which modernizes its forebear's substantive provisions and strengthens its enforcement capabilities, entered into force. Both charters have suffered from a notable lack of public awareness, however, and this fact, together with an increased emphasis on market-oriented economic policies in many European countries, threatens not only the ratification of the 1996 charter but, as well, the political commitment to the several and joint aims of each treaty.

INTER-AMERICAN HUMAN RIGHTS SYSTEM

In 1948, concurrent with its establishment of the Organization of American States (OAS), the Ninth Pan-American Conference adopted the American Declaration on the Rights and Duties of Man, which, unlike the Universal Declaration of the UN adopted seven months later, set out the duties as well as the rights of individual citizens. Subsequently, in 1959, a meeting of the American Ministers for Foreign Affairs created the Inter-American Commission on Human Rights, which has since undertaken important investigative activities in the region. Finally, in 1969, the Inter-American Specialized Conference on Human Rights adopted the American Convention on Human Rights, which, among other things, after entering into force in July 1978, made the existing Inter-American Commission an organ of the convention and established the Inter-American Court of Human Rights, which sits in San José, Costa Rica.

In November 1988, the OAS adopted the Additional Protocol to the American Convention on Human Rights in the Area of Economic, Social and Cultural Rights. Of the 26 Western Hemispheric states that so far have signed the convention, only the United States has yet to ratify it. Nor is the United States a party to the additional protocol, which entered into force in November 1999. The core structure of the Inter-American human rights system is similar to that of its European counterpart. Nevertheless, some noteworthy differences exist, and three stand out in particular. First, as noted above, the American convention, reflecting the influence of the American Declaration, acknowledges the relationship between individual duties and individual rights.

Second, the American convention reverses the priorities of the European convention prior to Protocol No. 11 by guaranteeing individual petitions while making interstate complaints optional. Finally, both the Inter-American Commission and the Inter-American Court operate beyond the framework of the American convention. The commission is as much an organ of the OAS Charter as of the American convention, with powers and procedures that differ significantly depending on the source of the commission's authority. The court, while primarily an organ of the convention, nonetheless has jurisdiction to interpret the human rights provisions of other treaties, including those of the OAS Charter.

AFRICAN HUMAN RIGHTS SYSTEM

In 1981 the Eighteenth Assembly of Heads of State and Government of the Organization of African Unity (replaced by the African Union [AU] in 2002) adopted the African Charter on Human and Peoples' Rights. Also known as the "Banjul Charter" for having been drafted in Banjul, Gambia, it entered into force on October 21, 1986, and boasts the vast majority of the states of Africa as parties. Like it's American and early European counterparts, the African Charter provides for a human rights commission, which has both promotional and protective functions. There is no restriction on who may file a complaint with it. In contrast to the European and American procedures, however, concerned states are encouraged to reach a friendly settlement without formally involving the investigative or conciliatory mechanisms of the commission.

Also, the African Charter does not, at present, call for a human rights court. African customs and traditions, it has been said, emphasize mediation, conciliation, and consensus rather than the adversarial and adjudicative procedures that are common to Western legal systems. Nevertheless, owing largely to political changes wrought by the end of the Cold War, planning for an African Court of Human Rights was begun in the late 1990s. As envisioned, the court would not replace the commission but would supplement and reinforce its mandate. Four other distinctive features of the African Charter are noteworthy. First, it provides for economic, social, and cultural rights as well as civil and political rights.

In this respect it resembles the American convention and differs from the European convention. Second, in contrast to both the European and American conventions, it recognizes the rights of groups in addition to the family, women, and children. The aged and the infirm are accorded special protection also, and the right of peoples to self-determination is elaborated in the right to existence, equality, and non domination. Third, it uniquely embraces two third-generation, or "solidarity," rights: the right to economic, social, and cultural development and the right to national and international peace and security. Finally, it is to date the only treaty instrument to detail individual duties as well as individual rights—to the family, society, the state, and the international African community. Nevertheless, in view of the turmoil that beset northern and sub-Saharan Africa at the end of the 20th century, it is fair to say that the African human rights system is still in its infancy.

MIDDLE EASTERN AND ASIAN HUMAN RIGHTS SYSTEMS

The Permanent Arab Commission on Human Rights, founded by the Council of the League of Arab States in September 1968, has been preoccupied primarily with the rights of Arabs living in Israeli-occupied territories. Functioning more to promote than to protect human rights, at the end of the 1990s it had yet to bring a proposed Arab Convention on Human Rights to a successful conclusion. Nevertheless, work by other intergovernmental and nongovernmental bodies manifested a continuing desire to establish human rights protection mechanisms in the Middle East. Building on the Universal Islamic Declaration of Human Rights (1981) and the Cairo Declaration on Human Rights in Islam (1990), the League of Arab States approved an Arab Charter on Human Rights in September 1994.

The charter provides for periodic reports to the league's Human Rights Committee by state parties and for an independent Committee of Experts apparently empowered to request and study reports and submits its own findings to the Human Rights Committee. No other institutions or procedures for monitoring human rights are specified in the charter, however. More so than in most other regions of the world (except Asia), the states of the Middle East were greatly divided over the need to enforce human rights law and the desirability of achieving a true regional system for the promotion and protection of human rights. In Asia, despite efforts by NGOs and the United Nations, the states of the region have been at best ambivalent—and at worst hostile—to human rights concerns, thus precluding agreement on almost all regional human rights initiatives.

In early 1993, anticipating the Vienna World Conference on Human Rights later that year, a conference of Asia-Pacific NGOs adopted an Asia-Pacific Declaration of Human Rights, and in 1997 another meeting of NGOs adopted an Asian Human Rights Charter. Both of these initiatives supported the universality and indivisibility of human rights. However, whereas the first initiative called for the creation of a regional human rights regime, the second—seemingly in deference to the cultural diversity and vastness of the region—urged instead the establishment of national human rights commissions and so-called "People's Tribunals," which would be based more on moral and spiritual foundations rather than on legal ones. The states of Asia were slow to respond to these recommendations.

Their positions were indicated at an UN-sponsored workshop in 1996, where the 30 participating states concluded that "it was premature ... to discuss specific arrangements relating to the setting up of a formal human rights mechanism in the Asian and Pacific region." The same states agreed, however, to "explore the options available and the process necessary for establishing a regional mechanism." It remains to be seen whether the economic and political crises that beset Asia at the end of the 20th century will stimulate efforts to ensure greater respect for human rights through regional cooperation.

INTERNATIONAL HUMAN RIGHTS IN DOMESTIC COURTS

Using domestic courts to clarify and safeguard international human rights is a new and still evolving approach to human rights advocacy. In addition to the inevitable interpretative problems involved in applying norms that are fashioned in multicultural settings, controversial theories about the interrelation of national and international law, as well as many procedural difficulties, burden the human rights claimant in this setting. To be sure, considerable progress has been made, as perhaps best evidenced in the far-reaching decision handed down by the U.S. Court of Appeals for the 2nd Circuit in

Filártiga v. *Peña-Irala* (1980), in which the court held that the international prohibition of torture, because it is unequivocally established in customary international law and applies regardless of the nationality of the victim or the perpetrator (at least in the case of private litigants), must be honoured in U.S. courts.

More recently, in 1998–99, the United Kingdom's highest tribunal, the Law Lords of the British House of Lords, captured international attention when, in response to an extradition request by a Spanish court, it upheld the arrest in England of former Chilean president Augusto Pinochet on charges of torture and conspiracy to commit torture in violation of international treaty law. Although Pinochet was later returned to Chile and declared by a Chilean court to be mentally unfit to stand trial, the Law Lords' ruling established the precedent that former heads of state do not enjoy immunity from prosecution, at least for systematic human rights crimes.

HUMAN RIGHTS AT THE TURN OF THE 21ST CENTURY

Whatever the current attitudes and policies of governments, the reality of popular demands for human rights including both greater economic justice and greater political freedom, is beyond debate. A deepening and widening concern for the promotion and protection of human rights on all fronts, hastened by the ideal of self-determination in a postcolonial era, is now unmistakably woven into the fabric of contemporary world affairs. Substantially responsible for this progressive development has been the work of the UN, its allied agencies, and such regional organizations as the Council of Europe, the OAS, and the AU. Also contributing to this development, particularly since the 1970s and '80s, have been five other salient factors:

1. The public advocacy of human rights as a key aspect of national foreign policies, made initially legitimate by the example of U.S. President Jimmy Carter,
2. The emergence and spread of civil society on a

transnational basis, primarily in the form of activist nongovernmental human rights organizations such as Amnesty International, Interights, and Human Rights Watch, the International Commission of Jurists, and diverse faith-based and professional groups,

3. A worldwide profusion of teaching and research devoted to the study of human rights in both formal and informal settings,
4. The proliferation of large UN conferences in areas such as children's rights, population, social development, women's rights, human settlements, and food production and distribution, and
5. A mounting feminist intellectual and political challenge regarding not only the rights of women worldwide, but also what feminists consider the paternalistic myths and myth structures that purport to define humane governance generally.

To be sure, because the application of international human rights law depends for the most part on the voluntary consent of nations, formidable obstacles attend the endeavours of human rights policy makers, activists, and scholars. Human rights conventions continue to be undermined by the failure of states to ratify them and by emasculating reservations and derogations, by self-serving reporting systems that outnumber objective complaint procedures, and by poor financing for the implementation of human rights prescriptions. In short, the mechanisms for the enforcement of human rights are still in their infancy. Nevertheless, it is certain that, out of necessity no less than out of realism, a palpable concern for the advancement of human rights is here to stay.

2

Universal Declaration on Human Rights

The Universal Declaration of Human Rights (UDHR) is a declaration adopted by the United Nations General Assembly (10 December 1948 at the Palais de Chaillot, Paris). The *Guinness Book of Records* describes the UDHR as the "Most Translated Document" in the world. The Declaration arose directly from the experience of the Second World War and represents the first global expression of rights to which all human beings are inherently entitled. It consists of 30 articles which have been elaborated in subsequent international treaties, regional human rights instruments, national constitutions and laws. The International Bill of Human Rights consists of the Universal Declaration of Human Rights, the International Covenant on Economic, Social and Cultural Rights, and the International Covenant on Civil and Political Rights and its two Optional Protocols.

In 1966 the General Assembly adopted the two detailed Covenants, which complete the International Bill of Human Rights; and in 1976, after the Covenants had been ratified by a sufficient number of individual nations, the Bill took on the force of international law. The ideas and values of human rights can be traced through history and in religious beliefs and cultures around the world. European philosophers of the enlightenment period developed theories of natural law that influenced the adoption of documents such as the Bill of

Rights of England, the Bill of Rights in the United States, and the Declaration of the Rights of Man and of the Citizen in France.

During World War II, the Allies adopted the Four Freedoms: freedom of speech, freedom of assembly, freedom from fear and freedom from want, as their basic war aims. The United Nations Charter "reaffirmed faith in fundamental human rights, and dignity and worth of the human person" and committed all member states to promote "universal respect for, and observance of, human rights and fundamental freedoms for all without distinction as to race, sex, language or religion". When the atrocities committed by Nazi Germany became apparent after the World War II, the consensus within the world community was that the United Nations Charter did not sufficiently define the rights it referenced. A universal declaration that specified the rights of individuals was necessary to give effect to the Charter's provisions on human rights. Such a declaration was proposed by Cuban diplomats Guy Pérez Cisneros and Ernesto Dihigo.

The history of human rights involves religious, cultural, philosophical and legal developments throughout recorded history. While the modern human rights *movement* hugely expanded in post-World War II era, the concept can be traced through all major religions, cultures and philosophies. Ancient Hindu law (Manu Smriti), Confucianism, the Qu'ran and the Ten Commandments all outline some of the rights now included in the Universal Declaration of Human Rights. The concept of natural law, guaranteeing natural rights despite varying human laws and customs, can be traced back to Ancient Greek philosophers, while Enlightenment philosophers suggest a social contract between the rulers and the ruled. The African concept of ubuntu is a cultural view of what it is to be human. Modern human rights thinking is descended from these many traditions of human values and beliefs.

EARLY HISTORY OF HUMAN RIGHTS

HUMAN RIGHTS IN THE ANCIENT WORLD

While it is known that the reforms of Urukagina of Lagash, the earliest known legal code (c. 2350 BC), must have addressed the concept of rights to some degree, the actual text of his decrees has not yet been found. The oldest legal codex extant today is the Neo-Sumerian *Code of Ur-Nammu* (ca. 2050 BC). Several other sets of laws were also issued in Mesopotamia, including the Code of Hammurabi (ca. 1780 BC), one of the most famous examples of this type of document. It shows rules and punishments if those rules are broken, on a variety of matters, including women's rights, men's rights, children's rights and slave rights. The prefaces of these codes invoked the Mesopotamian gods for divine sanction. Societies have often derived the origins of human rights in religious documents. The Vedas, the Bible, the Qur'an and the Analects of Confucius are also among the early written sources that address questions of people's duties, rights, and responsibilities.

MAURYA EMPIRE

The Maurya Empire of ancient India established unprecedented principles of civil rights in the 3rd century BC under Ashoka the Great. After his brutal conquest of Kalinga in circa 265 BC, he felt remorse for what he had done, and as a result, adopted Buddhism. From then, Ashoka, who had been described as "the cruel Ashoka" eventually came to be known as "the pious Ashoka". During his reign, he pursued an official policy of nonviolence (*ahimsa*) and the protection of human rights, as his chief concern was the happiness of his subjects.

The unnecessary slaughter or mutilation of animals was immediately abolished, such as sport hunting and branding. Ashoka also showed mercy to those imprisoned, allowing them outside one day each year, and offered common citizens free education at universities. He treated his subjects as equals regardless of their religion, politics or caste, and constructed free hospitals for both humans and animals. Ashoka defined the main principles of nonviolence, tolerance of all sects and opinions, obedience to parents, respect for teachers and priests, being liberal towards friends, humane treatment of servants, and generosity towards all.

These reforms are described in the Edicts of Ashoka. In the Maurya Empire, citizens of all religions and ethnic groups also had rights to freedom, tolerance, and equality. The need for tolerance on an egalitarian basis can be found in the Edicts of Ashoka, which emphasize the importance of tolerance in public policy by the government. The slaughter or capture of prisoners of war was also condemned by Ashoka. Some sources claim that slavery was also non-existent in ancient India. Other state, however, that slavery existed in ancient India, where it is recorded in the Sanskrit Laws of Manu of the 1st century BC.

EARLY ISLAMIC CALIPHATE

Many reforms in human rights took place under Islam between 610 and 661, including the period of Muhammad's mission and the rule of the four immediate successors who established the Rashidun Caliphate. Historians generally agree that Muhammad preached against what he saw as the social evils of his day, and that Islamic social reform in areas such as social security, family structure, slavery, and the rights of women and ethnic minorities improved on what was present in existing Arab society at the time. For example, according to Bernard Lewis, Islam "from the first denounced aristocratic privilege, rejected hierarchy, and adopted a formula of the career open to the talents."

John Esposito sees Muhammad as a reformer who condemned practices of the pagan Arabs such as female infanticide, exploitation of the poor, usury, murder, false contracts, and theft. Bernard Lewis believes that the egalitarian nature of Islam "represented a very considerable advance on the practice of both the Greco-Roman and the ancient Persian world." The Constitution of Medina, also known as the *Charter of Medina,* was drafted by Muhammad in 622. It constituted a formal agreement between Muhammad and all of the significant tribes and families of Yathrib (later known as Medina), including Muslims, Jews, and pagans. The document was drawn up with the explicit concern of bringing to an end the bitter inter tribal fighting between the clans of the Aws (Aus) and Khazraj within Medina. To this effect it instituted a number of rights and responsibilities for the Muslim, Jewish and pagan communities of Medina bringing them within the fold of one community-the Ummah.

The Constitution established the security of the community, freedom of religion, the role of Medina as a haram or sacred place (barring all violence and weapons), the security of women, stable tribal relations within Medina, a tax system for supporting the community in time of conflict, parameters for exogenous political alliances, a system for granting protection of individuals, a judicial system for resolving disputes, and also regulated the paying of blood-wite (the payment between families or tribes for the slaying of an individual in lieu of lex talionis). Muhammad made it the responsibility of the Islamic government to provide food and clothing, on a reasonable basis, to captives, regardless of their religion.

If the prisoners were in the custody of a person, then the responsibility was on the individual. Lewis states that Islam brought two major changes to ancient slavery which was to have far-reaching consequences. "One of these was the presumption of freedom; the other, the ban on the enslavement of free persons except in strictly defined circumstances," Lewis continues. The position of the Arabian slave was "enormously improved": the Arabian slave "was now no longer merely a chattel but was also a human being with a certain religious and hence a social status and with certain quasi-legal rights."

Esposito states that reforms in women's rights affected marriage, divorce, and inheritance. Women were not accorded with such legal status in other cultures, including the West, until centuries later. The Oxford Dictionary of Islam states that the general improvement of the status of Arab women included prohibition of female infanticide and recognizing women's full personhood. "The dowry, previously regarded as a bride-price paid to the father, became a nuptial gift retained by the wife as part of her personal property." Under Islamic law, marriage was no longer viewed as a "status" but rather as a "contract", in which the woman's consent was imperative. "Women were given inheritance rights in a patriarchal society that had previously restricted inheritance to male relatives."

Annemarie Schimmel states that "compared to the pre-Islamic position of women, Islamic legislation meant an enormous progress; the woman has the right, at least according to the letter of the law, to administer the wealth she has brought into the family or has earned by her own work." William Montgomery Watt states that Muhammad, in the historical context of his time, can be seen as a figure who testified on behalf of women's rights and improved things considerably. Watt explains: "At the time Islam began, the conditions of women were terrible - they had no right to own property, were supposed to be the property of the man, and if the man died everything went to his sons." Muhammad, however, by "instituting rights of property ownership, inheritance, education and divorce gave women certain basic safeguards." Haddad and Esposito state that "Muhammad granted women rights and privileges in the sphere of family life, marriage, education, and economic endeavors, rights that help improve women's status in society."

Sociologist Robert Bellah (*Beyond belief*) argues that Islam in its seventh-century origins was, for its time and place, "remarkably modern...in the high degree of commitment, involvement, and participation expected from the rank-and-file members of the community." This is because, he argues, and that Islam emphasized the equality of all Muslims, where leadership positions were open to all. Dale Eickelman writes that Bellah suggests "the early Islamic community placed a particular value on individuals, as opposed to collective or group responsibility."

There was an early emphasis on freedom of speech in the Caliphate, as summarized by al-Hashimi (a cousin of Caliph al-Ma'mun) in the following letter to one of the religious opponents he was attempting to convert through reason:

"Bring forward all the arguments you wish and say whatever you please and speak your mind freely. Now that you are safe and free to say whatever you please appoint some arbitrator who will impartially judge between us and lean only towards the truth and be free from the empery of passion, and that arbitrator shall be Reason, whereby God makes us responsible for our own rewards and punishments. Herein I have dealt justly with you and have given you full security and am ready to accept whatever decision Reason may give for me or against me. For "There is no compulsion in religion" (Qur'an 2:256) and I have only invited you to accept our faith willingly and of your own accord and have pointed out the hideousness of your present belief. Peace be with you and the blessings of God!"

MAGNA CARTA

Magna Carta is an English charter originally issued in 1215. Magna Carta was the most significant early influence on the extensive historical process that led to the rule of constitutional law today. Magna Carta influenced the development of the common law and many constitutional documents, such as the United States Constitution and Bill of Rights. Magna Carta was originally written because of disagreements amongst Pope Innocent III, King John and the English barons about the rights of the King. Magna Carta required the King to renounce certain rights, respect certain legal procedures and accept that his will could be bound by the law. It explicitly protected certain rights of the King's subjects, whether free or fettered — most notably the writ of habeas corpus, allowing appeal against unlawful imprisonment.

For modern times, the most enduring legacy of Magna Carta is considered the right of habeas corpus. This right arises from what are now known as clauses 36, 38, 39, and 40 of the 1215 Magna Carta. The Magna Carta also included the right to due process:

"No Freeman shall be taken or imprisoned, or be disseised of his Freehold, or Liberties, or free Customs, or be outlawed, or exiled, or any other wise destroyed; nor will we not pass upon him, nor condemn him, but by lawful judgment of his Peers, or by the Law of the Land. We will sell to no man; we will not deny or defer to any man either Justice or Right." — Clause XXIX of the Magna Carta

PHILOSOPHIES OF HUMAN RIGHTS

Several theoretical approaches have been advanced to explain how and why human rights become part of social expectations. One of the oldest Western philosophies on human rights is that they are a product of a natural law, stemming from different philosophical or religious grounds. Other theories hold that human rights codify moral behavior which is a human social product developed by a process of biological and social evolution (associated with Hume). Human rights are also described as a sociological pattern of rule setting (as in the sociological theory of law and the work of Weber). These approaches include the notion that individuals in a society accept rules from legitimate authority in exchange for security and economic advantage (as in Rawls) - a social contract.

NATURAL RIGHTS

Natural law theories base human rights on a "natural" moral, religious or even biological order this is independent of transitory human laws or traditions. Socrates and his philosophic heirs, Plato and Aristotle, posited the existence of natural justice or natural right (*dikaion physikon, äéêáéïí öõóéêïí,* Latin *ius naturale*). Of these, Aristotle is often said to be the father of natural law, although evidence for this is due largely to the interpretations of his work of Thomas Aquinas.

The development of this tradition of natural justice into one of natural law is usually attributed to the Stoics. Some of the early Church fathers sought to incorporate until then pagan concept of natural law into Christianity. Natural law theories have featured greatly in the philosophies of Thomas Aquinas, Francisco Suárez, Richard Hooker, Thomas Hobbes, Hugo Grotius, Samuel von Pufendorf, and John Locke. In the Seventeenth century Thomas Hobbes founded a contractualist theory of legal positivism on what all men could agree upon: what they sought (happiness) was subject to contention, but a broad consensus could form around what they feared (violent death at the hands of another). The natural law was how a rational human being, seeking to survive and prosper, would act.

It was discovered by considering humankind's natural rights, whereas previously it could be said that natural rights were discovered by considering the natural law. In Hobbes' opinion, the only way natural law could prevail was for men to submit to the commands of the sovereign. In this lay the foundations of the theory of a social contract between the governed and the governor. Hugo Grotius based his philosophy of international law on natural law. He wrote that "even the will of an omnipotent being cannot change or abrogate" natural law, which "would maintain its objective validity even if we should assume the impossible, that there is no God or that he does not care for human affairs." (*De iure belli ac pacis,* Prolegomeni XI). This is the famous argument etiamsi daremus (non esse Deum), that made natural law no longer dependent on theology.

John Locke incorporated natural law into many of his theories and philosophy, especially in *Two Treatises of Government.* Locke turned Hobbes' prescription around, saying that if the ruler went against natural law and failed to protect "life, liberty, and property," people could justifiably overthrow the existing state and create a new one. The Belgian philosopher of law Frank van Dun is one among those who are elaborating a secular conception of natural law in the liberal tradition. There are also emerging and secular forms of natural law theory that define human rights as derivative of the notion of universal human dignity. The term "human rights" has replaced the term "natural rights" in popularity, because the rights are less and less frequently seen as requiring natural law for their existence.

SOCIAL CONTRACT

The Swiss-French philosopher Jean-Jacques Rousseau suggested the existence of a hypothetical *social contract* where a group of free individuals agree for the sake of the common good to form institutions to govern themselves. This echoed the earlier postulation by Thomas Hobbes that there is a contract between the government and the governed - and led to John Locke's theory that a failure of the government to secure rights is a failure which justifies the removal of the government.

International equity expert Paul Finn has echoed this view:

"The most fundamental fiduciary relationship in our society is manifestly that which exists between the community (the people) and the state, its agencies and officials." —Paul Finn

The relationship between government and the governed in countries which follow the English common law tradition is a fiduciary one. In equity law, a politician's fiduciary obligations are not only duties of good faith and loyalty, but also include duties of skill and competence in managing a country and its people. Originating from within the Courts of Equity, the fiduciary concept exists to prevent those holding positions of power from abusing their authority. The fiduciary relationship between government and the governed arises from the governments' ability to control people with the exercise of its power. In effect, if a government has the power to abolish any rights, it is equally burdened with the fiduciary duty to protect such an interest because it would benefit from the exercise of its own discretion to extinguish rights which it alone had the power to dispose of.

RECIPROCITY

The Golden Rule, or the *ethic of reciprocity* states that one must do unto others as one would be treated themselves; the principle being that reciprocal recognition and respect of rights ensures that one's own rights will be protected. This principle can be found in all the world's major religions in only slightly differing forms, and was enshrined in the *Declaration Toward a Global Ethic* by the Parliament of the World's Religions in 1993.

OTHER THEORIES OF HUMAN RIGHTS

The philosopher John Finnis argues that human rights are justifiable on the grounds of their instrumental value in creating the necessary conditions for human well-being. Interest theories highlight the duty to respect the rights of other individuals on grounds of self-interest:

"Human rights law, applied to a State's own citizens serves the interest of states, by, for example, minimizing the risk of violent resistance and protest and by keeping the level of dissatisfaction with the government manageable"—Niraj Nathwani in *Rethinking Refugee Law.*

The biological theory considers the comparative reproductive advantage of human social behavior based on empathy and altruism in the context of natural selection.

MODERN HUMAN RIGHTS MOVEMENT

The conquest of the Americas in the 16th century by the Spanish resulted in vigorous debate about human rights in Spain. The debate from 1550-51 between Las Casas and Juan Ginés de Sepúlveda at Valladolid was probably the first on the topic of human rights in European history. Several 17th and 18th centuries European philosophers and most notably John Locke, developed the concept of *natural rights*, the notion that people are naturally free and equal. Though Locke believed natural rights were derived from divinity since humans were creations of God, his ideas were important in the development of the modern notion of rights. Lockean natural rights did not rely on citizenship or any law of the state, nor were they necessarily limited to one particular ethnic, cultural or religious group.

Two major revolutions occurred that century in the United States (1776) and in France (1789). The Virginia Declaration of Rights of 1776 sets up a number of fundamental rights and freedoms. The later United States Declaration of Independence includes concepts of natural rights and famously states "that all men are created equal, that they are endowed by their Creator with certain unalienable rights that among these are life, liberty and the pursuit of happiness." Similarly, the French Declaration of the Rights of Man and Citizen defines a set of individual and collective rights of the people. These are, in the document, held to be universal - not only to French citizens but to all men without exception.

1800 AD TO WORLD WAR I

Philosophers such as Thomas Paine, John Stuart Mill and Hegel expanded on the theme of universality during the 18th and 19th centuries. In 1831 William Lloyd Garrison wrote in a newspaper called The Liberator that he was trying to enlist his readers in "the great cause of human rights" so the term human rights probably came into use sometime between Paine's The Rights of Man and Garrison's publication. In 1849 a contemporary, Henry David Thoreau, wrote about human rights in his treatise On the Duty of *Civil Disobedience* which was later influential on human rights and civil rights thinkers.

United States Supreme Court Justice David Davis, in his 1867 opinion for Ex Parte Milligan, wrote "By the protection of the law, human rights are secured; withdraw that protection and they are at the mercy of wicked rulers or the clamor of an excited people." Many groups and movements have managed to achieve profound social changes over the course of the 20th century in the name of human rights. In Western Europe and North America, labour unions brought about laws granting workers the right to strike, establishing minimum work conditions and forbidding or regulating child labour. The women's rights movement succeeded in gaining for many women the right to vote. National liberation movements in many countries succeeded in driving out colonial powers.

One of the most influential was Mahatma Gandhi's movement to free his native India from British rule. Movements by long-oppressed racial and religious minorities succeeded in many parts of the world, among them the civil rights movement, and more recent diverse identity politics movements, on behalf of women and minorities in the United States. The foundation of the International Committee of the Red Cross, the 1864 Lieber Code and the first of the Geneva Conventions in 1864 laid the foundations of International humanitarian law, to be further developed following the two World Wars.

BETWEEN WORLD WAR I AND WORLD WAR II

The League of Nations was established in 1919 at the negotiations over the Treaty of Versailles following the end of World War I. The League's goals included disarmament, preventing war through collective security, settling disputes between countries through negotiation, diplomacy and improving global welfare. Enshrined in its Charter was a mandate to promote many of the rights which were later included in the Universal Declaration of Human Rights? The League of Nations had mandates to support many of the former colonies of the Western European colonial powers during their transition from colony to independent state.

Established as an agency of the League of Nations, and now part of United Nations, the International Labour

Organization also had a mandate to promote and safeguard certain of the rights later included in the UDHR:

"The primary goal of the ILO today is to promote opportunities for women and men to obtain decent and productive work, in conditions of freedom, equity, security and human dignity." Report by the Director General for the International Labour Conference 87th Session.

AFTER WORLD WAR II

RIGHTS IN WAR AND THE GENEVA CONVENTIONS

The Geneva Conventions came into being between 1864 and 1949 as a result of efforts by Henry Dunant, the founder of the International Committee of the Red Cross. The conventions safeguard the human rights of individuals involved in conflict, and follow on from the 1899 and 1907 Hague Conventions, the international community's first attempt to define laws of war. Despite first being framed before World War II, the conventions were revised as a result of World War II and readopted by the international community in 1949.

The Geneva Conventions are:

- First Geneva Convention *"for the Amelioration of the Condition of the Wounded and Sick in Armed Forces in the Field"* (first adopted in 1864, last revision in 1949).
- Second Geneva Convention *"for the Amelioration of the Condition of Wounded, Sick and Shipwrecked Members of Armed Forces at Sea"* (first adopted in 1949, successor of the 1907 Hague Convention X).
- Third Geneva Convention *"relative to the Treatment of Prisoners of War"* (first adopted in 1929, last revision in 1949).
- Fourth Geneva Convention *"relative to the Protection of Civilian Persons in Time of War"* (first adopted in 1949, based on parts of the 1907 Hague Convention IV).

In addition, there are three additional amendment protocols to the Geneva Convention:

- Protocol I (1977)- Protocol Additional to the Geneva Conventions of 12 August 1949, and relating to the Protection of Victims of International Armed Conflicts. As of 12 January 2007 it had been ratified by 167 countries.
- Protocol II (1977)- Protocol Additional to the Geneva Conventions of 12 August 1949, and relating to the Protection of Victims of Non-International Armed Conflicts. As of 12 January 2007 it had been ratified by 163 countries.
- Protocol III (2005)- Protocol Additional to the Geneva Conventions of 12 August 1949, and relating to the Adoption of an Additional Distinctive Emblem. As of May 20, 2008, it had been ratified by 28 countries and signed but not yet ratified by an additional 59 countries.

All four conventions were last revised and ratified in 1949, based on previous revisions and partly on some of the 1907 Hague Conventions. Later conferences have added provisions prohibiting certain methods of warfare and addressing issues of civil wars. Nearly all 200 countries of the world are "signatory" nations, in that they have ratified these conventions. The International Committee of the Red Cross is the controlling body of the Geneva conventions.

UNIVERSAL DECLARATION OF HUMAN RIGHTS

The Universal Declaration of Human Rights (UDHR) is a non-binding declaration adopted by the United Nations General Assembly in 1948, partly in response to the barbarism of World War II. The UDHR urges member nations to promote a number of human, civil, economic and social rights, asserting these rights are part of the "foundation of freedom, justice and peace in the world". The declaration was the first international legal effort to limit the behavior of states and press upon them duties to their citizens following the model of the rights-duty duality.

"...recognition of the inherent dignity and of the equal and inalienable rights of all members of the human family is the foundation of freedom, justice and peace in the world" — Preamble to the Universal Declaration of Human Rights, 1948

The UDHR was framed by members of the Human Rights Commission, with Eleanor Roosevelt as Chair, who began to discuss an International Bill of Rights in 1947. The members of the Commission did not immediately agree on the form of such a bill of rights, and whether, or how, it should be enforced. The Commission proceeded to frame the UDHR and accompanying treaties, but the UDHR quickly became the priority. Canadian law professor John Humprey and French lawyer Rene Cassin were responsible for much of the cross-national research and the structure of the document respectively, where the articles of the declaration were interpretative of the general principle of the preamble.

The document was structured by Cassin to include the basic principles of dignity, liberty, equality and brotherhood in the first two articles, followed successively by rights pertaining to individuals; rights of individuals in relation to each other and to groups; spiritual, public and political rights; and economic, social and cultural rights. The final three articles place, according to Cassin, rights in the context of limits, duties and the social and political order in which they are to be realized.. Humphrey and Cassin intended the rights in the UDHR to be legally enforceable through some means, as is reflected in the third clause of the preamble:

"Whereas it is essential, if man is not to be compelled to have recourse, as a last resort, to rebellion against tyranny and oppression, that human rights should be protected by the rule of law." —Preamble to the Universal Declaration of Human Rights, 1948.

Some of the UDHR was researched and written by a committee of international experts on human rights, including representatives from all continents and all major religions, and drawing on consultation with leaders such as Mahatma Gandhi. The inclusion of both civil and political rights and economic, social and cultural rights was predicated on the assumption that basic human rights are indivisible and that the different types of rights listed are inextricably linked. Though this principle was not opposed by any member states at the time of adoption (the declaration was adopted unanimously, with the abstention of the Soviet bloc, Apartheid South Africa and Saudi Arabia), this principle was later subject to significant challenges.

DRAFTING

Canadian John Peters Humphrey was called upon by the United Nations Secretary-General to work on the project and became the Declaration's principal drafter. At the time Humphrey was newly appointed as Director of the Division of Human Rights within the United Nations Secretariat. The Commission on Human Rights, a standing body of the United Nations, was constituted to undertake the work of preparing what was initially conceived as an International Bill of Rights. The membership of the Commission was designed to be broadly representative of the global community with representatives of the following countries serving: Australia, Belgium, Byelorussian Soviet Socialist Republic, Chile, China, Cuba, Egypt, France, India, Iran, Lebanon, Panama, Philippines, United Kingdom, United States, Soviet Union, Uruguay and Yugoslavia. Well known members of the Commission included Eleanor Roosevelt of the United States, who was Chairman, Jacques Maritain and René Cassin of France, Charles Malik of Lebanon and P. C. Chang of China, among others. Humphrey provided the initial draft which became the working text of the Commission.

According to *Globalizing Family Values*, the Declaration's pro-family phrases were the result of the Christian Democratic movement's influence on Cassin and Malik. The Universal Declaration of Human Rights was drafted from early 1947 to late 1948 by Canadian John Peters Humphrey of the United Nations Secretariat and representatives of countries which were members of the first United Nations Commission on Human Rights, which was until 2006, when it was replaced by the United Nations Human Rights Council, a standing body of the United Nations. Well known members of the Commission who contributed significantly to the creation of the Declaration included Eleanor Roosevelt of the United States, who was

Chairman, Jacques Maritain and René Cassin of France, Charles Malik of Lebanon, and P. C. Chang of China, among others.

MEMBERSHIP OF THE COMMISSION

The membership of the Commission was designed to be broadly representative of the global community with representatives of the following countries serving: Australia, Belgium, Byelorussian Soviet Socialist Republic, Chile, China, Egypt, France, India, Iran, Lebanon, Panama, Philippines, United Kingdom, United States, Union of Soviet Socialist Republics, Uruguay and Yugoslavia.

THE HUMPHREY DRAFT (THE FIRST DRAFT)

Humphrey was newly appointed as Director of the Division of Human Rights within the United Nations Secretariat. In this role he produced the first draft of a list of rights that were to form the basis of the Declaration.

THE CASSIN DRAFT (THE SECOND DRAFT)

The underlying structure of the Universal Declaration was introduced in its second draft which was prepared by Rene Cassin. Cassin worked from a first draft prepared by John Peters Humphrey. The structure was influenced by the Code Napoleon, including a preamble and introductory general principles. Cassin compared the Declaration to the portico of a Greek temple, with a foundation, steps, four columns and a pediment. Articles 1 and 2 are the foundation blocks, with their principles of dignity, liberty, equality and brotherhood.

The seven paragraphs of the preamble, setting out the reasons for the Declaration, are represented by the steps. The main body of the Declaration forms the four columns. The first column (articles 3-11) constitutes rights of the individual, such as the right to life and the prohibition of slavery. The second column (articles 12-17) constitutes the rights of the individual in civil and political society. The third column (articles 18-21) is concerned with spiritual, public and political freedoms such as freedom of religion and freedom of association. The fourth column (articles 22-27) sets out social, economic and cultural rights. In Cassin's model, the last three articles of the Declaration provide the pediment which binds the structure together. These articles are concerned with the duty of the individual to society and the prohibition of use of rights in contravention of the purposes of the United Nations.

SUBSEQUENT DRAFTING

The Cassin draft was submitted to the Commission on Human Rights and was to undergo editing in the Commission, then in further drafts considered by the Third Committee of the United Nations, and finally in a draft before the General Assembly of the United Nations, which ultimately adopted the Declaration on 10 December 1948.

ADOPTION

The Universal Declaration was adopted by the General Assembly on 10 December 1948 by a vote of 48 in favor, 0 against, with 8 abstentions (all Soviet Bloc states [i.e., Byelorussia, Czechoslovakia, Poland, Ukraine, and USSR] and Yugoslavia, South Africa and Saudi Arabia).

The following countries voted in favor of the Declaration: Afghanistan, Argentina, Australia, Belgium, Bolivia, Brazil, Burma, Canada, Chile, China, Colombia, Costa Rica, Cuba, Denmark, the Dominican Republic, Ecuador, Egypt, El Salvador, Ethiopia, France, Greece, Guatemala, Haiti, Iceland, India, Iran, Iraq, Lebanon, Liberia, Luxembourg, Mexico, Netherlands, New Zealand, Nicaragua, Norway, Pakistan, Panama, Paraguay, Peru, Philippines, Thailand, Sweden, Syria, Turkey, United Kingdom, United States, Uruguay and Venezuela. Despite the central role played by Canadian John Humphrey, the Canadian Government at first abstained from voting on the Declaration's draft, but later voted in favour of the final draft in the General Assembly.

STRUCTURE

The underlying structure of the Universal Declaration was introduced in its second draft which was prepared by Rene

Cassin. He worked from a first draft prepared by John Peters Humphrey. The structure was influenced by the Code Napoleon, including a preamble and introductory general principles. Cassin compared the Declaration to the portico of a Greek temple, with a foundation, steps, four columns and a pediment. Articles 1 and 2 are the foundation blocks, with their principles of dignity, liberty, equality and brotherhood. The seven paragraphs of the preamble, setting out the reasons for the Declaration, are represented by the steps. The main body of the Declaration forms the four columns.

The first column (articles 3–11) constitutes rights of the individual, such as the right to life and the prohibition of slavery. The second column (articles 12–17) constitutes the rights of the individual in civil and political society. The third column (articles 18–21) is concerned with spiritual, public and political freedoms such as freedom of religion and freedom of association. The fourth column (articles 22–27) sets out social, economic and cultural rights. In Cassin's model, the last three articles of the Declaration provide the pediment which binds the structure together. These articles are concerned with the duty of the individual to society and the prohibition of use of rights in contravention of the purposes of the United Nations.

PREAMBLE

The Universal Declaration begins with a preamble consisting of seven paragraphs followed by a statement "proclaiming" the Declaration. Each paragraph of the preamble sets out a reason for the adoption of the Declaration. The first paragraph asserts that the recognition of human dignity of all people is the foundation of justice and peace in the world. The second paragraph observes that disregard and contempt for human rights have resulted in barbarous acts which have outraged the conscience of mankind and that the four freedoms: freedom of speech, belief, freedom from want, and freedom from fear - which is "proclaimed as the highest aspiration" of the people.

The third paragraph states that so that people are not compelled to rebellion against tyranny, human rights should be protected by rule of law. The fourth paragraph relates human rights to the development of friendly relations between nations. The fifth paragraph links the Declaration back to the United Nations Charter which reaffirms faith in fundamental human rights and dignity and worth of the human person. The sixth paragraph notes that all members of the United Nations have pledged themselves to achieve, in cooperation with the United Nations, the promotion of universal respect for and observance of human rights and fundamental freedoms.

The seventh paragraph observes that "a common understanding" of rights and freedoms is of "the greatest importance" for the full realization of that pledge. These paragraphs are followed by the "proclamation" of the Declaration as a "common standard of achievement" for "all peoples and all nations", so that "all individuals" and "all organs of society" should by teaching and education, promote respect for these rights and freedoms and by progressive measures, national and international, secure their universal and effective recognition and observance.

The Preamble is:

- Whereas recognition of the inherent dignity and of the equal and inalienable rights of all members of the human family is the foundation of freedom, justice and peace in the world,
- Whereas disregard and contempt for human rights have resulted in barbarous acts which have outraged the conscience of mankind, and the advent of a world in which human beings shall enjoy freedom of speech and belief and freedom from fear and want has been proclaimed as the highest aspiration of the common people,
- Whereas it is essential, if man is not to be compelled to have recourse, as a last resort, to rebellion against tyranny and oppression, that human rights should be protected by the rule of law, and
- Whereas it is essential to promote the development of friendly relations between nations.
- Whereas the peoples of the United Nations have in the

Charter reaffirmed their faith in fundamental human rights, in the dignity and worth of the human person and in the equal rights of men and women and have determined to promote social progress and better standards of life in larger freedom,

- Whereas Member States have pledged themselves to achieve, in co-operation with the United Nations, the promotion of universal respect for and observance of human rights and fundamental freedoms,
- Whereas a common understanding of these rights and freedoms is of the greatest importance for the full realization of this pledge,

Now, Therefore the general assembly proclaims this universal declaration of human rights as a common standard of achievement for all peoples and all nations, to the end that every individual and every organ of society, keeping this Declaration constantly in mind, shall strive by teaching and education to promote respect for these rights and freedoms and by progressive measures, national and international, to secure their universal and effective recognition and observance, both among the peoples of Member States themselves and among the peoples of territories under their jurisdiction.

HUMAN RIGHTS SET OUT IN THE DECLARATION

The following reproduces the articles of the Declaration which set out the specific human rights that are recognized in the Declaration.

Article 1

All human beings are born free and equal in dignity and rights. They are endowed with reason and conscience and should act towards one another in a spirit of brotherhood.

Article 2

Everyone is entitled to all the rights and freedoms set forth in this Declaration, without distinction of any kind, such as race, colour, sex, language, religion, political or other opinion, national or social origin, property, birth or other status. Furthermore, no distinction shall be made on the basis of the political, jurisdictional or international status of the country or territory to which a person belongs, whether it be independent, trust, non-self-governing or under any other limitation of sovereignty.

Article 3

Everyone has the right to life, liberty and security of person.

Article 4

No one shall be held in slavery or servitude; slavery and the slave trade shall be prohibited in all their forms.

Article 5

No one shall be subjected to torture or to cruel, inhuman or degrading treatment or punishment.

Article 6

Everyone has the right to recognition everywhere as a person before the law.

Article 7

All are equal before the law and are entitled without any discrimination to equal protection of the law. All are entitled to equal protection against any discrimination in violation of this Declaration and against any incitement to such discrimination.

Article 8

Everyone has the right to an effective remedy by the competent national tribunals for acts violating the fundamental rights granted him by the constitution or by law.

Article 9

No one shall be subjected to arbitrary arrest, detention or exile.

Article 10

Everyone is entitled in full equality to a fair and public hearing by an independent and impartial tribunal, in the determination of his rights and obligations and of any criminal charge against him.

Article 11

1. Everyone charged with a penal offence has the right to be presumed innocent until proved guilty according to law in a public trial at which he has had all the guarantees necessary for his defence.
2. No one shall be held guilty of any penal offence on account of any act or omission which did not constitute a penal offence, under national or international law, at the time when it was committed. Nor shall a heavier penalty be imposed than the one that was applicable at the time the penal offence was committed.

Article 12

No one shall be subjected to arbitrary interference with his privacy, family, home or correspondence, nor to attacks upon his honour and reputation. Everyone has the right to the protection of the law against such interference or attacks.

Article 13

1. Everyone has the right to freedom of movement and residence within the borders of each state.
2. Everyone has the right to leave any country, including their own, and to return to their country.

Article 14

1. Everyone has the right to seek and to enjoy in other countries asylum from persecution.
2. This right may not be invoked in the case of prosecutions genuinely arising from non-political crimes or from acts contrary to the purposes and principles of the United Nations.

Article 15

1. Everyone has the right to a nationality.
2. No one shall be arbitrarily deprived of his nationality nor denied the right to change his nationality.

Article 16

1. Men and women of full age, without any limitation due to race, nationality or religion, have the right to marry and to found a family. They are entitled to equal rights as to marriage, during marriage and at its dissolution.
2. Marriage shall be entered into only with the free and full consent of the intending spouses.
3. The family is the natural and fundamental group unit of society and is entitled to protection by society and the State.

Article 17

1. Everyone has the right to own property alone as well as in association with others.
2. No one shall be arbitrarily deprived of his property.

Article 18

Everyone has the right to freedom of thought, conscience and religion; this right includes freedom to change his religion or belief, and freedom, either alone or in community with others and in public or private, to manifest his religion or belief in teaching, practice, worship and observance.

Article 19

Everyone has the right to freedom of opinion and expression; this right includes freedom to hold opinions without interference and to seek, receive and impart information and ideas through any media and regardless of frontiers.

Article 20

1. Everyone has the right to freedom of peaceful assembly and association.

2. No one may be compelled to belong to an association.

Article 21

1. Everyone has the right to take part in the government of their country, directly or through freely chosen representatives.
2. Everyone has the right of equal access to public service in their country.
3. The will of the people shall be the basis of the authority of government; this will shall be expressed in periodic and genuine elections which shall be by universal and equal suffrage and shall be held by secret vote or by equivalent free voting procedures.

Article 22

Everyone, as a member of society, has the right to social security and is entitled to realization, through national effort and international co-operation and in accordance with the organization and resources of each State, of the economic, social and cultural rights indispensable for his dignity and the free development of his personality.

Article 23

1. Everyone has the right to work, to free choice of employment, to just and favourable conditions of work and to protection against unemployment.
2. Everyone, without any discrimination, has the right to equal pay for equal work.
3. Everyone who works has the right to just and favourable remuneration ensuring for himself and his family an existence worthy of human dignity, and supplemented, if necessary, by other means of social protection.
4. Everyone has the right to form and to join trade unions for the protection of his interests.

Article 24

Everyone has the right to rest and leisure, including reasonable limitation of working hours and periodic holidays with pay.

Article 25

1. Everyone has the right to a standard of living adequate for the health and well-being of himself and of his family, including food, clothing, housing and medical care and necessary social services, and the right to security in the event of unemployment, sickness, disability, widowhood, old age or other lack of livelihood in circumstances beyond his control.
2. Motherhood and childhood are entitled to special care and assistance. All children, whether born in or out of wedlock, shall enjoy the same social protection.

Article 26

1. Everyone has the right to education. Education shall be free, at least in the elementary and fundamental stages. Elementary education shall be compulsory. Technical and professional education shall be made generally available and higher education shall be equally accessible to all on the basis of merit.
2. Education shall be directed to the full development of the human personality and to the strengthening of respect for human rights and fundamental freedoms. It shall promote understanding, tolerance and friendship among all nations, racial or religious groups, and shall further the activities of the United Nations for the maintenance of peace.
3. Parents have a prior right to choose the kind of education that shall be given to their children.

Article 27

1. Everyone has the right freely to participate in the cultural life of the community, to enjoy the arts and to share in scientific advancement and its benefits.
2. Everyone has the right to the protection of the moral and material interests resulting from any scientific, literary or artistic production of which he is the author.

Article 28

Everyone is entitled to a social and international order in

which the rights and freedoms set forth in this Declaration can be fully realized.

Article 29

1. Everyone has duties to the community in which alone the free and full development of his personality is possible.
2. In the exercise of his rights and freedoms, everyone shall be subject only to such limitations as are determined by law solely for the purpose of securing due recognition and respect for the rights and freedoms of others and of meeting the just requirements of morality, public order and the general welfare in a democratic society.
3. These rights and freedoms may in no case be exercised contrary to the purposes and principles of the United Nations.

Article 30

Nothing in this Declaration may be interpreted as implying for any State, group or person any right to engage in any activity or to perform any act aimed at the destruction of any of the rights and freedoms set forth herein.

INTERNATIONAL HUMAN RIGHTS DAY

The adoption of the Universal Declaration is a significant international commemoration marked each year on 10 December and is known as Human Rights Day or International Human Rights Day. The commemoration is observed by individuals, community and religious groups, human rights organisations, parliaments, governments and the United Nations. Decadal commemorations are often accompanied by campaigns to promote awareness of the Declaration and human rights. 2008 marks the 60th anniversary of the Declaration and is being accompanied by year long activities around the theme "Dignity and justice for all of us". Human Rights Day is celebrated annually across the world on 10 December.

The date was chosen to honour the United Nations General Assembly's adoption and proclamation, on 10 December 1948, of the Universal Declaration of Human Rights

(UDHR), the first global enunciation of human rights. The commemoration was established in 1950, when the General Assembly invited all states and interested organizations to celebrate the day as they saw fit. The day is a high point in the calendar of UN headquarters in New York City, United States, and is normally marked by both high-level political conferences and meetings and by cultural events and exhibitions dealing with human rights issues. In addition, it is traditionally on 10 December that the five-yearly United Nations Prize in the Field of Human Rights and Nobel Peace Prize are awarded.

Many governmental and nongovernmental organizations active in the human rights field also schedule special events to commemorate the day, as do many civil and social-cause organisations. The theme for 2006 was the struggle against poverty, taking it as a human rights issue. Several statements were released on that occasion, including the one issued by 37 United Nations Special Procedures mandate holders.

"Today, poverty prevails as the gravest human rights challenge in the world. Combating poverty, deprivation and exclusion is not a matter of charity, and it does not depend on how rich a country is. By tackling poverty as a matter of human rights obligation, the world will have a better chance of abolishing this scourge in our lifetime....Poverty eradication is an achievable goal." —UN High Commissioner for Human Rights Louise Arbour, 10 December 2006.

The 60th anniversary of the Universal Declaration of Human Rights occurs on December 10, 2008, and the UN Secretary-General has launched a year-long campaign to lead up to this anniversary. Because the UDHR holds the world record as the most translated document (with more than 360 language versions available), organizations around the globe will be able to use the year to focus on helping people everywhere learn about their rights.

SIGNIFICANCE AND LEGAL EFFECT

Significance

In the preamble, governments commit themselves and their

peoples to progressive measures to secure the universal and effective recognition and observance of the human rights set out in the Declaration. Eleanor Roosevelt supported the adoption the UDHR as a declaration, rather than as a treaty, because she believed that it would have the same kind of influence on global society as the United States Declaration of Independence had within the United States. In this she proved to be correct. Even though not formally legally binding, the Declaration has been adopted in or influenced most national constitutions since 1948. It also serves as the foundation for a growing number of international treaties and national laws and international, regional, national and sub-national institutions protecting and promoting human rights.

Legal Effect

While not a treaty itself, the Declaration was explicitly adopted for the purpose of defining the meaning of the words "fundamental freedoms" and "human rights" appearing in the United Nations Charter, which is binding on all member states. For this reason, the Universal Declaration is a fundamental constitutive document of the United Nations. Many international lawyers, in addition, believe that the Declaration forms part of customary international law and is a powerful tool in applying diplomatic and moral pressure to governments that violate any of its articles. The 1968 United Nations International Conference on Human Rights advised that it "constitutes an obligation for the members of the international community" to all persons.

The declaration has served as the foundation for two binding UN human rights covenants, the International Covenant on Civil and Political Rights and the International Covenant on Economic, Social and Cultural Rights and the principles of the Declaration are elaborated in international treaties such as the International Convention on the Elimination of All Forms of Racial Discrimination, the International Convention on the Elimination of Discrimination Against Women, the United Nations Convention on the Rights of the Child, the United Nations Convention Against Torture and many more. The

Declaration continues to be widely cited by governments, academics, advocates and constitutional courts and individual human beings who appeal to its principles for the protection of their recognised human rights.

REACTION

Praise

The Universal Declaration has received praise from a number of notable people. Charles Malik, Lebanese philosopher and diplomat, called it "an international document of the first order of importance," while Eleanor Roosevelt, first chairwoman of the Commission on Human Rights (CHR) that drafted the Declaration, stated that it "may well become the international Magna Carta of all men everywhere." 10 December 1948. In a speech on 5 October 1995, Pope John Paul II called the UDHR "one of the highest expressions of the human conscience of our time". And in a statement on 10 December 2003 on behalf of the European Union, Marcello Spatafora said that "it placed human rights at the centre of the framework of principles and obligations shaping relations within the international community."

Censorship

The Cuban regime has ordered copies of the Universal Declaration of Human Rights to be burned or otherwise destroyed. In one instance, an entire shipment of books - which included children's literature and medical textbooks - was destroyed because State Security found that it contained 8,000 copies of the declaration.

CRITICISM

Islamic Criticism

Predominantly Islamic countries such as Sudan, Pakistan, Iran, and Saudi Arabia have criticized the Universal Declaration of Human Rights for its perceived failure to take into the account the cultural and religious context of Islamic countries. In 1982, the Iranian representative to the United Nations, Said Rajaie-

Khorassani, articulated the position of his country regarding the Universal Declaration of Human Rights, by saying that the UDHR was "a secular understanding of the Judeo-Christian tradition", which could not be implemented by Muslims without trespassing the Islamic law.

On 30 June 2000, Muslim nations that are members of the Organization of the Islamic Conference officially resolved to support the Cairo Declaration on Human Rights in Islam, an alternative document that says people have "freedom and right to a dignified life in accordance with the Islamic Shari'ah".

Property Rights Criticism

Libertarians and some conservatives believe the positive rights that must be provided by others through forceful extraction (for example taxation) negate other peoples' inalienable rights.

Education

Some proponents of alternative education, particularly unschooling, take issue with the right to compulsory education stated in Article 26. In the philosophies of John Holt and others, compulsory education itself violates the right of a person to follow their own interests:

No human right, except the right to life itself, is more fundamental than this. A person's freedom of learning is part of his freedom of thought, even more basic than his freedom of speech. If we take from someone his right to decide what he will be curious about, we destroy his freedom of thought. We say, in effect, you must think not about what interests you and concerns you, but about what interests and concerns us. – *John Holt, Escape from Childhood.*

THE RIGHT TO REFUSE TO KILL

Groups such as Amnesty International and War Resisters International have advocated for "The Right to Refuse to Kill" to be added to the UDHR. War Resisters International has stated that the right to conscientious objection to military service is primarily derived from, but not yet explicit in, Article 18 of the UDHR: the right to freedom of thought, conscience and religion. Steps have been taken within the UN to make this right more explicit; but those steps have been limited to secondary, more "marginal" UN documents. That is why Amnesty International would like to have this right brought "out of the margins" and explicitly into the primary document, namely the UDHR itself.

To the rights enshrined in the Universal Declaration of Human Rights one more might, with relevance, be added. It is "The Right to Refuse to Kill." - Assistant Secretary General of the United Nations, and Nobel Peace Laureate, Sean MacBride, 1974 Nobel Lecture.

BANGKOK DECLARATION

In the Bangkok Declaration adopted by Ministers of Asian states meeting in 1993 in the lead up to the World Conference on Human Rights, Asian governments reaffirmed their commitment to the principles of the United Nations Charter and the Universal Declaration of Human Rights. They stated their view of the interdependence and indivisibility of human rights and stressed the need for universality, objectivity and non-selectivity of human rights.

3

Promotion of Human Rights

The promotion of human rights is charitable by analogy principally with charitable purposes concerned with moral or spiritual welfare and improvement. There are many ways in which a charity might seek to promote human rights, including:

- Monitoring abuses of human rights;
- Otaining redress for the victims of human rights abuse;
- Relieving need among the victims of human rights abuse;
- Research into human rights issues;
- Educating the public about human rights;
- Providing technical advice to government and others on human rights matters;
- Contributing to the sound administration of human rights law;
- Commenting on proposed human rights legislation;
- Raising awareness of human rights issues;
- Promoting public support for human rights;
- Promoting respect for human rights by individuals and corporations;
- International advocacy of human rights;
- Eliminating infringements of human rights.

The purposes of a charity must be clear, unambiguous and exclusively charitable. An organisation seeking to establish itself as a charity to promote human rights must therefore identify the code or codes of human rights which it is seeking to promote. If it will operate only in one country or region, it must identify that country or region. We recommend that it should also specify in its stated purposes the ways in which it will promote human rights.

At the end of this publication we give an example of how a human rights charity with very wide purposes might draw up its object. The promotion of human rights will often involve engagement with the political process and a human rights charity is able to engage in a very wide range of political activity within the parameters which are described in this guidance. Organisations set up for political purposes (or partly for political purposes) cannot be charities and we examine the extent to which this legal principle affects the scope for promoting human rights as a charitable purpose.

AS A CHARITABLE PURPOSE

For a purpose to be recognised as charitable, it must be shown that the purpose is (1) analogous to a purpose which has already been accepted as charitable and (2) beneficial to the community. The purpose must also be sufficiently clear for the Court (and the Commission) to be able to control and give effect to it.

AN EXISTING CHARITABLE PURPOSE

The Commissioners have decided that, when asked to draw an analogy with existing charitable purposes, they should take a constructive and imaginative approach, adapting the concept of charity to meet constantly evolving social needs.

Depending upon the means by which human rights are promoted, there are many existing charitable purposes which might be regarded as appropriate analogies. Given that respect for human rights is widely regarded as a moral imperative, the well-established charitable purpose of promoting the moral or spiritual welfare and improvement of the community provides a sufficient (but not the only) analogy for treating the promotion of human rights generally as charitable.

It is by analogy with moral improvement that we have registered as charities bodies which are concerned

- To promote good race relations, to eliminate discrimination on grounds of race and to encourage equality of opportunity between persons of different racial groups;
- To promote equal rights for women and for homosexuals;
- To promote ethical standards of conduct and compliance with the law in the workplace;
- To promote religious harmony; and
- To promote equality and diversity.

BENEFIT TO THE COMMUNITY

Human rights are rights which:

- Are fundamental in the sense of being essential to our humanity or to our functioning as human beings;
- Accordingly have a moral dimension;
- Extend to everyone; and
- Prescribe what the State must do for us, and what it must not do (or allow others to do) to us.

The concept of human rights is virtually unanimously endorsed by the countries of the world (even if strict observance of these rights is intermittent). The United Nations Convention on the Rights of the Child, for example, has been ratified by 191 countries (only two countries have failed to do so). The United Kingdom government has incorporated the European Convention for the Protection of Human Rights and Fundamental Freedoms into domestic law.

There is an obvious public benefit in promoting human rights. For individuals whose human rights are thereby secured, the benefit is immediate and tangible. There is also a less tangible, but nonetheless significant, benefit to the whole community that arises from our perception that the fundamental rights of all members of the community are being protected. That provides sufficient benefit to the community to justify treating the promotion of human rights as a charitable purpose in its own right.

CLARITY OF PURPOSE

There are several different codes of human rights. The most widely accepted are the Universal Declaration of Human Rights and subsequent United Nations human rights conventions and declarations. Outside the auspices of the UN, there are other international and regional codes, as well as codes which have been established by individuals and NGOs. In order to achieve the degree of certainty in the expression of its objects that is necessary for charitable status, individuals creating charities for the promotion of human rights need to specify the body of rights that they seek to promote. In practice, given the primacy of the Universal Declaration, that is likely to involve reference to the Declaration and subsequent UN-sponsored standards.

The purposes of a charity must be exclusively charitable. Hence an organisation established for purposes some of which are charitable and some of which are non-charitable cannot be a charity. The promotion of human rights is a broad concept which can include non-charitable purposes (especially, of course, political purposes). We therefore recommend that a human rights organisation seeking to establish itself as a charity should set out its purpose in its governing document as precisely as possible. If the organisation's purpose is very wide, we recommend that it should set out the ways in which it will promote human rights.

The following paragraphs describe some of the ways (there may well be others) in which a charity might promote human rights. Each of these ways of promoting human rights is, of course, also capable of being a charitable purpose in its own right. At the end of this guidance we provide an example of a very widely-drawn object for a human rights charity.

WAYS OF PROMOTING HUMAN RIGHTS

PROMOTING HUMAN RIGHTS AT HOME AND ABROAD

Generally, for an organisation set up to operate abroad to be a charity under the law of England and Wales, it must be the case that the objects of the organisation would be charitable according to English law if its purposes were to be carried out in England and Wales. The following list of various ways in which a charity might promote human rights is not exhaustive.

MONITORING ABUSES OF HUMAN RIGHTS

A charity concerned with promoting human rights may engage in monitoring and reporting breaches of a country's human rights obligations, whether those obligations arise under domestic legislation or international standards.

OBTAINING REDRESS FOR VICTIMS OF HUMAN RIGHTS ABUSE

A human rights charity may bring pressure to bear in individual cases (including through the mobilisation of public opinion) to encourage a government to respect its own human rights legislation. A charity may provide support for attempts to obtain redress through the courts of the country concerned, whether by way of specialist legal advice and representation or by less direct means. The availability of that option will, of course, depend upon whether or not the country's legal code enables the victims of human rights abuse to obtain redress.

Even if the legal code of the country in which the abuse takes place does not expressly provide redress, it may still be possible to attempt to obtain compensation or a public inquiry or an acknowledgement of responsibility. A human rights charity may also support the investigation and prosecution before international tribunals of individuals and organisations accused of human rights abuse.

RELIEVING NEED AMONG THE VICTIMS

It is charitable to relieve needy 'prisoners of conscience' or their dependants. Assistance can include financial, educational and rehabilitation help. We have registered as charities bodies concerned with relieving the suffering and distress of individuals who have suffered human rights abuses. We have also accepted that it is charitable to provide financial assistance to victims of torture who are in financial need to enable them to obtain compensation or redress.

RESEARCH INTO HUMAN RIGHTS ISSUES

Human rights are an appropriate subject for research. The Court has held that promoting and commissioning research into the maintenance and observation of human rights is a subject of study which is capable of adding usefully to the store of human knowledge.

EDUCATING THE PUBLIC ABOUT HUMAN RIGHTS

Human rights are an established subject of study in schools and colleges. A human rights charity may advance education in human rights through support for such studies or through less formal types of education.

TECHNICAL ADVICE TO GOVERNMENTS AND OTHERS ON HUMAN RIGHTS MATTERS

A human rights charity may provide technical advice to governments, NGOs and other relevant bodies on the creation, improvement and implementation of legal, regulatory and administrative systems for the not-for-profit sector in countries abroad. A charity with appropriately-worded objects may also provide technical advice to governments and to domestic and foreign public authorities on the adoption and implementation of human rights legislation, including training for administrators in the application of that legislation.

CONTRIBUTING TO THE SOUND ADMINISTRATION OF HUMAN RIGHTS LAW

A wide range of activities revolves around contributing to the sound administration of human rights law. This includes providing the essential material for the study of a country's human rights law (such as reports of judicial decisions). It also includes acquiring and passing on knowledge about what the law is at any given time, how it is developing and how it is being administered and applied.

COMMENTING ON PROPOSED HUMAN RIGHTS LEGISLATION

A charity for the promotion of human rights may participate in government consultations about changes in the law. It may also recommend improvements in human rights law and provide objective comment on the adequacy of legislation to implement human rights (whether or not it is invited by government to do so).

RAISING AWARENESS OF HUMAN RIGHTS ISSUES

A charity may raise awareness of human rights issues by facilitating debate and discussion. However, a charity established to promote human rights does not need to limit itself to balanced, educational activities. It can promote awareness of human rights issues by distributing material which does not present both sides of the argument but simply promotes its own point of view.

PROMOTING POPULAR SUPPORT FOR HUMAN RIGHTS

Cultivation of particular opinions or sentiments among the public is charitable where the reason for doing so is to promote mental or moral improvement. It is on this basis that we have accepted as charitable "the promotion of ethical standards of conduct". And on this basis promoting popular support for human rights is charitable. In the last century, in the United States, the promotion of a "public sentiment that will put an end to Negro slavery" was held to be charitable.

The Court took the view that the bequest would not have been charitable had it been directed towards political agitation and attempts to alter the law. In fact, however, the method specified in the gift was to apply pressure not to government, but to private individuals with a view to obtaining voluntary manumission. That purpose was charitable by analogy with a line of cases that showed that the peaceable redemption or manumission of slaves in any manner not prohibited by law was charitable. In this country, the Court has accepted that the exercise of moral influence and the cultivation of public sentiment in ways which do not involve seeking to change the law or government policy change can be legitimate means of pursuing recognised charitable objects.

PROMOTING RESPECT FOR HUMAN RIGHTS BY INDIVIDUALS AND CORPORATIONS

Although human rights are defined primarily by reference to the appropriate treatment of individuals by the State, the concept of human rights also has implications for the way that individuals treat each other. Discrimination on grounds of race or religion, for example, may be combated by legislation or by trying to influence the way in which individuals treat each other. There seems to be no reason therefore why an organisation set up to promote human rights should not encourage individuals to respect each other's human rights. The absence of effective human rights legislation in a country can be exploited by individuals and corporations for their own economic advantage. It is open to a human rights charity to address this issue and to challenge such exploitation, for example by campaigning.

INTERNATIONAL ADVOCACY OF HUMAN RIGHTS

Promoting human rights includes advocating adoption of, and compliance with, international and regional codes of human rights, the incorporation of human rights into domestic law is a legitimate objective of a charity promoting human rights. Advocacy of this kind is conducted primarily in international fora and depends on well-researched material for its effectiveness. It extends also to contributing to international and State-sponsored conferences and seminars concerned with the adoption and implementation of human rights. A political campaign to press the government of a particular country to adopt particular human rights legislation (or particular policies) would be open to a charity provided that it fell within the principles discussed in paragraphs below.

ELIMINATING INFRINGEMENTS OF HUMAN RIGHTS

A charity may seek to eliminate infringements of human rights. Some of the means that may be available for doing so have been mentioned in this guidance, such as monitoring and raising awareness of abuse, obtaining redress, and promoting respect for human rights among individuals and corporations. We have accepted that it is charitable "to procure the abolition of torture by all lawful means" and to procure the abolition of torture, extra-judicial killing and 'disappearance'. We have also registered as charities organisations concerned with the elimination of slavery, the slave trade and other forms of unlawful forced labour.

Infringements of human rights of this kind are, almost by definition, contrary to the domestic law of the country in which they take place (particularly when considered in the context of its international treaty obligations) and hence trying to eliminate them will not generally involve trying to change domestic law. However, even where a country's domestic law is inconsistent with international standards, a charity may campaign for legislation or changes in government policy provided that it does so within the principles discussed below.

POLITICAL ACTIVITIES

Charities are able to engage in political campaigning in order to further their charitable purposes. Charity law draws a distinction between political purposes and political activities. An organisation which has purposes which include the promotion of human rights by seeking a change in the law or a shift in government policy, or a reversal of a government decision has (at least in part) political purposes and cannot be a charity. However, the trustees of a charity may nonetheless use political means without jeopardising charitable status. What is important for charitable status is that political means should not be the dominant method by which the organisation will pursue its apparently charitable objects.

Charities are able to engage in political activities in furtherance of their charitable purposes, provided that:

- There is a reasonable expectation that the proposed activities will further the purposes of the charity to an extent justified by the resources committed; and
- The activities will not be allowed to dominate the activities which the charity carries out in order to further its objects directly.

The charity trustees must also have assessed any reputation and other risks and they must comply with the general law and any other regulatory requirements. The form of object which is given by way of example at the end of this guidance contains a power to engage in political activity. Although it is not strictly necessary for a charity to have an express power of this kind, our example usefully reminds trustees of the constraints on political activity by a charity. The principles discussed above have general application. Their effect is that a charity for the relief of poverty abroad, for example, may campaign in favour of the adoption of human rights in a particular country if it can show that the adoption of those rights would tend to relieve poverty in that country.

Inevitably, a charity concerned with promoting human rights will have considerable scope for engaging in ancillary, incidental political activities. Where a charity is concerned with relieving the victims of human rights abuse, for example, in the course of doing so it may well identify measures which might be taken by the government in question (or by other governments) to prevent that abuse. It may properly undertake ancillary political activity to that end. Provided that it's political activities are not the dominant means by which it carries out its charitable objects, a human rights charity may engage in political activity which is unrelated to its other activities.

EXAMPLE: OBJECT FOR A HUMAN RIGHTS CHARITY

"To promote human rights (as set out in the Universal Declaration of Human Rights and subsequent United Nations conventions and declarations) throughout the world by all or any of the following means:

- Monitoring abuses of human rights;
- Obtaining redress for the victims of human rights abuse;
- Relieving need among the victims of human rights abuse;
- Research into human rights issues;
- Educating the public about human rights;
- Providing technical advice to government and others on human rights matters;
- Contributing to the sound administration of human rights law;
- Commenting on proposed human rights legislation;
- Raising awareness of human rights issues;
- Promoting public support for human rights;
- Promoting respect for human rights among individuals and corporations;
- International advocacy of human rights;
- Eliminating infringements of human rights.

In furtherance of that object but not otherwise, the trustees shall have power:

- To engage in political activity provided that the trustees are satisfied that the proposed activities will further the purposes of the charity to an extent justified by the resources committed and the activity is not the dominant means by which the charity carries out its objects...".

Promotion of Human Rights Issues of Mentally ill Persons With experience gained in 14 mental health pilot projects Gujarat State, Vardaan Foundation with the support of Government of Gujarat and Ministry of Health and Family Welfare Government of India, organized a two day National level workshop on "Developing Guidelines for Promotion of Human Rights Issues of Mentally ill Person". The workshop was attended by participants from all over India and included subject experts, psychiatrists, clinical psychologists, activists, NGOs, policy makers, lawyers, judges, government representatives, academicians, and SHG members consisting of patients and family members. A total of 55 participants attended the workshop.

The workshop discussed the issues and challenges related to human rights violations at institutional level (for both treatment and rehabilitation); programme level (in the community for identification and prevention); at family level (for basic, essential, civil, and political right) at work place; reforms in legal procedure and existing Acts, and the role of media to minimize the human right violation. Eminent experts and former Consultants of Mental Health in Ministry of Health and Family Welfare, New Delhi, Emeritus Professor Shridhar Sharma (IHBAS, New Delhi); Professor, S.C. Malik (LHMC); Professor of Emeritus S.M. Channabasavanna (Former Director and Vice Chancellor, NIMHANS, Bangalore); Shri S.K.Verma (Former Director, B.M. Institute of Mental Health, Ahmedabad and Managing Trustee, Vardaan Foundation, Vadodara); and Professor Nimesh G. Desai (Head and Medical Superintendent, IHBAS, New Delhi) gave their viewpoints for making guidelines on identified themes.

Representative of Government Dr. S.K. Sinha (GOI); Dr. R. H. Bakre and Mr. I.B. Chaudary (GOG) also took active part in discussion. Beside NGO representatives Dr. Harshit Sinha (Vardaan Foundation, Vadodara); Dr. Bakul Buch (Ashadeep, Junagadh), Bipin Maliya (Atma Vishwas, Valsad) and Mr. Avinash Bhatija (Samarpan, Indore) gave their views on human rights in running rehabilitation programmes. Activist Mr. Nilesh Singit, and high court lawyer Mr. Bhushan Oza; Mrs. Laila Ollapally (legal consultant, Bangalore), and Shri R.H. Sharma (District and Session Judge, Vadodara) shared viewpoints relating to reforms in legal procedure and amendments to be made in the Mental Health Act and other laws.

The chief guest at valedictory function, Dr. Amarjit Singh (Commissioner of Health, GOG) shared his concern for the subject matter and described the state government strategy of allocating resources Rs. 6.00 crore to the mental health activities for the first time in the state budget and promised continuing support to all fourteen pilot projects. The major strategies identified by the group were related to the definition of human rights (HR) violation/abuse need to be evolved, framework for understanding HR concern in different settings requires to be developed and all type of HR violence/abuse need to be identified and listed for active monitoring by the agencies in the community.

All the sectors, including the organized and unorganized (Public- Private) sectors, of mental health services requires to be monitored for HR violations. Gender perspective and concerns have to be built into all possible strategies so that the situation of homeless persons, specifically women, about HR violations and corrective measures can be attended. Promotion of HR issues by different methods - users who have already benefited from their experience should encourage and motivate the self help groups and parent groups. Besides, awareness about the rights of the mentally ill persons requires being enhanced - in general public, media personnel, law enforcement personnel, and caregivers.

It also becomes essential for demystification of mental illness to be followed actively with involvement of media, and public education strategies. The guidelines should also emphasize media advocacy for the promotion of human rights of mentally ill persons. The group unanimously decided to make treatment a positive right with the full spectrum of care as the right of mentally ill patients Taking account of the legal reforms, amendment to the Mental Health Act (1987) should provide for contemporary needs and human rights concerns, with active involvement of all the stakeholders, specifically users. It was also recommended to utilize all possible opportunities in the policy and judicial review procedures (including the PILs), for active advocacy HR concerns.

Overall it was recommended that HR concerns should get central position in all mental health policy and programs. Important recommendations of the workshop are as follows:

- Major strategies identified - Active monitoring for prevention of violation of human rights, monitoring for negation of rights, and intervention for all possible discrimination on ground of mental illness, active promotion of human rights.
- The definition of HR violations/abuse needs to be

evolved. Not all experiences of negative nature are seen and construed as HR violations.

- The framework for understanding HR concerns in different settings needs to be developed.
- All types of HR violations/abuse need to be recognized. These occur in different ways, and active monitoring agencies are vital in the community.
- All the sectors, including the unorganized sector, of mental health services require to be monitored for HR violations.
- The situation of homeless persons, specifically women, about HR violations and corrective measures needs to be attended.
- Gender perspective has to be built into all possible strategies.
- Promotion of HR issues by different methods- those who have already benefited from their experiences should be encouraged to share their experiences.
- Encourage and motivate user groups, self help groups and parent groups about the rights of mentally ill persons so that it is enhanced- in the general public, media personnel, law enforcement personnel, caregivers.
- Demystification of mental illness needs to be done with the active involvement of media, and public education strategies.
- Media advocacy for promotion of human rights of mentally ill persons needs to be put into place.
- Development of mental health services needs to be actively followed in all aspects- reform mental health institutions, and offer more community outreach programs.
- Make treatment a positive right- with the full spectrum of care (treatment and rehabilitation) being a right.
- Amend the Mental Health Act, 1987- to provide for contemporary needs and human rights concerns, with active involvement of all stake holders, specifically users.
- Utilize all possible opportunities in policy and judicial review situations (including PILs), for active advocacy of HR concerns and all the above issues.

- HR concerns should get central position in all considerations of mental health policy and programs.
- Good practices examples/case studies examples (including some of the pilot projects of the Government of Gujarat & available from other places (like Delhi, Indore, Baroda, Bangalore etc) should be documented and their recommendations should be implemented.

The promotion of human rights and democracy has become an extremely well integrated element of EU external relations policy, with multiple references to it at various institutional levels. The Treaties of Maastricht, Amsterdam and Nice, agreed and signed at bi-annual European Council summit meetings, have successively built on each other. Most recently, the Nice Treaty (signed in December 2000, and remaining subject to ratification) extends the objective of promoting human rights and fundamental freedoms from development co-operation to all forms of co-operation with third countries (Article 181bis TEC), thus covering trade and association agreements. Additionally, the EU Charter of Fundamental Rights, also officially proclaimed at the Nice European Council summit in December 2000, aims at promoting coherence between internal and external policy. The Council of Ministers and European Commission have been similarly active in this area.

The Council of Ministers' landmark Resolution of November 1991, at which the promotion of human rights and democracy was made both an objective and condition of development co-operation, has been progressively followed-up over the past decade by the introduction of human rights and democracy elements into the Council Regulations that govern the array of regional co-operation agreements that the EU retains, for example with Asia and Latin America. The new Cotonou Agreement with the now 77 ACP (African, Caribbean and Pacific) countries, the successor to the Lomé Convention, includes 'good governance' as a 'fundamental and positive element', in addition to respect for human rights, democratic principles and the rule of law as essential elements of the Agreement (Art. 9).

The latter essential elements were established in Lomé

IV (revised), but the inclusion of good governance in the Cotonou agreement was one of the most controversial aspects of the negotiations between the ACP states and the EU. The ACP objected to good governance as an 'essential element', subject to a non-execution or suspension clause. The resultant compromise of good governance as a 'fundamental and positive element' entails linguistic contortions, with good governance becoming the subject of regular dialogue and an area for positive support, but not subject to a non-execution clause, except in "serious cases of corruption" where significant funds provided by the Community are involved (Art. 97).

A 'Joint Statement on EC Development Policy' by the Council of Ministers and the European Commission in November 2000 incorporated the promotion of human rights, democracy, the rule of law and good governance as an integral part of development co-operation, signalling an intent to concentrate resources on this sector. It was subsequently declared that this policy statement represents a "new framework for the European Commission's activities in support of human rights and democratisation". Numerous European Commission communications on development co-operation, both of a general nature and region or country specific, have incorporated discussion of the political dimension.

For instance, Commission proposals for reviews of regional development co-operation agreements invariably involve an upgrading of the human rights and democracy dimension, as is evident in the case of both Latin America and Mediterranean countries, with a Communication on relations with Asia forthcoming in late 2001. A significant element of policy implementation has been the inclusion since 1992 of human rights and democracy clauses as essential elements in agreements with 'third countries' standardised from May 1995. Such clauses are essentially a conditionality mechanism, enabling suspension of agreement in the event of perceived violations of human rights and democratic principles.

The EU annual report on human rights for 2000, the second such report published by the Council, congratulates itself for the insertion of such clauses in agreements with "more than

120 countries", though 77 of these are covered by the Lomé (now Cotonou) Convention. The annual report does not mention, however, that a human rights and democracy clause remains outstanding in the agreement with ASEAN (the Association of Southeast Asian Nations), nor the manipulation involved by the Council and Commission in avoiding a new agreement that would require the approval of the European Parliament, with ratification unlikely precisely due to the lack of such a clause. The forthcoming Communication on relations with Asia will be interesting in this respect.

At the general level, a new policy document was released in May 2001 on 'The European Union's Role in Promoting Human rights and Democratisation in Third Countries' (European Commission 2001). Focusing on the role of Commission-managed external assistance programmes in this field, the document emphasises the current prioritisation of human rights and democracy strategies and aims "to ensure that these issues permeate all Community policies, programmes and projects". It identifies three areas for greater effectiveness of activity:

- Promoting coherent and consistent policies both within European Community activities, and between those and other EU actions, especially the CFSP, as well as Member State activities;
- Placing a higher priority on human rights and democratisation in relations with third countries and taking a more pro-active approach , using opportunities offered by political dialogue, trade and external assistance;
- Developing a more strategic approach to the European Initiative on Democracy and Human Rights.

Moreover, in this document, the Commission explicitly states that it "wants to be judged on its performance in meeting the EU's policy goals" in the area of human rights and democracy promotion. This chapter aims to contribute to such an assessment through combining a critical examination of recent evaluation reports, inclusive of their shortcomings, along with discussion of an appropriate evaluation methodology by which to judge the EU's performance in this field.

EVALUATION STUDIES OF EU DEMOCRACY AND HUMAN RIGHTS PROMOTION

As outlined, the EU is high on rhetoric with regard to democracy promotion, but what are its achievements in practice? How can we judge its performance? Of course, the traditional way in which aid performance is judged is through evaluation. To date, four evaluation studies have been conducted on European Commission assistance to democracy and human rights, each evaluation restricted to a particular budget line(s) or regional programme. An initial report on positive measures to support human rights and democracy in developing countries was undertaken by the German Development Institute and published in 1995, followed by three studies concentrating on different regions. An evaluation of the PHARE and TACIS Democracy Programmes in Central and Eastern Europe was undertaken by ISA Consult and the European Institute, University of Sussex (European Commission 1997).

An evaluation of the MEDA Democracy Programme (MDP) from 1996 to1998 was undertaken for the European Commission by Nadim Karkutli and Dirk Bützler and most recently, an evaluation of 'positive actions in the field of human rights and democracy' (1995-99) in the African, Caribbean and Pacific (ACP) nations was undertaken by Franklin Advisory Services. The latter three regional evaluations are examined here, undertaking a comparative analysis that focuses on evaluation objectives, methodological approaches, and findings. Additionally, the shortcomings and limitations of the studies are identified.

The three evaluation studies are characterised by difference. There is no consistency or uniformity in the evaluation approach, objectives or methodologies, in line with the general fragmentation and incoherence of Commission activities in this field. The PTDP study is the most ambitious of the three. Its objective is an ex-post impact evaluation, investigating the contribution of the PTDP to democratisation processes in nine selected countries (out of 26), i.e. an impact evaluation at the macro, national level.

Objectives of the MDP study are two-fold: an analysis of the general intervention strategy at country level, and an evaluation of 34 (out of 124) selected projects in six (out of 12) countries. It is described as "an objective ex-post examination" of the strategy used and of the impact of projects. Thus, impact evaluation is at the micro level of selected projects only. The ACP evaluation is different again. Its stated objectives are to evaluate the adequacy and coherence of the EC's policy 'instruments', and the relevance, effectiveness, efficiency, impact and sustainability of its 'positive actions'.

Like the MDP study, impact is investigated at the micro level only, examining projects in seven selected country cases (out of the 77 ACP countries), namely Senegal, Rwanda, Nigeria, Malawi, Haiti, Ethiopia and the Great Lakes region (Congo-Tanzania). Additionally, this study entailed a thematic focus on conflict prevention and electoral assistance. One interesting element of commonality, however, is that all three evaluation studies themselves added a further objective: an assessment of programme management by the Commission.

Methodological approaches likewise vary, partly reflecting the differing objectives, though with some similarities, particularly between the MDP and ACP studies. The PTDP study adopts a two-stage approach to macro-level impact evaluation. The first stage involves a democracy assessment of the strengths and weaknesses of the nine countries, using a methodology developed previously by Kaldor and Vejvoda. The second stage entails an examination of projects and programmes to assess their contribution to democratisation in each country that is, investigating to what extent they have contributed to the strengths and addressed the weaknesses. Eight evaluation criteria were invoked, fairly traditional in character: relevance, consistency, adequacy of procedures, cost-effectiveness, and impact (both intended and unintended), sustainability, replicability, visibility.

A combination of quantitative and qualitative methods was used, with statistical analysis complemented by qualitative background studies (stage one above) and fieldwork interviews and roundtable discussions. The methodology of the MDP study was divided into two aspects, corresponding to the two distinct objectives. First, background studies of the six country cases were completed and priority issues of democratisation ascertained for each country, pertinent to the evaluation of the intervention strategy. Second, as required by the terms of reference, project evaluation was based on the logical framework approach (LFA), with each project's logframe used to assess the relevance, efficiency, effectiveness, impact and sustainability at project level.

Fieldwork methods included questionnaires, interviews and roundtable discussions. Interestingly, reservations were expressed as to the appropriateness of the logical framework approach. It was emphasised that such political programmes have "many 'soft' components with regard to project results, objectives and impact... very difficult to measure in terms of the logical framework". Notwithstanding the terms of reference, the study intriguingly cites support from the Commission itself, quoting the statement that "human rights projects are quite different from infrastructure construction programmes, and the evaluation and selection criteria should therefore be based on a different approach". It would appear; however, that little progress has been made in developing such an approach.

In contrast, the ACP study enthusiastically adopted the logical framework "as the cornerstone of its methodology", describing it as "the most widely accepted planning tool" and a "useful quality assessment tool". Although the authors clearly state that "the evaluation formulated its analysis...in logical framework categories", the precise way in which this methodology was employed is neither well explained nor appears unproblematic, with log frames having to be reconstructed at both project and programme levels. At project level, it is stated that the logframe "often has to be reconstructed *a posteriori* from the project documentation", presumably due to absence or inadequacy.

A programme logframe was also constructed in order to evaluate the positive measures as a single project, thus enabling general conclusions to be made without relying on an aggregation of "variable individual project results". Somewhat bewilderingly, two programme logframes were then drawn up. One is described as the 'de facto' or 'restored' framework, based on existing Regulations and other Commission documents. While the other is labelled as the 'optimal' or 'recommended' framework, "as defined by the evaluation findings". What is clear is the authors' commitment to a logframe-based evaluation study.

What remains unclear is not only how this methodology was operationalised, but also its appropriacy in this context, which remains unquestioned. Additionally, the role played by the country case studies in the report and what research methods were used are not clearly elucidated. One aspect common to all three studies is the relative lack of participatory methods. Participation by stakeholders and beneficiaries of assistance is not completely absent, but limited and instrumental, used more as a means of gathering information, than valued as a essential and dynamic feature of evaluation in itself. The PTDP and MDP studies both use roundtables in the country studies as a method by which to ascertain opinions, while the ACP report uses stakeholder interviews for general validation purposes.

FINDINGS

The findings of the PTDP and the MDP studies are generally positive, while the ACP evaluation is more mixed in its overall findings. The most critical comments in each report are reserved for management and procedural issues.

PTDP

The overall finding is that "the PTDP has been of considerable value for the development of democracy and civil society in Central and Eastern Europe". The most significant impact is judged as its contribution to the growth of a lively NGO sector in all nine countries examined, regarded in turn as crucial to the democratisation process. It is noted that it is difficult to distinguish the impact of the PTDP from other Western democracy assistance, and that democracy assistance itself is a "comparatively minor instrument in assisting the process of democratisation". Nevertheless, it is held that such assistance has been important financially, psychologically and politically to non-governmental groups. It is believed that foreign funds have helped create "a moral community" essential to the construction of a democratic political culture.

Findings on management of the programme were more mixed, noting delays in financial disbursements and the potential adverse effect on impact. Programme management up to the selection of projects is deemed relatively satisfactory, contracted out to the European Human Rights Foundation, but subsequent procedures for issuing contracts and making payments, in the hands of the Commission, are severely criticised for serious delays, undermining projects and damaging the reputation of the programme. One interesting recommendation pertains to the formalising of a participatory dimension to programme planning.

It is noted that NGOs in recipient countries have helped shape priorities informally, sometimes through their Western partners, alerting the EU to new issues. It is recommended that discussion of priorities for democratisation in each country should be formalised through regular round tables, like those organised for the study, involving recipients, EU delegations and outside experts. If implemented, two outstanding issues would concern the relative weight of internal and external personnel and the question of who participates from the recipient side.

MDP

The finding concerning the intervention strategy was basically that there wasn't one: "there has been no official formulation of a particular strategy". In other words, project selection had been reactive and application-led, thus relatively *ad hoc*. Yet, rather than being critical of the lack of country-based strategies, the evaluators attempt to turn this into a positive. Such a 'reactive strategy' (as generously described) is "not to be seen as being negative" as "it guarantees a bottom-up approach" and "usually the human rights and democracy organisations on the ground have the best judgement on priorities for their country".

Whilst acknowledging that this latter statement appears to correspond to the approach favoured in this chapter, which itself emphasises the essential contribution of local actors to developing a democratisation strategy, there are potential dangers in such a positive perception of a reactive, application-driven approach. Responding to applications remains a relatively arbitrary process and does not 'guarantee' the inclusion of the range of local actors, both government and non-governmental, who may perform key functions in the democratisation process.

The strengthening of civil society is again highlighted as the main positive contribution of the programme, unsurprising given that 96 per cent of projects were to NGOs. Such concentration of assistance is not only noted satisfactorily, but also the "continuation and expansion of the support to local civil society" is recommended, perceived as playing "a crucial role" in the "long and hard road to democratisation in the Arab World". Whilst the significance of civil society to democratisation is not questioned here, an almost exclusive focus on channelling support to NGOs contains an inherent danger. It disregards the importance of democratising government institutions, of supporting pro-reform elements within government, and of strengthening government-related organisations that perform 'watchdog' and accountability functions, for instance, parliament, a human rights ombudsman, the auditor general.

Specific findings with regard to the 34 selected projects were generally positive for each of the five criteria, though with some qualifications. Impact at micro level was perceived as mainly good, though variable between different types of projects. One exception to the positive picture, however, was the negative findings with regard to the adequacy of procedures and management. Substantial delays were common due to understaffing and over extensive procedures, viewed as not only having adverse effects on the efficiency, effectiveness and impact of projects but also on the credibility of the EU as a donor.

ACP

The findings of this study are more mixed, though again it is issues of Commission management that receive the harshest criticism, viewed as having had a particularly adverse effect on achievements. Such difficulties are not presented separately but integrated into the overall conclusions on the five stated criteria, as follows. Findings are closely related to the logical framework approach which both pervades and limits this study. *Relevance* of measures is generally very good, though with qualifications that a longer-term strategy is needed to replace short-term preoccupations and that some areas are relatively neglected, for example, governance, conflict, economic, social and cultural rights.

As regards project impact, the country studies generally note positive contributions, but it is recognised that impact is difficult to ascertain due to the attributional problems associated with single projects as triggering a particular change, as well as the lack of specific and realistic objectives by which to assess impact.

Coherence, understood as the quality of the linkages between results achieved and objectives, is perceived as particularly problematic, due to:

- Weaknesses in the logical framework, focusing again on poorly defined specific objectives (or project purpose), often insufficiently related to the particular country context or a particular aspect of the EU's programme, resulting in a "problematic gap between the stated immediate objectives of the projects, and the general objectives".
- Weaknesses in programme management, with the Commission's ability to set abstract goals not matched by its ability to put these goals in practice. The authors find that poor management affects all stages of the programme cycle, from project selection and planning, to monitoring and evaluation. It is noteworthy that, unlike the PTDP, the Commission dealt with all aspects of programme management with ACP countries, with no contracting out

of parts of the programme cycle. Importantly, the study also found evidence of good project management on the ground, underlining that problems lay principally in Brussels. This leads to recommendations for greater involvement of EU Delegations in the identification of projects and in programming generally. Whether this would lead to greater participation by domestic actors in the development of country strategies remains an open question, apparently not one addressed in the evaluation report.

Efficiency and effectiveness are found to be difficult to assess due to the lack of specific programme/project objectives, as referred to above. Again, the harshest critique is reserved for poor project management at the Commission level. While project management is relatively good at country level, the process of internal reform in Commission structures has led to a shift of emphasis in programming away from Delegations to specialised units in Brussels, contrary to the report's recommendations. The report concludes that this trend has led in fact to a *decrease* in the effectiveness and efficiency of individual projects since late 1998.

In summary, especially compared with the other two regional studies, the authors of the ACP study identify considerable problems with EC interventions in the field of democracy and human rights. Predominantly, however, these pertain to design (logframe approach) and management issues (Commission structures and division of labour), rather than more major questions such as the development of coherent democratisation strategies at country level and the respective roles of internal and external actors in this task.

SHORTCOMINGS AND LIMITATIONS

While these evaluation studies provide important and useful insights, they also display some shortcomings, limiting their value as a rigorous assessment of European Community performance in this field. Five such limitations are identified here. Excepting the PTDP study, the inherent methodological problems of conducting evaluations in this field, especially with regard to issues of impact, are not addressed. Robinson noted that "donors lack a systematic approach to evaluation of democracy assistance and political aid and there is no generally accepted methodology or set of indicators". The two main methodological difficulties identified are, firstly, the specification of criteria and indicators for judging success, and, secondly, the establishment of causal linkages between democracy and governance assistance and national democratic changes.

Neither the MDP report nor the ACP study engages with these difficulties, relying on the logical framework approach, though with some reluctance on the part of the former. It is posited here that the LFA is not suitable for the evaluation of democracy and human rights programmes. LFA is based on a rigidly preconceived framework and hierarchy of objectives, inverting evaluation inwards towards project documents and programme management, most evident in the ACP study. While such an approach may be appropriate for 'blueprint' type projects, for instance, infrastructural projects, it is wholly unsuited to the evaluation of programmes in the political domain. Evaluation here requires an outward orientation and an ability to capture the dynamic political context in which such interventions are embedded.

The PTDP study does engage more usefully with methodological problems, especially those associated with impact evaluation. First, democratisation is acknowledged as a complex process influenced by a multitude of interrelated factors, including democratic institutions and processes, economic development and political culture. Second, it is recognised that the impact of a single programme (PTDP, for instance), far less that of a single project, can never be measured exactly, given that it is very difficult to single out its influence from the range of factors affecting the democratisation process. Four main problems concerning 'attribution' are identified.

- 'With and without' situations or issues of counter factuality: rarely is it possible to gauge what would have happened without the external support, given complex and turbulent political contexts.

- Intangible lines of causality, with indirect performance indicators (for example, increased number of legal drafts) which could have happened anyway.
- Outputs of a specific donor or programme (for example, PTDP) can be indistinguishable from those of other donors.
- Possible outcomes of donor efforts maybe contradicted or cancelled out if not supported by other local policies and processes.

Nevertheless, despite recognition of such methodological problems in the PTDP study, only a limited attempt was made to address and potentially resolve such issues, perhaps due to the exacting time constraints under which the evaluation was undertaken. The study's findings of a significant impact on strengthening the NGO sector fall back on a relatively unsophisticated and self-evident linkage between projects and their contribution to national-level democratisation, given the overwhelming focus of the PTDP on the non-government sector.

Political Analysis

The importance of background studies for country evaluations, analysing the political context with regard to changes towards (or away from) democratisation, is recognised to some extent by the PTDP and MDP evaluations. The former places most emphasis on this as an essential part of its methodology for determining the extent to which projects and programmes have contributed to democratisation in each country. However, greater use could be made of the background studies, with their function limited to evaluating one criterion out of the eight listed (i.e. the relevance of projects and programmes). The MDP study only uses the background studies for its assessment of intervention strategy, not for impact evaluation.

Micro-macro Linkages

Robinson stated that "most evaluations either focus on measurable project outputs or seek evidence of impact in terms of the contribution of donors to macro-level political change".

In the reports examined here, the PTDP study attempts impact evaluation at micro and macro levels, while the MDP and ACP studies investigate impact at the micro, project level only. Micro level evaluations are perceived by Schmitter and Brouwer as generally limited, examining "only short-term visible and intended effects, while ignoring long-term processes...as well as unintended effects".

Additionally, the gulf between micro level projects and macro level political change means that lines of causality are often intangible, with Schmitter and Brouwer noting a tendency "to assume rather than to prove the impact of individual projects on the entire process of democratisation, even in the absence of any clear causal relationship between the two", and in fact cite the PTDP evaluation as an example. Additionally, although timely evaluation is desirable, impact evaluation of projects and programmes that have only recently been completed may be more an act of faith than certainty, especially given that democratic change is a long-term process. This applies in particular to the MDP study, where some projects remained relatively new and ongoing.

Unintended Impact

Does the search for positive impact ignore the possibility of negative, unintended impact? Schmitter and Brouwer address this issue head-on: "it is not sufficient just to measure the extent to which a specific goal has been reached. The 'complete evaluator' has to deal with the entire array of changes emanating from a specific programme or project". External intervention involves a dynamic, inter-active process and can have unintended side effects, with an intensification of ethnic divisions one of the greatest concerns.

Less dramatically, a distorting effect on the nature of civil society can occur as some NGOs "adapt to the discourse of the donors" in order to "enjoy funding, visibility and a certain influence", developing upward linkages and accountability to donors, with downward linkages and accountability to members detrimentally affected. Of the three studies examined here, the PTDP study does fleetingly acknowledge the issue of unintended impact, yet with no evidence that such effects were seriously looked for in the country cases. A participatory approach to evaluation aims to address such issues.

Critical Analysis

Although criticisms are made of the management of democracy and human rights assistance, ones that are common to all Commission development programmes, the findings of all three studies are generally positive in relation to the substantive issues of democracy promotion, with limited critical analysis. This would seem to be a function of evaluation studies that are contracted by donor agencies, to which various key actors may exist in a behoven relationship. Donors determine the terms of reference and thus limit the framework of study.

Consultants may be independent in theory, but dependent on ongoing donor contracts in practice. Similarly, beneficiaries of assistance are unlikely to 'bite the hand that feeds them'. Such scenarios can contribute to a lack of critical analysis and the failure to learn more fundamental lessons about the inadequacies of democracy assistance and how it could be improved. Again, a participatory approach is posed as a more critical alternative. Thus, in sum, the consequences of such limitations are that the judgements made concerning the value of EU human rights and democracy assistance are themselves undermined by the shortcomings of the evaluation studies themselves. They have not provided reliable and adequate assessments of the performance of EU efforts in meeting its stated policy goal of promoting human rights and democracy. Thus, an alternative approach to evaluation is proposed.

EVALUATING DEMOCRACY AND HUMAN RIGHTS ASSISTANCE

In developing an alternative approach to evaluation in this field, aims are two-fold. One is to contribute to resolving the methodological difficulties and therefore provide a more accurate assessment of democracy assistance activities. The other is to learn lessons from past efforts more effectively and thus to improve future strategy, notably at country level. The methodology aims to evaluate the impact of external actors' contribution to the democratisation process in individual countries, including at the meso level that is the thematic or partial regime level. Meso level evaluation could also contribute to comparative thematic studies, with analysis from a number of country case-studies examining different aspects of democracy promotion, for example, legislative strengthening or support for independent media.

There are three main elements to the proposed methodology:

- Political context studies: i.e. background political analysis of the particular country context and the trends towards (or regression from) democratisation.
- Following Schmitter and Brouwer (1999), a three-fold linkage between micro, meso and macro levels as an appropriate means for achieving impact evaluation.
- A participatory approach to evaluation. This latter proposition is the most central to the proposed methodology and is discussed in greatest detail.

POLITICAL CONTEXT STUDIES

Prior to an impact assessment of the contribution of EU democracy promotion efforts in a particular country context, it is necessary to gauge the political reforms that have occurred in that country over a given time period, covering at least the period of the assistance programme. Such background analysis was undertaken in the case of the PTDP and MDP studies, though not fully utilised, but apparently not in the ACP evaluation. Political context studies would concentrate on general democratisation trends, in both progressive and regressive directions, at the regime and partial regime levels. Partial regimes are the various sectors, as well as linkages between them, that make up the political regime as a whole.

Instances of partial regimes include: electoral systems, the division of power between the executive, legislature and judiciary, civil-military relations the NGO environment and so forth. Political context studies would also focus on the opportunities for and challenges to democratisation. Such studies would be undertaken by local academic specialists and could make use of democratic audit methodology, as well as surveys of academic literature and other sources.

Political context studies are invaluable not only as essential background to the assessment of the contribution of external actors to democratic reform processes, but also for future strategic planning, indicating priority themes and emerging issues.

Impact Assessment and the 'Missing Link' at Meso Level

The impact of a project or programme can be assessed at three distinct levels: micro, meso and macro.

- Micro is the impact of the project /programme at the local level, i.e. the impact on single organisations and institutions (e.g. a specific NGO or legislature strengthened), often corresponding to the fulfilment of project / programme objectives, at times as stated in the project's logical framework.
- Meso is the impact at sectoral or thematic level, e.g. the impact on civil society (rather than on a specific NGO); on the legal system (rather than on the judiciary or police); on democratic decentralisation; on women's role in politics, and so forth. The meso level is sometimes referred to as the partial regime level.
- Macro is the impact at the national level in terms of the overall political regime and its progress towards (or regression from) democratisation.

The benefits of a meso perspective are its recognition that "even if donors provide assistance to a single NGO, this affects a large part or even the entire NGO community and the relationship between the community and the state/government".

Meso level analysis goes beyond the impact of a single project and examines changes that have occurred to a specific and limited set of organisations and institutions, while avoiding the more speculative leaps of faith regarding the influence of external assistance on national processes of democratisation. Thus, given the wide gap between analysis at micro and macro levels, the meso level can act as an important linkage (ibid.), enabling a more reliable assessment of the impact of external interventions generally. Evidence of micro-level outcomes and impact can contribute to pictures of meso level impact. In turn, macro level analysis can be based more credibly on impact analyses of a variety of partial regimes.

PARTICIPATORY EVALUATION

The significance of a participatory approach within evaluation is increasingly recognised. Indeed, Cracknell recently stated that, "The trend towards the use of participatory methods in monitoring and evaluation is undoubtedly the most significant change currently taking place in the field of evaluation". Participatory evaluation (PE) is not a new concept, however, and its own history can be traced back at least twenty years to discussion by contributors in the volume edited by Fernandes and Tandon (1981) of participatory research and evaluation in India.

More recently, UNDP have provided a useful definition and summary of PE. It "involves the stakeholders and beneficiaries of a programme or project in the collective examination and assessment of that programme or project. It is people-centered: project stakeholders and beneficiaries are the key actors of the evaluation process and not the mere objects of the evaluation." Its key characteristics include:

- Drawing on local resources and capacities;
- Recognising the innate wisdom and knowledge of end-users;
- Demonstrating that end-users are creative and knowledgeable about their environment;
- Ensuring that stakeholders are part of the decision-making process;
- Using facilitators who act as catalysts and who assist stakeholders in asking key questions.

Although PE is not new, it has not been applied in the field of democracy and governance assistance by the European Commission or by other international donor agencies. A recent study of evaluation reports in this area found that only two reports out of sixty could be regarded as participatory. This finding is confirmed in Estrella and Gaventa's (1998) review of participatory monitoring and evaluation. Their selection of 20 case examples to illustrate the types of projects and programme using PM&E did not include a single one from the political aid sector.

Nevertheless, it is asserted here that a participatory approach to evaluation is appropriate and beneficial in evaluating democracy and governance assistance for the following reasons:

- PE addresses some of the shortcomings of evaluations in this area;
- The process of PE is akin to the process of democratisation itself;
- The principles of PE relate closely to the principles of democracy.

These perceived advantages are examined in more detail in turn.

CHALLENGES IN EVALUATING DEMOCRACY

A number of problematic issues can be outlined, including some identified in the studies examined here:

- How to determine the main opportunities for and obstacles to democratic development and to assess the relevance of external actors' efforts?
- How to untangle the multiplicity of actors and factors involved in democratisation trends and to single out the contribution of external assistance?
- How to assess the impact of donor activities at micro and meso levels and to construct the linkages in order to evaluate impact at the macro level of regime change?
- How to disentangle external – internal relations and to ascertain the extent to which perceived donor success is dependent on local support, or, conversely, the extent to which donor efforts are undermined by countervailing, internal forces?
- How to determine whether there have been unintended,

negative effects on the democratisation process through external activities?

It is proposed here that these difficult questions can be most satisfactorily addressed and answered by the reflections and analysis of well-informed national actors, engaged in a collective process of dialogue and negotiation.

The principles of PE relate closely to the principles of democracy. Estrella and Gaventa define the four characteristic features of PE as: participation, learning, negotiation and flexibility. All four are closely associated with the principles of democracy. Participation itself is clearly central to democratic processes. The democratic principles of popular control and political equality are realised precisely through political participation, minimally in electoral processes, as well as more substantially through a variety of democratic practices, both to influence policy-making and to hold government to account, from local community level upwards to national level. Regarding the other principles of PE, there is a clear resonance with democratic values.

Democracy is precisely about resolving differences and taking decisions through negotiation, dialogue and compromise, in contrast to rule through coercion and control over the means of violence. In democratic processes and practices, the need for flexibility and the degree of learning are both at a premium. It is therefore asserted that a participatory approach to evaluation is especially appropriate, given that its own defining features are closely associated with those of the very democratic processes that are being examined and assessed.

The process of PE is akin to the process of democratisation itself. There is general consensus that democratisation is essentially an internal or autochthonous process. From an actor-oriented theoretical perspective in particular, democracy is constructed and crafted (and resisted and undermined) by various coalitions of domestic actors and interest groups, inclusive of elite groups. Frequently, it is local knowledge of rapidly changing regime circumstances and the alliances between national, pro-democratic actors that are central to processes of democratic transition and consolidation. Despite the contemporary (and historically unprecedented) phenomena of democracy promotion from outside, there is agreement that internal actors and activities are key to democratisation, and that the contribution of external actors, while frequently not insignificant, remains marginal.

Nevertheless, one problem identified with the democracy and governance assistance activities of agencies such as the European Commission is the limited involvement of recipient organisations, both government and non-government, in the design and implementation of projects and programmes. At worst, this can be perceived as the notion that 'donors know best'. Such ideas are underlined by the application of a standard model of democratisation and menu of democracy assistance activities, with little consideration of the particular country context. Evaluation provides an opportunity for reflection on and analysis of democracy promotion activities, as well as consideration of issues such as the degree of recipient involvement.

If evaluation studies are themselves donor-focused and conducted by external consultants, then this can become an opportunity lost as the moment for critical thinking descends into mere corroboration and affirmation of donor efforts, as mainly found here. In contrast, PE not only provides that essential input of local knowledge and critical analysis, but also the very process of a participatory evaluation is akin to the process of democratisation itself. PE entails a group of well-informed representatives of local groups who discuss the strengths and limitations of donor activities in the context of the prospects for and constraints upon sustained democratisation in the particular country context.

The anticipated outcome of such negotiation and consensus-seeking is a learning process for both participants and donor organisations: past and current efforts are examined and reflected upon, objectives are revisited and future strategies determined. Knowledge is enhanced, as is the capacity to take appropriate action in pursuit of democratic change, both by internal and external actors. EU promotion of democracy and human rights through development co-operation is high on rhetoric but low on achievement. The European Commission has stated it "wants to be judged on its performance". Yet, evaluation studies thus far have been limited in both the degree of critical analysis achieved and in their engagement with the methodological difficulties in this field.

In order to address such shortcomings, an alternative methodology is proposed here for undertaking impact evaluations of country programmes, comprised of three main elements. Political context studies, undertaken by national academic experts, provide the background picture of movement along the democratisation continuum, both at the national regime level and at the partial regime or thematic levels, highlighting both opportunities for and constraints upon sustained democratic reform. The addition of meso level analysis provides the 'missing link' between micro and macro level analyses, enabling more grounded and credible impact evaluations. Finally, a participatory approach entails control of the evaluation process being placed in the hands of well-informed, national actors, representative of a range of pro-democratic groups and organisations.

Advantages are claimed as two-fold, with both intended to re-assert domestic control over EU assistance. First, external activities are subject to a more rigorous critique, in which the perceptions of knowledgeable domestic actors are regarded as essential to judgements on the relevance, effectiveness and impact of external activities. Second, lessons learned are based on detailed knowledge of a country's political context and the overall prospects for and constraints on democratisation. In turn, the European Commission can integrate such lessons into revised programmes, guided by internal forces and in which domestic authorship is maximised (in contrast to 'ownership' of external schemes), as appropriate to processes of democratisation.

4

United Nations and Human Rights

The United Nations Charter sets forth the "inherent dignity" and the "equal and inalienable rights of all members of the human family." Upholding these human rights principles as "the foundation of freedom, justice, and peace in the world" is fundamental to every undertaking of the United Nations. The United Nations (UN) has created a global structure for protecting human rights, based largely on its Charter, non-binding declarations, and legally binding treaties and on various activities aimed at advancing democracy and human rights throughout the world.

The UN often finds it necessary to define rights in a cautious manner, as it is host to an extremely diverse group of member states, with varying economic, social, cultural and political histories. Subsequently, the UN must accommodate these differences in its mechanisms for protecting the human rights it has outlined in treaties and declarations. Thus, these methods may be less substantive or lack in strict enforcement as compared to those of regional institutions. Broad agreements allow the UN to accommodate a spectrum of different viewpoints. The UN thus affects more nations and many more individuals than any regional institution could.

The UN's system of human rights protection has three main components: first, it establishes international standards through its Charter, legally binding treaties, non-binding declarations, agreements, and documents; next, it mandates Special Rapporteurs and experts, and groups, such as working groups, committees and treaty bodies, to work in various manners for the promotion and protection of human rights; finally, it offers technical assistance through the Voluntary Fund for Advisory Services and Technical Assistance in the field of Human Rights. International legal agreements and organizations pre-date the formation of the United Nations. At the International Peace Conference in The Hague in 1899 over 25 nations met for ten weeks to codify the laws of war, both on land and at sea. In addition to this monumental agreement, they also formulated instruments for peaceful crisis settlement and war prevention.

This formal statement on the desirability of international peace laid the foundation for such organizations as the League of Nations and the United Nations. Twenty years later, the League of Nations was founded. At the Treaty of Versailles in 1919, the victors of the First World War convened to negotiate a peace settlement. At this conference, the League, the UN's predecessor, was formed "to promote international cooperation and to achieve peace and security" throughout the world. Member states agreed not to go to war with one another without first submitting complaints to any offending state; and for offending states who were not members of the League, its members pledged not to go to war without an enquiry to the state. The League had originally been proposed by the president of the United States (US) Woodrow Wilson, but domestic pressure prevented the US from ever joining. The League of Nations lasted only until 1946; it dissolved after it failed to prevent the outbreak of World War II.

The trauma and violence of World War II (WWII) inspired the Allied Nations to try to establish a peace-keeping organization for the prevention of the recurrence of such horrors. On June 12, 1941, a preliminary move toward the establishment of the United Nations occurred with the signing of the Inter-Allied Declaration. Signed in London, the Inter-Allied Declaration pledged that the Allied powers would "work together, with other free peoples, both in war and in peace".

Two months later, President of the United States Franklin Delano Roosevelt of the United States and Prime Minister of the United Kingdom Winston Churchill agreed upon a doctrine upon which to base international cooperation. The two main principles behind the UN, the establishment of both world peace and global security, are found in the Atlantic Charter. Roosevelt and Churchill signed this document while on board the HMS Prince of Wales on August 14, 1941.

The signing signaled that the Allied Powers intended to form a stronger, more effective organization than the League of Nations had proven to be. On January 1, 1942, representatives from the 26 Allied nations gathered in Washington, DC to sign the Declaration by United Nations. This document reaffirmed the goals set by the Atlantic Charter. It also first contained the term "United Nations", which had been suggested by President Roosevelt. In 1943, two conferences were held during which nations recognized that the goals set forth in the Declaration by United Nations regarding international peace and security should be upheld within an international organization.

The governments of the Soviet Union (USSR), the UK, the US and China signed such an agreement to this end in Moscow on October 30; leaders of the US, the USSR and the UK renewed this intention at Teheran on December 1, 1943. From these agreements, leaders from the United States, the United Kingdom, the Soviet Union and China met for several months in the fall of 1944 in Washington, DC, to determine the goals, structure, and methods of functioning for the United Nations. These meetings held between September 21 and October 7 became known as the Dumbarton Oaks Conference. On February 11, 1945, President Roosevelt, Prime Minister Churchill and Premier Joseph Stalin met at Yalta and announced their resolution to form "a general international organization to maintain peace and security".

The San Francisco Conference of 1945 propelled the United Nations into reality. On April 25, delegates from fifty nations across the globe gathered in San Francisco, where they negotiated and drew up the 111-article Charter of the United

Nations; the Charter was then unanimously adopted on June 25 and signed on June 26. Poland was not represented at the conference, but soon signed the Charter to become the 51st and last original member state.

The Charter's preamble states the purpose in founding such an institution: "We the peoples of the United Nations determined...to reaffirm faith in fundamental human rights, in the dignity and worth of the human person, in the equal rights of men and women and of nations large and small ..." The Charter itself includes the following goals: "...To achieve international co-operation in solving international problems of an economic, social, cultural or humanitarian character, and in promoting and encouraging respect for human rights and for fundamental freedoms for all without distinction as to race, sex, language, or religion..."

The United Nations officially became an institution with the ratification of the UN Charter on October 24, 1945. From then on, it quickly became an active international body. On January 10, 1946, the first General Assembly met at Westminster, London. There were 51 nations represented at this first meeting. One week later, on January 17, the Security Council first met, also in London. The following week, on January 24, the General Assembly adopted its first resolution, focusing on peaceful uses of atomic energy and the elimination of weapons of mass destruction. February 1 of that year saw the appointment of the first Secretary-General, Trygve Lie, from Norway. The UN Headquarters were first established in New York City on October 24, 1949.

MAIN BODIES OF THE UNITED NATIONS

The United Nations is composed of six major bodies: the General Assembly, the Secretariat, the Security Council, the International Court of Justice, the Trusteeship Council and the Economic and Social Council. Although the United Nations was divided into these six spheres, they are of unequal size (some possess many subsidiary bodies and committees while others have very few), status (some are quite powerful while others have become almost obsolete), and relevance to human rights (some focus extensively on the issue while others bear little or no relevance for the protectin and promotion of human rights).

GENERAL ASSEMBLY

The General Assembly is the legislative body of the UN. It currently consists of 191 member states, all of which must take part in its sessions and none of which may have more than five representatives. The General Assembly has established Permanent Committees, such as the seven Main Committees, the Procedural Commissions and the Permanent Commissions, that meet between General Assembly sessions. It is also responsible for appointing the Secretary-General, upon recommendation from the Security Council, to a renewable five year term.

SECRETARIAT

The Secretariat is headed by the UN Secretary-General, who is recommended by the Security Council and then appointed to a five-year term by the General Assembly. It is in charge of carrying out programs designed by other branches of the United Nations, such as peacekeeping missions, international dispute mediation, and studying economic, cultural, human rights, or social trends. It also handles administrative details, such as speech and documents translations, UN news and information releases, and international conference co-ordinations. The Secretariat hosts around 9,000 staff members.

SECURITY COUNCIL

The Security Council possesses the power to draft resolutions providing for the use of force against states, with an emphasis on non-violent conflict resolution and preventative measures. In order to pass a resolution permitting the use of arms against a state, it must gain at least nine "yea" votes from its fifteen members with no vetoes. Only its permanent members hold veto power. Its composition was established in the UN Charter, and consists of five permanent members,

China, France, Russia, the United Kingdom and the United States. Additionally, ten non-permanent members serve on the Council who are elected to two year terms. Non-members may participate in hearings and meetings, but may not vote. The Security Council is an important branch of the UN, developed for the maintenance of peace and security in the world.

INTERNATIONAL COURT OF JUSTICE

The International Court of Justice (ICJ), the judicial branch of the UN, is based in The Hague, the Netherlands, and was established in 1945 by the Charter of the United Nations. All states that have signed the UN Charter are members of the ICJ. Its jurisdiction extends to international conflicts, with the exception of political ones. Its responsibilities include: giving opinions on concrete topics; ruling on cases; and clarifying international legal norms.

The ICJ is the latest step in the continuing evolution of international courts. The first such court, Permanent Court of Arbitration, was founded in 1899 and still exists today. The Permanent Court of International Justice was created by the League of Nations and existed between 1922 and 1946. It served as the model on which the International Court of Justice is based.

ECONOMIC AND SOCIAL COUNCIL (ECOSOC)

The Economic and Social Council (ECOSOC) makes recommendations to the General Assembly on human rights issues. It reviews the reports submitted by the Commission on Human Rights and submits the amended versions to the General Assembly. ECOSOC is composed of 54 members serving three year terms; members meet twice a year.

Additionally, it oversees several committees and commissions, such as the Commission on Human Rights, the Sub-Commission on the Promotion and Protection of Human Rights, the Commission on the Status of Women and the Commission on Crime Prevention and Criminal Justice, as well as UN specialized agencies, such as the International Labor

Organization (ILO) and the World Health Organization (WHO).

TRUSTEESHIP COUNCIL

This council was originally established to preside over the so-called "dependent areas" within the international Trusteeship System, under Article 75 of the UN Charter. However, the goals for and tasks of the Council have largely been fulfilled, and it is therefore now mostly obsolete. Currently, the Trusteeship Council only meets if and when a scenario requires it.

HUMAN RIGHTS PROTECTION AND PROMOTION

The type of protection provided by the United Nations on issues of human rights is based on either Charter-based or treaty-based mechanisms. Those mechanisms based on the UN Charter include: the Universal Declaration of Human Rights; the Commission on Human Rights; and the Sub-Commission on the Promotion and Protection of Human Rights.

UNIVERSAL DECLARATION OF HUMAN RIGHTS

The Universal Declaration of Human Rights (UDHR) is one of the first international documents to be based on the idea that rights are guaranteed to each human being. Most previous international declarations and treaties were based on the idea of positivism, whereby rights are only recognized once they have been set forth in national legislation. Like the UN itself, the UDHR was written with the aim of establishing world peace by promoting human rights. Originally, the UDHR brought together 58 distinct geographic, cultural and political backgrounds in the formation of one universal document.

Although the UDHR is not legally binding it has created international human rights standards that are codified in various international treaties. The Universal Declaration of Human Rights was drafted between January 1947 and December 1948. Its text was composed by the then eight-member Commission on Human Rights headed by Eleanor Roosevelt, and sought to include the whole spectrum of human rights: from cultural, social and economic to civil and political rights. Following over 1,400 votes modifying the document's text, the UN General Assembly unanimously passed the Declaration on December 10, 1948, with eight abstentions to the vote, coming from Belarus, Czechoslovakia, Poland, Saudi Arabia, South Africa, the Soviet Union, Ukraine, and Yugoslavia.

The UDHR consists of 30 articles specifying basic rights guaranteed to each individual. The first two articles establish the document's premise, that all humans share universal equality, and that this equality is based on the fundamental dignity bestowed upon humanity. This equality of human dignity translates to universality of human rights. Included in the notion of universality is the idea that these rights are automatically extended to everyone and may not be denied for any reason or because of any action an individual may commit. Article 1 states: "All human beings are born equal in dignity and rights. They are endowed with reason and conscience and should act towards one another in a spirit of brotherhood."

Article 2 continues: "Everyone is entitled to all the rights and freedoms set forth in this Declaration, without distinction of any kind such as race, colour, sex, language, religion, political or other opinion, national or social origin, property, birth or other status."

Articles 3 through 21 specify civil and political rights. In these articles, rights set forth include the right to life, liberty, a fair trial, free speech, privacy, of personal security, and of movement, as well as freedom from slavery, torture, and arbitrary arrest. Articles 22 through 27 provide for economic, social and cultural rights. These rights are specified as an indispensable aspect of an individual's life, being necessary for one's dignity and personal development, and include economic rights such as the right to social security, economic work-related rights, fair payment and leisure; social rights such as the right to an adequate standard of health, well-being and education; and cultural rights, such as the right to participate in cultural life.

Finally, Articles 28 through 30 establish a general framework to provide for the enjoyment of human rights: the recognition of the right to a social and international system that promotes human rights; a statement that humans have obligations to the community along with fundamental rights; and a reminder that no state or individual may utilize the Declaration to promote goals contrary to the mission or goals of the UN.

COMMISSION ON HUMAN RIGHTS

Composed of 53 member states, the Commission on Human Rights is the Charter-based body that most directly deals with the area of human rights. It is assisted by the Sub-Commission on the Promotion and Protection of Human Rights, individual experts, representatives, and Special Rapporteurs. The Commission on Human Rights meets for six weeks each year in Geneva, although it may also meet in majority-endorsed "Special Sessions" in order to provide the most expeditious manner of dealing with human rights abuses. In evaluating a situation, the Commission may choose to monitor a situation itself or may request for an outside body to do so. Its jurisdiction of human rights protection was expanded by ECOSOC in the 1970s to include the entire globe.

From its inception, the Commission has influenced international human rights standards, working to set as well as to enforce rights standards. It helped author the Universal Declaration of Human Rights in 1948. Since then, it has formed standards relating to the right to development, civil and political rights, economic, social and cultural rights, the elimination of racial discrimination, torture, the rights of the child and the rights of human rights defenders.

MONITORING HUMAN RIGHTS

The Commission on Human Rights also devotes much time to monitoring the implementation of the standards it has set. It may turn to any number of permanent or special procedures when examining a specific area of human rights. Its two permanent procedures are the 1503 Procedure and the 1235 Procedure; its special procedures include fact-finding missions, thematic mechanisms or mandates and advisory services. The 1503 Procedure is a confidential procedure named after ECOSCO Resolution 1503 by which it was established. It is activated when the Commission receives a communication about a consistent pattern of gross human rights violations.

Violations considered under this procedure include genocide, apartheid, racial or ethnic discrimination, torture, forced mass migrations and mass imprisonment without a trial. The report of consistent gross human rights violations to the Commission may not be an anonymous one, yet does not require the consent of the state concerned for an investigation to take place. This regulation gives the Commission great leeway in deciding how to best approach a situation. Following its investigation, the Commission then decides what action to take. When a 1503 Procedure has failed to stop a human rights violation it has investigated, the Commission on Human Rights may invoke the 1235 Procedure under which it can hold an annual public debate about the gross violations of human rights in question. If this also fails to adequately affect the situation, the Commission may move to have ECOSOC pass a resolution condemning the violators.

This public condemnation tarnishes the reputation of the leaders in the state in question and discredits their legitimacy as political elites. Among the special procedures available to the Commission on Human Rights, fact-finding missions are a useful tool. In a fact-finding mission, an expert or group of experts studies the human rights situation and looks for violations in a given state with the purpose of gathering information for a 1503 or a 1235 procedure. However, a fact-finding mission may only occur with the consent of the state whose human rights recored is being questioned. As of April 2003, 47 countries had extended standing invitations to the Thematic Special Procedures of the United Nations Commission on Human Rights to investigate human rights issues, meaning that the Commission may initiate a fact-finding mission to any one of those countries at any time.

For all other nations, the Commission must first seek and gain approval before dispatching its experts to the country. Another special procedure available to the Commission on Human Rights is a thematic mechanism or mandate. Working groups and/or Special Rapporteurs investigate human rights violations and the problems they have caused on a multi-state level. Recently, there has been an increase in the number of Special Rapporteurs investigating human rights issues. Lastly, the Commission on Human Rights offers advisory services to nations that request it. The Commission provides educational and informational assistance to states in order to help them observe a high level of human rights protection. Additionally, the Commission on Human Rights may request assistance from the Office of the High Commissioner for Human Rights in the form of seminars, training courses, and clinics as well as advice from experts.

SUB-COMMISSION ON THE PROMOTION AND PROTECTION OF HUMAN RIGHTS

The Sub-Commission was established by the Commission on Human Rights at its first meeting in 1947, and was titled the Sub-Commission on Prevention of Discrimination and Protection of Minorities before a 1999 vote to change its name. It serves as the main subsidiary body to the Commission on Human Rights. The Sub-Commission is comprised of 26 member experts acting independently, without affiliation to their state of origin, though they are elected by the Commission proportionally according to geographical population distribution. Presently, member experts are divided as follows: seven from Africa, six from Western Europe and other States, five from Asia, five from Latin America and three from Eastern Europe.

Each member has one alternate; half the members and their alternates are elected every two years and each serves for a term of four years. The Sub-Commission meets for three weeks each year in Geneva; government officials, staff of UN specialized agencies and NGO observers may also attend their meetings. The Sub-Commission's mission is to undertake studies under the guidance of the UDHR and to make recommendations to the Commission on Human Rights concerning the prevention of discrimination of any kind relating to human rights and fundamental freedoms and the protection of racial, national, religious and linguistic minorities.

The Sub-Commission also undertakes work assigned to it by the Commission or ECOSOC, and distributes these assignments between its six working groups: the Working Group on Communications (which considers complaints regarding a consistent pattern of gross and verifiable violations of human rights within the scope of communications, together with any existing replies from governments), the Working Group on Contemporary Forms of Slavery, the Working Group on Indigenous Populations, the Working Group on Minorities, the Working Group on Administration of Justice and the Working Group on Transnational Corporations.

HIGH COMMISSIONER FOR HUMAN RIGHTS

The position of the High Commissioner for Human Rights was established by the General Assembly of the United Nations in December 1993. The High Commissioner carries out the Secretary-General's "good offices" duties relating to human rights, and is accountable to the Economic and Social Council as well as the Secretary-General. The Commissioner holds the principal position of promoting human rights and dealing with human rights activities in the UN, and must also maintain dialogue with all member states on the subject of human rights. Responsibilities of the High Commissioner include: crisis management; prevention and early warning of abuses; assistance to states in periods of political transition; promotion of substantive rights to governments; and coordination and rationalization of human rights programs.

The Commissioner is assisted by a Deputy to the United Nations High Commissioner for Human Rights, a staff for dealing with substantive issues, and an administrative staff. The Deputy, who assists the Commissioner in fulfilling assignments, is the Officer-In-Charge when the Commissioner is absent. The policies of the High Commissioner are implemented by the Office of the High Commissioner for Human Rights (OHCHR), is "to protect and promote human rights for all." OHCHR fulfills its goals through a variety of activities, including: emphasizing the significance of human rights globally and locally; providing education and resources regarding human rights; supporting human rights organs and treaty monitoring bodies; and responding to serious human rights violations. The post of High Commissioner for Human Rights was first held by Mr. José Ayala-Lasso of Ecuador.

International law takes precedence over the domestic law of a state. Thus, when a nation signs a treaty, it is pledging to adopt the provisions set forth within the treaty into the domestic law of a state. In this way, treaty-based mechanisms vary from Charter-based ones. Whereas the UN Charter's mechanisms are at times either not legally binding or require permission to be executed, treaties are backed by the norms regulating international law and are therefore legally binding. International legal instruments take the form of a treaty (also called agreement, convention, protocol) which may be binding on the contracting states. When negotiations are completed, the text of a treaty is established as authentic and definitive and is "signed" to that effect by the representatives of states. There are various means by which a state expresses its consent to be bound by a treaty. The most common are ratification or accession.

A new treaty is "ratified" by those states that have negotiated the instrument. A state which has not participated in the negotiations may, at a later stage, "accede" to the treaty. The treaty enters into force when a pre-determined number of states have ratified or acceded to the treaty. When a state ratifies or accedes to a treaty, that state may make reservations to one or more articles of the treaty, unless reservations are prohibited by the treaty. Reservations may normally be withdrawn at any time. In some countries, international treaties take precedence over national law; in others, a specific law may be required to give an international treaty, although ratified or acceded to, the force of a national law. Practically all states that have ratified or acceded to an international treaty must issue decrees, amend existing laws or introduce new legislation in order for the treaty to be fully effective on the national territory.

The UN currently has seven human rights treaties: the International Covenant on Economic, Social and Cultural Rights (ICESCR); the International Covenant on Civil and Political Rights (ICCPR); the International Convention on the Elimination of All Forms of Racial Discrimination (ICERD); the Convention on the Elimination of All Forms of Discrimination against Women (CEDAW); the Convention against Torture and Other Cruel, Inhuman or Degrading Treatment or Punishment (CAT); the Convention on the Rights of the Child (CRC); and the International Convention on the Protection of the Rights of All Migrant Workers and Members of their Families.

Each of these seven human rights treaties has a monitoring body, composed of independent experts who examine the reports that signatory nations submit under the treaty. These committees are also in charge of issuing "concluding observations/comments", where they summarize their concerns about certain states and also give recommendations for the future. Four of the treaty committees have mechanisms to deal directly with individual complaints of human rights violations under their respective treaties. These four bodies are: the Human Rights Committee, for the ICCPR; the Committee on the Elimination of Racial Discrimination, for the ICERD; the Committee on the Elimination of all forms of Discrimination against Women, for CEDAW; and the Committee against Torture, for CAT. Strict regulations exist regarding when an individual may formally issue a complaint to one of the monitoring bodies.

All domestic options for settling the violation must have been previously exhausted. Additionally, the individual issuing the complaint must be under the jurisdiction of a state that is a party to the relevant treaty. No complaint may be made anonymously; it must come from either the victim, a representative of the victim, or, in rare circumstances in which it is impossible for either of these people to complain, a third, non-anonymous party may issue a complaint. The event in question must have occurred on or after the later date of either the treaty's entrance into force or the date the state in question signed the treaty.

INTERNATIONAL COVENANT ON ECONOMIC, SOCIAL AND CULTURAL RIGHTS (ICESCR)

This International Covenant on Economic, Social and Cultural Rights (ICESCR) was adopted by the United Nations in 1966 and entered into force one decade later, in 1976. Along with the International Covenant on Civil and Political Rights, the amount of time that it took the ICESCR to enter into force may be partly attributed to the Cold War, in which Communist regimes, who advocated for economic, social and cultural rights, stood squarely against Western capitalist democracies, who embraced the civil and political rights codified in the International Covenant on Civil and Political Rights. The ICESCR is monitored by the Committee on Economic, Social and Cultural Rights.

COMMITTEE ON ECONOMIC, SOCIAL AND CULTURAL RIGHTS

The Covenant itself did not provide for the creation of a monitoring body, so in the early days of ICESCR, states that had ratified the treaty reported to a working group of ECOSOC. In 1986, the Committee on Economic, Social and Cultural Rights (CESCR) took over the role as an independent expert committee to monitor the implementation of the Covenant. Currently, the Committee does not have a mechanism for processing individual complaints, although in 1996, CESCR sent to the Commission on Human Rights a draft of a proposed optional protocol that would provide for this kind of complaints procedure. It meets three times a year in Geneva.

INTERNATIONAL COVENANT ON CIVIL AND POLITICAL RIGHTS (ICCPR)

The International Covenant on Civil and Political Rights, like the ICESCR, was adopted by the UN in 1966, but did not enter into force until 1976. Also like the ICESCR, the ICCPR saw a great deal of delay in its ratification due to the Cold War conflicts. These two treaties were signed separately because of the thought that political and civil rights could and must be guaranteed from the moment a nation signs on to the Covenant listing them, but that, while it was desirable for the same to be true of economic, social and cultural rights, it was not feasible. Implementation of social and economic rights was expected to take much time and thus could not be forced upon a nation merely because it has ratified the Covenant.

This application theory is recognized in the respective second articles of each Covenant: In Article 2, paragraph 1 of the ICCPR, the Covenant obliges a state "...to respect and to ensure to all individuals...the rights recognized in the present Covenant." Meanwhile, a state "undertakes to take steps...to the maximum of its available resources, with a view to achieving progressively the full realization of the rights recognized in the present Covenant..." according to Article 2, paragraph 1 of the ICESCR. The ICCPR is monitored by the Human Rights Committee. These two treaties account for most of the provisions listed under the Universal Declaration of Human Rights; further, they make the provisions binding for those nations who are parties to the covenants. The two covenants along with their optional protocols and the Universal Declaration of Human Rights are known as the International Bill of Human Rights.

HUMAN RIGHTS COMMITTEE

The Human Rights Committee was established to ensure that the rights listed under the ICCPR were protected. It is composed of 18 elected representatives, who serve four-year terms as independent and not representatives of their state of origin, and is based in Geneva. Its role is comprised of four main duties: to review reports submitted by states on their domestic actions taken to comply with the treaty; to consider information submitted from one member state accusing another member state of violating the treaty in some manner; to consider individuals' complaints against states that have signed the treaty, as well as reports written also by NGO; and to issue "General Comments".

Each member state of the ICCPR is required to submit a report to the Human Rights Committee each year "on the measures they have adopted which give effect to the rights recognized herein and on the progress made in the enjoyment of those rights." (ICCPR, Article 40). These reports must contain both a general and a specific component to them. The general aspect of the report must include data and statistics on the nations' frameworks in place that protect the rights listed in the treaty, whereas the report's specific aspect must include information addressing each article in the ICCPR as well as information about court rulings and the extent to which rights are being enjoyed in the member state.

Member states may report on other member states not abiding by the treaty's provisions. If such a circumstance were to arise, the report would first be sent to the offending state. Then, if it were not addressed adequately by the state, it could be sent to the Human Rights Committee for review. Despite the availability of this mechanism, it has never been utilized. In the case of the ICCPR, the state in question must be a party to the treaty's optional protocol, which allows for the registering of individual complaints.

If all these preconditions are met, the complaint proceeds through three stages: the registration of the complaint, an examination of whether or not the complaint satisfactorily meets the preconditions, and a communication on whether the complaint falls under the ICCPR and may therefore be given consideration. When the Human Rights Committee considers a complaint, the Committee will submit "views" on the issue in an annual publication. Although these views may condemn a government or state sector, the Committee has no means of sanctioning the guilty party or of enforcing its views.

International Convention on the Elimination of All Forms of Racial Discrimination (ICERD)

The International Convention on the Elimination of All Forms of Racial Discrimination was adopted in 1965 and entered into force in 1969. It seeks to eliminate all forms of racial discriminations, and is monitored by the Committee on the Elimination of Racial Discrimination.

Committee on the Elimination of Racial Discrimination

The Committee on the Elimination of Racial Discrimination (CERD) exists to monitor state parties to the CERD. It has 18 independent experts who are elected to CERD by state parties to the Convention. They meet in Geneva each year for two three-week sessions. CERD's four main duties are the same as Human Rights Committee's: to review reports submitted by states on their domestic actions taken to comply with the treaty; to consider information submitted from one member state accusing another member state of violating the treaty in some manner; to consider individuals' complaints against states that have signed the treaty; and to issue written "General Comments".

Convention on the Elimination of all forms of Discrimination against Women (CEDAW)

The Convention on the Elimination of All Forms of Discrimination against Women was adopted 1979 and entered into force in 1981. It focuses on the areas of education, employment, health, marriage, and the family as each area relates specifically to women. CEDAW calls for the elimination of discrimination against women within society as well as the adoption of legislation to further women's rights. It is monitored by the Committee on the Elimination of all forms of Discrimination against Women.

Committee on the Elimination of all forms of Discrimination against Women

The Committee on the Elimination of all forms of Discrimination against Women (the CEDAW Committee) monitors the CEDAW treaty. It consists of 23 independent experts who are elected by those states that are parties to the Convention. It is one of the four monitoring committees that may undertake confidential inquiries into individual complaints.

As the Committee on the Elimination of Racial Discrimination and the Human Rights Committee, the CEDAW Committee has four main duties: to review reports submitted by states on their domestic actions taken to comply with the treaty; to consider information submitted from one member state accusing another member state of violating the treaty in some manner; to consider individuals' complaints against states that have signed the treaty; and to issue Committee written "General Comments" on each state's compliance with the treaty, taking into account reports written also by NGOs, to present to the Secretary General.

Convention against Torture and Other Cruel, Inhuman or Degrading Treatment or Punishment (CAT)

The Convention against Torture and Other Cruel, Inhuman or Degrading Treatment or Punishment was adopted in 1984 and entered into force in1987. Among other provisions, it bans torture and rape as weapons during wartime. It is monitored by the Committee against Torture.

Committee against Torture

The Committee against Torture exists to monitor the Convention against Torture treaty. Its membership includes ten independent experts, elected by parties to the Convention. The Committee meets twice a year in Geneva for two to three weeks at a time, and submits an annual report to the UN General Assembly. The Committee against Torture shares four of its five main duties with the Human Rights Committee, the Committee on the Elimination of Racial Discrimination, and the CEDAW Committee.

Its mission includes: reviewing reports submitted by states on their domestic actions taken to comply with the treaty; considering information submitted from one member state accusing another member state of violating the treaty in some manner; considering individuals' complaints against states that have signed the treaty; issuing Committee written "General Comments" on each state's compliance with the treaty, taking into account reports written also by NGOs, to present to the

Secretary General. In addition to these four shared goals; CAT also investigates into allegations of general systematic forms of torture.

Convention on the Rights of the Child (CRC)

The Convention on the Rights of the Child was adopted in November of 1989 and entered into force less than a year later, in September of 1990. It is the UN's most universally ratified human rights convention. It protects children from economic and sexual exploitation, among other things, and is monitored by the Committee on the Rights of the Child.

Committee on the Rights of the Child

The Committee on the Rights of the Child monitors the Convention on the Rights of the Child. While the Committee engages in many of the same practices as do other committees, there is no individual complaints mechanism associated with the Convention, nor is there one associated with either of its two optional protocols, the Optional Protocol to the Convention on the Rights of the Child on the sale of children, child prostitution and child pornography and the Optional Protocol to the Convention on the Rights of the Child on the involvement of children in armed conflict. However, the Committee still examines state reports submitted and makes general recommendations to the General Assembly on state parties and their compliance with the Convention.

International Convention on the Protection of the Rights of All Migrant Workers and Members of their Families

The latest of the UN's human rights treaties, the International Convention on the Protection of the Rights of All Migrant Workers and Members of their Families, was adopted in 1990 and entered into force July 1, 2003. It is monitored by the Committee on the Protection of the Rights of All Migrant Workers and Members of their Families.

Committee on the Protection of the Rights of All Migrant Workers and Members of Their Families

The Committee on the Protection of the Rights of All Migrant Workers and Members of Their Families monitors the treaty under the same name. It is composed of 10 members, and its roles are: to examine state reports submitted and to make general recommendations. Under the treaty, it will be possible to address individual complaints once a minimum of ten states have agreed to the practice.

THE UN GENERAL ASSEMBLY

The United Nations currently comprises 185 member states, all of which belong to the General Assembly. The General Assembly controls the UN's finances, makes non-binding recommendations, and oversees and elects members of other UN organs. It is the General Assembly that ultimately votes to adopt human rights declarations and conventions, which are also called 'treaties or covenants'. For example, in 1948 when the UN Commission on Human Rights had completed its draft of the Universal Declaration of Human Rights, the General Assembly voted to adopt the document.

OTHER UN BODIES

In addition to the General Assembly, in which all member states are represented, there are five other main bodies of the United Nations that deal with different types of international concerns and administrative tasks.

Although human rights are fundamental to all functions of the UN, human rights issues mainly fall under the Economic and Social Council (ECOSOC). This council of fifty-four members elected by the General Assembly is responsible for coordinating all economic and social work of the UN and its affiliated institutions. The Economic and Social Council oversees the work of many intergovernmental organizations (IGOs) and certain UN commissions, such as the UN Commission on Human Rights.

THE UN COMMISSION ON HUMAN RIGHTS

Made up of fifty-three member states elected by ECOSOC the UN Commission on Human Rights initiates studies and fact-finding missions and discusses specific human rights issues. It has responsibility for initiating and drafting human rights declarations and conventions. ECOSOC also supervises intergovernmental organizations (IGOs), which are specialized agencies that function independently with their own charter, budget, and staff but are affiliated with the UN by special agreements. IGOs report to the ECOSOC and may be asked to review reports from certain UN bodies that are relevant to their area of focus.

Some intergovernmental organizations that work to protect human rights include:

- International Labor Organization (ILO)- Develops international labor standards and provides technical assistance training to governments.
- United Nations Children's Fund (UNICEF)- Works with other UN bodies, governments, and nongovernmental organizations to provide community-based services in primary healthcare, basic education, and safe water and sanitation for children in developing countries. Human rights are fundamental to its programming.
- United Nations Development Fund for Women (UNIFEM)- Promotes economic and political empowerment of women in developing countries, working to ensure their participation in development planning and practices, as well as their human rights.
- United Nations Educational, Scientific, and Cultural Organization (UNESCO)- Pursues intellectual cooperation in education, science, culture, and communications and promotes development through social, cultural, and economic projects.
- World Health Organization (WHO)- Conducts immunization campaigns, promotes and coordinates research, and provides technical assistance to countries that are improving their health systems.

OTHER UN BODIES AND HUMAN RIGHTS

The UN Security Council, comprising fifteen member states, is responsible for making decisions regarding international peace and security. It can make recommendations and decisions for action, including providing humanitarian aid, imposing economic sanctions, and recommending peacekeeping operations.

The Security Council has been responsible for establishing international tribunals to prosecute serious violations of humanitarian law. For example, special tribunals have been set up to prosecute war crimes in the former Yugoslavia and acts of *genocide* in Rwanda. The Secretariat is the administrative arm of the UN, responsible for overseeing the programs and policies established by the other UN organs. The position of UN High Commissioner on Human Rights, currently held by Mary Robinson, the former President of Ireland, is part of the UN Secretariat.

Human rights are recognized as fundamental by the United Nations and, as such, feature prominently in the Preamble of the Charter of the United Nations: "... to reaffirm faith in fundamental human rights, in the dignity and worth of the human person, in the equal rights of men and women and of nations large and small...". One of the early acts of the General Assembly was to draft and adopt the Universal Declaration of Human Rights (resolution 217 A of 10 December 1948). As an indication of the continuing importance of this vast field, the General Assembly created the Human Rights Council in 2006. This new body is charged, inter alia, to review and improve the mechanisms of human rights monitoring; UN documentation related to human rights is evolving to reflect the new practices.

The Organization's prominent role in this area is carried out by a number of human rights bodies. When researching human rights issues, a distinction must be made between Charter-based and treaty-based human rights bodies.

Charter-based bodies:

- Derive their establishment from provisions contained in the Charter of the United Nations,
- Hold broad human rights mandates,
- Address an unlimited audience, and

- Take action based on majority voting.

Treaty-based bodies:

- Derive their existence from provisions contained in a specific legal instrument,
- Hold more narrow mandates (i.e., the set of issues codified in the legal instrument involved),
- Address a limited audience (i.e., only those countries that have ratified the legal instrument in question), and
- Base their decision-making on consensus.

Reflecting this distinction, the human rights documentation posted on the website of the Office of the High Commissioner is organized into two databases: Charter-based bodies and Treaty bodies. A third database, the Universal Human Rights Index, provides access to human rights information by country, by rights, or by body.

By resolution 48/141 of 20 December 1993, the General Assembly created the post of United Nations High Commissioner for Human Rights. The Office of the High Commissioner for Human Rights provides secretariat support for all UN human rights bodies.

- Each year the High Commissioner reports on the activities carried out by the Office of the High Commissioner; this report is issued as Supplement No. 36 to the Official Records of the General Assembly (e.g., A/63/36). A complete list of the annual reports, can be found in the UN-I-QUE database.
- Statements made by the High Commissioner can be retrieved through the OHCHR Media Centre.
- The Office of the High Commissioner also administers the communications/complaints procedures available under the various human rights bodies.

HUMAN RIGHTS COUNCIL

The Human Rights Council was established by General Assembly resolution 60/251 of 15 March 2006. The Council meets at least three times annually and reports to the General Assembly.

- Working documents are issued under the series symbol A/HRC/-.
- Summary records of meetings are issued under the series symbol A/HRC/[session]/SR.[meeting number] (e.g., A/HRC/6/SR.27: summary record of the 27th meeting of the 6th session on 11 December 2007).
- The sessional reports are published as Supplement 53 to the Official Records of the General Assembly (e.g., A/63/53 + Add.1). They provide summaries of the work concluded and contain the texts of resolutions and decisions adopted by the Council. A complete list of the sessional reports (2006 onwards) can be found in the UN-I-QUE database.
- Resolutions and decisions are not released as separate documents in paper format but may be retrieved as individual items through the Charter-based bodies' database.
- Full text documents of the Council are retrievable from the Charter-based bodies' database, UNBISnet, and the Official Document System of the UN (ODS).
- UN Headquarters press releases for the Council, issued under the series symbol HRC/-, are accessible through the search option at the Press Releases website. Press releases from the Office of the High Commissioner can be retrieved through the OHCHR Media Centre website.

The Council has responsibility for the special procedures originally established by the Commission on Human Rights. The special procedures include special rapporteurs, special representatives, independent experts, and working groups, that investigate, discuss, and report on specific human rights issues under a country mandate or thematic mandate.

- A complete listing of these reports can be found in the UN-I-QUE database (e.g., reports on extrajudicial, summary and arbitrary executions).
- The full text of recent reports can be retrieved from the Charter-based bodies' database, UNBISnet and the Official Document System of the United Nations (ODS).

- The Universal Human Rights Index database provides access to documents by country, by rights, or by body (including the special procedures of the Human Rights Council).

In addition, by General Assembly resolution resolution 60/251 of 15 March 2006, the Human Rights Council is mandated to undertake a universal periodic review of each state's fulfillment of its human rights obligations and commitments. The modalities of the universal periodic review were decided in the fifth session of the Council. The Secretary-General has compiled guidelines on the form and content of reports to be submitted by States parties to the international human rights treaties (HRI/GEN/2/Rev.5, as at August 2008 only English, Russian and Spanish have been issued).

COMMISSION ON HUMAN RIGHTS

The Commission on Human Rights was established by Economic and Social Council resolution 5 (I) of 16 February 1946. The Commission met in annual and, when required, special sessions and reported to the Economic and Social Council (ECOSOC). The Commission on Human Rights concluded its 62nd and final session on 27 Mar. 2006; its work is continued by the Human Rights Council.

- Working documents were issued under the series symbol E/CN.4/-. The full text of recent documents can be retrieved from the Charter-based bodies' database, UNBISnet and the Official Document System of the United Nations (ODS).
- Summary records of meetings were issued under the series symbol E/CN.4/[year]/SR.[meeting number] (e.g., E/CN.4/1997/SR.52: summary record of the 52nd meeting of the 53rd session on 9 April 1997). The full text of recent meeting records can be retrieved from the Charter-based bodies' database, UNBISnet and the Official Document System of the United Nations (ODS).
- The sessional reports carried a double symbol (series E/- and E/CN.4/-) and were published as Supplements to the Official Records of the Economic and Social Council (e.g.,

E/2006/23-E/CN.4/2006/122 [final report]). They provide summaries of the work concluded and contain the texts of resolutions and decisions adopted by the Commission (resolutions and decisions are not released as separate documents in paper format but may be retrieved as individual items through the Charter-based bodies database). A complete listing of the sessional reports (1947-2006) can be found in the UN-I-QUE database. The full text of recent reports is retrievable from the Charter-based bodies' database, UNBISnet and the Official Document System of the United Nations (ODS).

- UN Headquarters press releases for the Commission, issued under the series symbol HR/CN/-, are accessible through the search option at the Press Releases website. Press releases from the Office of the High Commissioner can be retrieved through the OHCHR Media Centre website.

The Commission had established special procedures: special rapporteurs, representatives or experts and working groups that investigated, discussed and reported on specific human rights issues under a country mandate or thematic mandate. A complete listing of these reports can be found in the UN-I-QUE database (e.g., reports on extrajudicial, summary and arbitrary executions). The full text of recent reports can be retrieved from the Charter-based bodies' database, UNBISnet and the Official Document System of the United Nations (ODS).

HUMAN RIGHTS COUNCIL ADVISORY COMMITTEE

The Human Rights Council Advisory Committee was established by Human Rights Council resolution 5/1 of 18 June 2007; General Assembly resolution 62/219 of 22 December 2007, inter alia, endorses the decision of the Human Rights Council to adopt resolution 5/1. This is a new body and the pattern of documentation has not yet been established. The Advisory Committee supercedes the Subcommission on the Promotion and Protection of Human Rights.

THE PROMOTION AND PROTECTION OF HUMAN RIGHTS

The Subcommission on the Promotion and Protection of Human Rights was established by the Commission on Human Rights under the authority of Economic and Social Council resolution 9 (II) of 21 June 1946. The name was changed from Subcommission on Prevention of Discrimination and Protection of Minorities by ECOSOC decision 1999/256 of 27 July 1999. The Subcommission met in annual sessions from 1947 - 2006. Prior to 19 June 2006, the Subcommission reported to the Commission on Human Rights; its final report was submitted to the Human Rights Council. A complete listing of the sessional reports (1947-2006) can be found in the UN-I-QUE database. The work of the Subcommission is continued by the Human Rights Council Advisory Committee.

- From 1947 to 19 June 2006, working documents were issued under the series symbol E/CN.4/Sub.2/-. The working documents of the final session were issued under the series symbol A/HRC/Sub.1/-.
- From 1947 to 19 June 2006, summary records were issued under the series symbol E/CN.4/Sub.2/[year]/SR.[meeting number] (e.g., E/CN.4/Sub.2/2001/SR.4: summary record of the 4th meeting of the 53rd session on 1 August 2001). The summary records of the meetings of the final session were issued under the series symbol A/HRC/Sub.1/[session]/SR.[meeting number] (e.g., A/HRC/Sub.1/58/SR.1: summary record of the 1st meeting of the 58th session on 7 August 2006; as at 30 July 2008 most of the summary records of these meetings have been issued in English only).
- The sessional reports carried a double symbol (series E/CN.4/- and E/CN.4/Sub.2/-; e.g., E/CN.4/2006/2-E/CN.4/Sub.2/2005/44; the final report has the symbol A/HRC/2/2-A/HRC/Sub.1/58/36 + Corr.1). They provide summaries of the work concluded and contain the text of resolutions and decisions adopted by the Subcommission (resolutions and decisions are not released as separate documents in paper format but may be retrieved as

individual items through the Charter-based bodies database). A complete listing of these reports (1947-2006) can be found in the UN-I-QUE database.

- UN Headquarters press releases for the Subcommission, issued under the series symbol HR/CN/-, are accessible through the search option at the Press Releases website. Press releases from the Office of the High Commissioner can be retrieved through the OHCHR Media Centre website.

Reports were also presented to the Subcommission by working groups and special rapporteurs. A complete listing of these reports can be found in the UN-I-QUE database (e.g., reports on contemporary forms of slavery). The full text of recent reports can be retrieved from the Charter-based bodies' database, UNBISnet and the Official Document System of the United Nations (ODS).

COMMITTEE AGAINST TORTURE

The Committee against Torture was established pursuant to Article 17 of the Convention against Torture and Other Cruel, Inhuman or Degrading Treatment or Punishment to supervise the implementation of the Convention. The current status of the Convention is posted on the website of the High Commissioner. The Committee meets in two sessions each year in Geneva.

- Working documents are issued under the series symbol CAT/C/.
- Summary records of meetings are issued under the series symbol CAT/C/SR.[meeting number] (e.g., CAT/C/SR.382: summary record of the 382nd meeting on 7 May 1999). The full text of recent meeting records can be retrieved from the Treaty body database, UNBISnet and the Official Document System of the United Nations (ODS).
- The sessional reports are issued as Supplement No. 44 to the Official Records of the General Assembly (e.g., A/63/44). A complete listing of these reports (1988 onwards) can be found in the UN-I-QUE database.

- UN Headquarters press releases for the Committee, issued under the series symbol HR/-, are accessible through the search option at the Press Releases website. Press releases from the Office of the High Commissioner can be retrieved through the OHCHR Media Centre website.

States Parties to the Convention are required by Article 19 to submit an initial report on the measures taken to give effect to their undertakings under the Convention within one year after its entry into force for the State Party concerned and thereafter every four years. A complete listing of these reports can be found in the UN-I-QUE database (e.g., reports submitted by Canada). The full text of recent reports as well as report preparation guidelines can be retrieved from the Treaty body database, UNBISnet and the Official Document System of the United Nations (ODS).

COMMITTEE ON ECONOMIC, SOCIAL AND CULTURAL RIGHTS

The Committee on Economic, Social and Cultural Rights was established by Economic and Social Council resolution 1985/17 to supervise the implementation of the International Covenant on Economic, Social and Cultural Rights but functions like a treaty body. The current status of the Covenant is posted on the website of the High Commissioner. The Committee currently meets in three sessions each year in Geneva.

- Working documents are issued under the series symbol E/C.12/-.
- Summary records of meetings are issued under the series symbol E/C.12/[year]/SR.[meeting number] (e.g., E/C.12/1999/SR.37: summary record of the 37th meeting of the 21st session on 19 November 1999).
- The sessional reports carry a double symbol (E/- and E/C.12/-) and are issued as Supplements to the Official Records of the Economic and Social Council (e.g., E/2008/22-E/C.12/2007/3). A complete listing of these reports (1987 onwards) can be found in the UN-I-QUE database.
- UN Headquarters press releases for the Committee, issued under the series symbol HR/-, are accessible through the

search option at the Press Releases website. Press releases from the Office of the High Commissioner can be retrieved through the OHCHR Media Centre website.

States Parties to the Covenant are required by Economic and Social Council resolution 1988/4 to submit an initial report on the measures they have adopted and the progress made in achieving the observance of the rights recognized within the Covenant within two years of its entry into force for the State Party concerned and thereafter every five years. A complete listing of these reports can be found in the UN-I-QUE database (e.g., reports submitted by Denmark). The full text of recent reports as well as report preparation guidelines can be retrieved from the Treaty body database, UNBISnet and the Official Document System of the United Nations (ODS).

THE ELIMINATION OF DISCRIMINATION AGAINST WOMEN

The Committee on the Elimination of Discrimination against Women was established pursuant to Article 17 of the Convention on the Elimination of All Forms of Discrimination against Women to supervise the implementation of the Convention. The current status of the Convention is posted on the website of website of the High Commissioner. The Committee meets in two sessions each year. Beginning in 2008, the meetings are held in Geneva; previously all meetings were held in New York.

- Working documents are issued under the series symbol CEDAW/C/-.
- Summary records of meetings are issued under the series symbol CEDAW/C/SR.[meeting number] (e.g., CEDAW/C/SR.827: summary record of the 827th meeting on 5 January 2008).
- The sessional reports are issued as Supplement No. 38 to the Official Records of the General Assembly (e.g., A/63/38). A complete listing of these reports (1982 onwards) can be found in the UN-I-QUE database. The reports are also issued cumulatively in the series The Work of CEDAW.

- Press releases, issued under the series symbol WOM/-, are accessible through the search option at the at the Press Releases website.

States Parties to the Convention are required by Article 18 to submit an initial report on the legislative, judicial, administrative or other measures which they have adopted and which give effect to the provisions of the Convention within one year after its entry into force for the State Party concerned and thereafter every four years. A complete listing of these reports can be found in the UN-I-QUE database (e.g., reports submitted by Costa Rica). The full text of recent reports as well as report preparation guidelines can be retrieved from the website, the Treaty body database, UNBISnet and the Official Document System of the United Nations (ODS).

COMMITTEE ON THE ELIMINATION OF RACIAL DISCRIMINATION

The Committee on the Elimination of Racial Discrimination was established pursuant to Article 8 of the International Convention on the Elimination of All Forms of Racial Discrimination to supervise the implementation of the Convention. The current status of the Convention is posted on the website of the High Commissioner. The Committee meets in two sessions each year in Geneva.

- Working documents are issued under the series symbol CERD/C/-.
- Summary records of meetings are issued under the series symbol CERD/C/SR.[meeting number] (e.g., CERD/C/SR.1346: summary record of the 1346th meeting on 10 August 1999).
- The sessional reports are issued as Supplement No. 18 to the Official Records of the General Assembly (e.g., A/63/18). A complete listing of these reports (1970 onwards) can be found in the UN-I-QUE database.
- UN Headquarters press releases for the Committee, issued under the series symbol RD/-, are accessible through the search option at the at the Press Releases website.

States Parties to the Convention are required by Article 9 to submit an initial report on the legislative, judicial, administrative or other measures which they have adopted and which give effect to the provisions of the Convention within one year after its entry into force for the State Party concerned and thereafter every two years. A complete listing of these reports can be found in the UN-I-QUE database (e.g., reports submitted by Botswana).

Committee on the Protection of the Rights of All Migrant Workers and Members of Their Families

The Committee on the Protection of the Rights of All Migrant Worker and Members of Their Families was established pursuant to Article 72 of the Convention on the Protection of the Rights of All Migrant Workers and Members of Their Families to supervise the implementation of the Convention. The current status of the Convention is posted on the website of the High Commissioner. The Committee meets in Geneva.

- Working documents are issued under the series symbol CMW/C/-.
- Summary records of meetings are issued under the series symbol CMW/C/SR.[meeting number] (e.g., CMW/C/SR.12: summary record of the 12th meeting on 26 Apr. 2005).
- The sessional reports are issued as Supplement No. 48 to the Official Records of the General Assembly (e.g., A/63/48). A complete listing of these reports (2004 onwards) can be found in the UN-I-QUE database.
- UN Headquarters press releases for the Committee, issued under the series symbol HR/-, are accessible through the search option at the at the Press Releases website.

States Parties to the Convention are required by Article 73 to submit an initial report on measures adopted which give effect to the rights recognized therein and on the progress made on the enjoyment of those rights within one year of its entry into force for the State Party concerned and thereafter every five years. A complete listing of these reports can be found in the UN-I-QUE database (e.g., report submitted by Mali).

COMMITTEE ON THE RIGHTS OF THE CHILD

The Committee on the Rights of the Child was established pursuant to Article 43 of the Convention on the Rights of the Child to supervise the implementation of the Convention. The current status of the Convention is posted on the website of the High Commissioner. The Committee meets in three sessions each year in Geneva.

- Working documents are issued under the series symbol CRC/C/-.
- Summary records of meetings are issued under the series symbol CRC/C/SR.[meeting number] (e.g., CRC/C/SR.391: summary record of the 391st meeting on 2 June 1997).
- Sessional reports of the Committee are issued as Supplement No. 41 to the Official Records of the General Assembly (e.g., A/63/41). A complete listing of these reports (1991 onwards) can be found in the UN-I-QUE database.
- UN Headquarters press releases for the Committee, issued under the series symbol HR/-, are accessible through the search option at the Press Releases website.

States Parties to the Convention are required by Article 44 to submit an initial report on measures adopted which give effect to the rights recognized therein and on the progress made on the enjoyment of those rights within two years of its entry into force for the State Party concerned and thereafter every five years. A complete listing of these reports can be found in the UN-I-QUE database (e.g., reports submitted by Thailand).

HUMAN RIGHTS COMMITTEE

The Human Rights Committee was established pursuant to Article 28 of the International Covenant on Civil and Political Rights. The current status of the Covenant is posted on the website of the High Commissioner. The Committee meets in three sessions each year in New York and Geneva.

- Working documents are issued under the series symbol CCPR/C/-.
- Summary records of meetings are issued under the series symbol CCPR/C/SR.[meeting number] (e.g., CCPR/C/SR.1690: summary record of the 1690th meeting on 24 July 1998).
- The sessional reports are issued as Supplement No. 40 to the Official Records of the General Assembly (e.g., A/62/40 (Vol.I) and A/62/40 (Vol.II)). A complete listing of these reports (1977 onwards) can be found in the UN-I-QUE database.
- From 1977-1987, the Committee published a Yearbook; since 1987, this publication has been continued by the Official Records of the Human Rights Committee.
- UN Headquarters press releases for the Committee, issued under the series symbol HR/CT/-, are accessible through the search option at the Press Releases website.

States Parties to the Covenant are required by Article 40 to submit an initial report on the measures they have adopted which give effect to the rights recognized within the Covenant and on the progress made in the enjoyment of those rights within one year of its entry into force for the State Party concerned and thereafter every five years. A complete listing of these reports can be found in the UN-I-QUE database (e.g., reports submitted by Jordan).

The Committee also considers communications under the Optional Protocol received from individuals who assert that their rights (as enumerated in the Covenant) have been violated without domestic redress. The texts of the Committee's final decisions under the Protocol are included in its annual reports (e.g., A/62/40 (Vol. II)), as well as periodically cumulated on a selective basis.

5

Human Rights and Responsibilities

Human rights are universal, meaning that each person possesses certain human rights by the mere fact of this person's humanity. What does not matter - or at least what should not matter - is where a person lives, how much money a person has (or does not have), whether that person's country has (or has not) became a party to any particular international human rights treaties, and so on. Who has the responsibility for meeting these "universal" rights? The (universal) response of states has been that each country is responsible for protecting human rights within its own borders - but that no state has human rights obligations that extend outside of its own territorial jurisdiction. But what if a country is not able or is not willing to protect the human rights of its citizens? Or what if human rights are being violated, in large part due to the actions of outside states? It is here that the silence of the international community has been deafening.

Thus, notwithstanding near-universal declarations of the "universality" of human rights, the responsibility for protecting human rights has been based almost exclusively on territorial considerations. What has this territorial approach to human rights given us? Unfortunately, not nearly enough. Looking at violations of economic rights alone, we live in a world where an average of 50,000 people die every single day due to preventable causes. Yet, notwithstanding this incredible level of human rights atrocities, the territorial approach to human rights has essentially gone unchallenged. However, this has started to change and it has come from the most unlikely of sources: the "war on terror." To state matters bluntly, the reason why "enemy combatants" are being held at Guantanamo Bay, Cuba and not in some location in this country is that American government officials are of the mind that U.S. obligations under international law do not extend outside the territorial boundaries of the United States.

Under this (territorial) approach to human rights, the U.S. government is not bound by the Torture Convention and the Covenant on International Civil and Political Rights (both of which the U.S. is a party to) when it is operating outside the territorial borders of the United States. This same kind of rationale is behind the policy of "extraordinary rendition." The idea is that the U.S. has not done anything wrong or unlawful when individuals outside the United States are being kidnapped and sent to some third country for "interrogation" purposes - albeit at the behest of, and under the direction and control of, American authorities. Again, the argument is that American obligations under international law are only applicable to actions within the United States.

Fortunately, most people have been able to see behind this façade. That is, they have recognized that territorial considerations should not be used in this manner to demarcate where a country's human rights obligations begin - but, more importantly, where they end. Most people seem to believe that torture is illegal whether it takes place in Fort Benning, Georgia, or Guantanamo Bay, Cuba, or at the Abu Ghraib prison in Iraq. In that way, the "war on terror" has helped us see that territorial considerations oftentimes make little sense in the context of protecting human rights. This is not to suggest that "territory" does not matter at all or that states have the same human rights obligations outside their borders as they do domestically. Neither of these propositions happens to be true.

Rather, each state has the primary responsibility for protecting human rights within its own domestic borders. However, what we have completely failed to recognize are the secondary responsibilities that the rest of the international community has when the territorial state has not been willing or able to offer human rights protection. And what also has to be said is that this is not simply a moral obligation - wouldn't it be a nice gesture if we provided some assistance to starving children in some other land - rather, it is a legal obligation. This is most clearly seen in the language of the International Covenant on Economic, Social and Cultural Rights, one of the so-called International Bill of Rights, whereby each state party to the Covenant has (legally) obligated itself to protect the economic rights of "everyone" by means of "international assistance and cooperation."

What does "international assistance and cooperation" mean? What it means is that when children in a particular country are being denied an education (to choose one example), this not only constitutes a violation of human rights by the territorial state - but this also constitutes a human rights violation on the part of the rest of the international community, which has pledged to protect those rights. The point is that human rights are universal, but so are the duties and responsibilities to meet those rights. This is what the framers of the International Bill of Rights, and all of the other international human rights treaties, sought to achieve. This is the only way that the notion of human rights makes any sense.

If human rights protection were something that individual states could (and would) do individually, there would be no need for any international conventions. Stripped to their barest essentials, what each one of these treaties represents is nothing less than this: that everyone has an ethical as well as a legal obligation to protect the human rights of all other people. Sadly enough, our inability to recognize the extent of our own human rights obligations has constituted the greatest human rights failure of all. Human rights are the basic rights that belong to all of us just because we are human beings. They have been recognised around the world as the basic standards required for governments, societies and communities to operate in a respectful and peaceful manner.

Human rights are the foundation for freedom, justice, peace and respect, and are an essential part of any democratic and inclusive society that respects the rule of law, human dignity and equality. Everyone has the same human rights: men, women, and children, rich and poor, and all nationalities and faiths. Human rights are about recognizing and respecting the dignity of other people.

Our human rights entitlements include:

- Civil and political rights.
- Economic and social rights.
- Environmental and cultural rights.

THE VICTORIAN CHARTER OF HUMAN RIGHTS AND RESPONSIBILITIES

The Charter is an Act of Parliament that clearly sets out our rights and freedoms, and the responsibilities that go with them, in one document. The Charter focuses on civil and political rights, and includes well known democratic rights such as the right to vote and freedom of expression. Other rights protected by the Charter include:

- Protection from forced work.
- The right to privacy.
- The right to a fair trial.
- Cultural rights.

The Charter is an agreed set of human rights, freedoms and responsibilities protected by law. Government departments and public bodies must observe these rights when they create laws, set policies and provide services. This means that Government, public servants, local councils, Victoria Police and others are required to act in a way that is consistent with the human rights protected under the Charter. These bodies will have to comply with the Charter and take human rights into account in their day-to-day operations.

All new laws require a Statement of Compatibility to tell Parliament whether they meet the standards set by the Charter. New laws are required to be checked against the Charter. In the rare circumstance that a law does not meet human rights standards then the Government is expected to explain how and why. In exceptional circumstances Parliament may strike down a law that does not uphold human rights. From 1 January 2008, the Supreme Court can issue a Declaration of Incompatibility requiring the Government to reconsider legislation but it does not have the power to strike down legislation. Parliament has the final say over what laws are in place in Victoria.

There is no additional right to legal action just for a breach of the Charter. The focus of the Charter is about getting things right at a planning and policy stage, rather than awarding compensation. It is designed to ensure the Government anticipates and prevents potential human rights infringements. However, the Charter allows a person to raise a human rights argument in a court or tribunal in an existing case. When complaint handling bodies such as the Health Services Commissioner and the Victorian Equal Opportunity & Human Rights Commission deal with existing complaints, they also need to give consideration to human rights. Additionally, the Victorian Ombudsman investigates complaints about the Victorian government departments, most statutory authorities and local government. Under the Charter, the Ombudsman's office has the power to investigate whether any administrative action is incompatible with a human right.

The Charter is essentially a form of insurance to ensure that human rights are a priority for present and future governments. Experience in other countries shows that when human rights are considered when making laws, developing policies and delivering services, the community is more united and people can participate fully and equally in society. The Charter will ensure that the State Government respects our basic rights when it provides services such as healthcare, education and law enforcement. New policies and laws will also take into account human rights and people who work for the Government must also observe human rights so that people are not treated unfairly.

Although some human rights were protected in various other laws, several other basic and important rights, such as freedom of speech, freedom from forced work, and freedom from degrading treatment, had no clear legal protection. The Charter's main purpose is to ensure that the State Government makes laws fairly. In that sense, everyone will benefit. Over time the Charter will help to change attitudes so that we all understand that rights come with responsibilities - including the responsibility to respect other people's rights.

Most parts of the Charter of Human Rights and Responsibilities came into effect from 1 January 2007. The public sector will be bound by the Charter from 1 January 2008. This extra time is to allow for practices and procedures to be changed if necessary. The Charter protects the group of rights referred to as civil and political rights. These can be grouped under four key principles of Freedom, Respect, Equality and Dignity.

FREEDOM

Freedom of Movement, Expression, Assembly and Association

People who are in Victoria lawfully have the right to enter and leave the State, to move around freely within it and to freely choose where they live. People have the right to hold opinions without interference from the government or from other people. People have the right to seek out, receive and pass on information and ideas of all kinds whether orally, in writing, in print, as an artistic expression or in any other way of their choosing. People have the right to assemble and meet peacefully, to freely associate with others and to form and join trade unions.

Right to Liberty and Security

Everyone has the right to freedom (liberty) and security. This means a person must not be arrested or detained arbitrarily. A person must not be deprived of his or her freedom, except when it is lawful and according to procedures established by law. For example, when someone has been arrested and charged with a crime. If a person is arrested or detained, he or she must be told the reason at the time of their arrest or detention and promptly told about charges to be laid.

A person must be quickly brought before a court and tried without unreasonable delay. Otherwise, that person must be released.

A person who is awaiting trial must not be automatically kept in custody. They may be released with conditions, guaranteeing they appear in court (for example, bail). Any person who is deprived of their freedom by arrest or detention has the right to apply to a court for a declaration on whether the detention is lawful. The court must make a decision on this application without delay and order the release of the person if it finds that the detention is against the law.

Children in the Criminal Process

A child charged with committing a crime who is being detained or a child who has been detained without charge must be held separately from all detained adults; brought to trial as quickly as possible; and treated in a way that is appropriate for his or her age.

A Fair Hearing

A person has a right to a fair hearing. This means the right to have criminal charges or civil proceedings decided by a competent, independent and impartial court or tribunal after a fair and public hearing. A court or tribunal can exclude the media and the public from a hearing if a law other than the Charter allows it to do so. All judgments or decisions made by a court or tribunal must be made public unless doing so would not be in the best interests of a child, or a law other than the Charter allows it to be kept secret.

Rights in Criminal Proceedings

A person who is charged with a crime has the right to be presumed innocent until proved guilty according to the law.

A person charged with a crime is entitled without discrimination to a number of minimum guarantees, such as:

- To be promptly informed about the detail and reason for the charge.
- Access to legal representation (a lawyer).

- The help of an interpreter.
- Enough time and facilities to prepare a defence and communicate with a lawyer or advisor.
- To be tried without unreasonable delay.
- To be present at the trial.
- To choose to access legal representation or have legal aid, if eligible. There is no right to legal aid beyond the eligibility set out in the Legal Aid Act 1978 (Vic).
- To examine prosecution witnesses, and to call witnesses on his or her behalf.
- The right not to testify against oneself and the right not to be compelled to confess guilt.

These guarantees are set out to ensure that the person charged fully understands the process taking place and has the opportunity to answer the charges brought against them. A child who is charged with a crime has the right to a process that takes into account their age and the desirability of promoting their rehabilitation. Any person convicted of a crime has the right to have the conviction and sentence reviewed by a higher court in accordance with law.

Right not to be Tried or Punished more than once

A person cannot be tried or punished for the same offence twice if he or she has already been convicted or acquitted of that offence in a court.

Retrospective Criminal Laws

A person must not be found guilty of a crime if the behaviour was not against the law at the time they engaged in it. If a penalty is imposed for a crime, it must not be greater than the penalty that applied at the time the offence was committed. If a penalty for an offence is reduced after a person committed the offence, that person must be eligible for the reduced penalty. These points do not apply to offences under international law.

Freedom of Thought, Conscience, Religion and Belief

People have the freedom to have or choose a religion or

belief, and the freedom to demonstrate their religion or belief. They can do this privately or publicly - at home, at work or in a place of worship - as part of a group or alone. For example, banning the wearing of religious symbols could be a breach of freedom of religion.

Property Rights

A person must not be deprived of his or her property except in accordance with law. For example, if there has been a breach of a mortgage contract, it may be lawful to deprive a person of their property as long as proper processes are followed.

Freedom from Forced Work

A person must not be held in slavery or servitude, or forced to work, except as part of normal civil obligations (such as jury duty), or as part of a court order, or during emergency situations. For example, forced work does not include court ordered community service.

RESPECT

Right to Life

Every person has the right to life and the right not to be arbitrarily deprived of life.

Protection of Families and Children

Families are entitled to be protected by society and the State. Public authorities should keep this in mind when carrying out their duties. Children have the right to protection according to their best interests, without discrimination.

Cultural Rights, including recognition that Human Rights have a special importance for the Aboriginal people of Victoria

People of all cultural, religious, racial or linguistic backgrounds have the right to enjoy their culture, declare and practise their religion and use their languages. Aboriginal people have the right to enjoy their identity and culture. They have the right to maintain their language, kinship ties and their distinctive essential relationship with the land, waters and other resources to which they have a connection under traditional laws and customs.

EQUALITY

Equal Recognition before the Law

Every person has the right to equal recognition and protection before the law. Everyone is entitled to equal and effective protection against discrimination, and to enjoy human rights without discrimination. This applies regardless of a person's age, gender, race, disability, religion, marital status and a range of other personal characteristics. Some groups or individuals, such as people with a disability or members of minority groups may be disadvantaged by discrimination they experience. Measures taken to help people who are disadvantaged by discrimination will not be considered unlawful under the Charter. For example, government funded programs may be directed to particular disadvantaged groups.

Entitlement to Participate in Public Life (including voting)

Every person has the right to take part in public affairs without discrimination. Every eligible person has the right to vote, be elected and to have equal access to the Victorian public service and public office.

DIGNITY

Protection from Torture and Cruel, inhuman or Degrading Treatment, Medical or Scientific Experimentation or Treatment without Consent

A person must not be tortured, treated or punished in a cruel, inhuman or degrading way. A person must not be subjected to medical or scientific experimentation or treatment without his or her full, free and informed consent.

Protection of Privacy and Reputation

A person has a right to privacy. This means that someone's personal privacy, family, home or correspondence can not be unlawfully or arbitrarily interfered with. The Charter also prohibits unlawful attacks on a person's reputation.

Humane Treatment when Deprived of Liberty

All people deprived of their freedom (liberty) must be treated with humanity and respect for their dignity. An accused person or someone who is detained without charge must be held separately from people who have been convicted of offences, except where reasonably necessary. They must be treated in a way that is appropriate for someone who has not been convicted.

Limiting Human Rights

The Charter recognises that human rights are not absolute but may be limited in certain circumstances. Under the Charter rights may be limited but only when justified in a free and democratic society, taking into account relevant factors. These factors involve the following types of questions:

- Which right is to be limited? Is the right very important in international law, for example, freedom from torture?
- Is the purpose for wanting to limit the human right very pressing and important to society?
- What sort of limitation is being imposed? *How* could it infringe human rights?
- Is the limitation likely to achieve its purpose? Is the limitation excessive or out of proportion to its purpose?
- Are there any less restrictive means reasonably available to achieve the purpose that the limitation seeks to achieve?

For example, the right to freedom of expression may be restricted in order to respect the rights and reputation of other people or for the protection of national security, public order, health or morality. This allows a balance to be struck between people's rights and a need for Government departments and other public organisations to protect the broader public interest.

The role of the Victorian Equal Opportunity and Human Rights Commission

Under the Charter, the Victorian Equal Opportunity and Human Rights Commission (formerly the Equal Opportunity Commission Victoria) is responsible for:

- Ensuring Victorians understand their human rights protections and obligations.
- Providing an independent assessment of how well State and local governments comply with the Charter.

To meet these responsibilities, the Commission will:

- Report to the Attorney-General about how the Charter is operating in relation to new legislation and the courts.
- Work with community organisations to promote human rights and raise awareness about the Charter.
- Report to the Attorney-General about community perspectives on how the Charter is operating.
- Investigate particular human rights issues and concerns.
- Review the policies and practices of public authorities to ensure they comply with the Charter.

These responsibilities are in addition to the Commission's existing responsibilities which include:

- Resolving complaints of discrimination, sexual harassment, and racial and religious vilification through its free, impartial conciliation process.
- Conducting education, consultancy services and research
- Providing legal and policy advice.
- Informing Victorians about equal opportunity and racial and religious vilification laws.

Our world is becoming smaller and ever more interdependent with the rapid growth in population and increasing contact between people and governments. In this light, it is important to reassess the rights and responsibilities of individuals, peoples and nations in relation to each other and to the planet as a whole. This World Conference of organizations and governments concerned about the rights and freedoms of people throughout the world reflects the appreciation of our interdependence. No matter what country or continent we come from we are all basically the same human beings. We have the common human needs and concerns. We all seek happiness and try to avoid suffering regardless of our race, religion, sex or political status.

Human beings, indeed all sentient beings, have the right to pursue happiness and live in peace and in freedom. As free human beings we can use our unique intelligence to try to understand ourselves and our world. But if we are prevented from using our creative potential, we are deprived of one of the basic characteristics of a human being. It is very often the most gifted, dedicated and creative members of our society who become victims of human rights abuses. Thus the political, social, cultural and economic developments of a society are obstructed by the violations of human rights. Therefore, the protection of these rights and freedoms are of immense importance both for the individuals affected and for the development of the society as a whole.

It is my belief that the lack of understanding of the true cause of happiness is the principal reason why people inflict suffering on others. Some people think that causing pain to others may lead to their own happiness or that their own happiness is of such importance that the pain of others is of no significance. But this is clearly shortsighted. No one truly benefits from causing harm to another being. Whatever immediate advantage is gained at the expense of someone else is short-lived. In the long run causing others misery and infringing upon their peace and happiness creates anxiety, fear and suspicion for oneself. The key to creating a better and more peaceful world is the development of love and compassion for others. This naturally means we must develop concern for our brothers and sisters who are less fortunate than we are.

In this respect, the non-governmental organizations have a key role to play. You not only create awareness for the need to respect the rights of all human beings, but also give the victims of human rights violations hope for a better future. We need to think in global terms because the effects of one nation's actions are felt far beyond its borders. The acceptance of universally binding standards of Human Rights as laid down in the Universal Declaration of Human Rights and in the International Covenants of Human Rights is essential in today's shrinking world. Respect for fundamental human rights should not remain an ideal to be achieved but a requisite foundation for every human society.

When we demand the rights and freedoms we so cherish we should also be aware of our responsibilities. If we accept that others have an equal right to peace and happiness as ourselves do we not have a responsibility to help those in needs? Respect for fundamental human rights is as important to the people of Africa and Asia as it is to those in Europe or the Americas. All human beings, whatever their cultural or historical background, suffer when they are intimidated, imprisoned or tortured. The question of human rights is so fundamentally important that there should be no difference of views on this. We must therefore insist on a global consensus not only on the need to respect human rights world wide but more importantly on the definition of these rights.

Recently some Asian governments have contended that the standards of human rights laid down in the Universal Declaration of Human Rights are those advocated by the West and cannot be applied to Asia and others parts of the Third World because of differences in culture and differences in social and economic development. The majority of Asian people do not support this view either, for it is the inherent nature of all human beings to yearn for freedom, equality and dignity, and they have an equal to achieve that. I do not see any contradiction between the need for economic development and the need for respect of human rights. The rich diversity of cultures and religions should help to strengthen the fundamental human rights in all communities. Because underlying this diversity are fundamental principles that bind us all as members of the same human family. Diversity and traditions can never justify the violations of human rights. Thus discrimination of persons from a different race, of women, and of weaker sections of society may be traditional in some regions, but if they are inconsistent with universally recognized human rights, these forms of behavior must change. The universal principles of equality of all human beings must take precedence.

It is mainly the authoritarian and totalitarian regimes who are opposed to the universality of human rights. It would be absolutely wrong to concede to this view. On the contrary, such regimes must be made to respect and conform to the universally accepted principles in the larger and long term interests of their own peoples. The dramatic changes in the past few years clearly indicate that the triumph of human rights is inevitable. There is a growing awareness of peoples' responsibilities to each other and to the planet we share. This is encouraging even though so much suffering continues to be inflicted based on chauvinism, race, religion, ideology and history. A new hope is emerging for the downtrodden, and people everywhere are displaying a willingness to champion and defend the rights and freedoms of their fellow human beings.

Brute force, no matter how strongly applied, can never subdue the basic human desire for freedom and dignity. It is not enough, as communist systems have assumed, merely to provide people with food, shelter and clothing. The deeper human nature needs to breathe the precious air of liberty. However, some governments still consider the fundamental human rights of its citizens an internal matter of the state. They do not accept that the fate of a people in any country is the legitimate concern of the entire human family and that claims to sovereignty are not a license to mistreat one's citizens. It is not only our right as members of the global human family to protest when our brothers and sisters are being treated brutally, but it is also our duty to do whatever we can to help them.

Artificial barriers that have divided nations and peoples have fallen in recent times. With the dismantling of Berlin wall the East - West division which has polarized the whole world for decades has now come to an end. We are experiencing a time filled with hope and expectations. Yet there still remains a major gulf at the heart of the human family. By this I am referring to the North-South divide. If we are serious in our commitment to the fundamental principles of equality, principles which, I believe, lie at the heart of the concept of human rights, today's economic disparity can no longer be ignored. It is not enough to merely state that all human beings must enjoy equal dignity. This must be translated into action. We have a responsibility to find ways to achieve a more equitable distribution of world's resources.

We are witnessing a tremendous popular movement for the advancement of human rights and democratic freedom in the world. This movement must become an even more powerful moral force, so that even the most obstructive governments and armies are incapable of suppressing it. This conference is an occasion for all of us to reaffirm our commitment to this goal. It is natural and just for nations, peoples and individuals to demand respect for their rights and freedoms and to struggle to end repression, racism, economic exploitation, military occupation, and various forms of colonialism and alien domination. Governments should actively support such demands instead of only paying lip service to them.

As we approach the end of the Twentieth Century, we find that the world is becoming one community. We are being drawn together by the grave problems of over population, dwindling natural resources, and an environmental crisis that threaten the very foundation of our existence on this planet. Human rights, environmental protection and great social and economic equality, are all interrelated. I believe that to meet the challenges of our times, human beings will have to develop a greater sense of universal responsibility. Each of us must learn to work not just for one self, one's own family or one's nation, but for the benefit of all humankind. Universal responsibility is the best foundation for world peace.

This need for co-operation can only strengthen humankind, because it helps us to recognize that the most secure foundation for a new world order is not simply broader political and economic alliances, but each individual's genuine practice of love and compassion. These qualities are the ultimate source of human happiness, and our need for them lies at the very core of our being. The practice of compassion is not idealistic, but the most effective way to pursue the best interests of others as well as our own. The more we become interdependent the more it is in our own interest to ensure the well-being of others.

Today sees the 60th anniversary of the Universal Declaration of Human Rights and it's good to see that Justice Secretary Jack Straw is commemorating the event by and planning to water down human rights laws. The Justice Secretary's admission that he is 'frustrated' by the way the Act has sometimes been interpreted by the courts alarmed campaigners. He told the Mail there were genuine public concerns about the way it is being exploited by criminals and extremists to hide from the law. The Justice Secretary sympathises with those who complain that the act has become used by prisoners to avoid punishment or by Islamic extremists to avoid deportation. He tells the Mail that he wants to 'rebalance' the rights set out in the Human Rights Act by adding explicit 'responsibilities', specifically to obey the law and to be loyal to the country. He said: 'I fully understand that Mail readers have concerns about the Human Rights Act. There is a sense that it's a villains charter or that it stops terrorists being deported or criminals being properly given publicity. I am greatly frustrated by this, not by the concerns, but by some very few judgments that have thrown up these problems.'

There are three main planks to his argument. Firstly he buys in to the Mail's "villain's charter" line by complaining that the act is often used by criminals. Well that's the thing about human rights - we possess them by virtue of being human, not by being law-abiding and they apply to the worst of us as well as the best. In fact an essential part of any charter or bill of rights is how we are treated when suspected of a crime (guilty or not) and if we are subsequently convicted.

Furthermore, given the squalid state of our prison system it is hardly surprising that the government is found to be in breach of the HRA in the way some prisoners are treated. Of course there may be individual rulings which seem perverse (although it's important to separate these from myths such as rioting prisoners being given KFC meals because of the HRA) but there is no evidence that there is any widespread abuse of the HRA which would require it to be amended.

Secondly he bemoans the government's inability to deport Islamic extremists, which is probably the area which causes most controversy. The most notorious case of course is Abu Qatada, whose extradition to Jordan was blocked on the basis that he would not receive a fair trial. The issue more commonly arises when the government wants to deport those whom it considers extremists and who have no right to remain in the country, but cannot because of likelihood they will be tortured in the countries to which they are sent. As for "memoranda of understanding" that the people concerned will not be tortured, well the notion that these would be worth the paper they are written on is laughable.

Finally, Straw claims that he wants to rebalance' the rights set out in the Human Rights Act by adding explicit 'responsibilities', specifically to obey the law and to be loyal to the country." First of all the specifics he mentions are nonsense; there are already penalties for those who do not obey the law, this hardly needs to be pointed out. As people living in a complex society we do have some kinds of responsibilities towards each other and society in general, but the point of the HRA is that it is enforceable in law - even if you could codify the kinds of behaviour which make us responsible citizens (but are not subject to the law already) how is the government going to enforce them, by making our rights stated in the HRA conditional on them? But human rights are not conditional - as stated above we possess them merely by virtue of being human. If you attach conditions then they cease to become rights at all, so the government would either be tearing up the ECHR or be left with a list of nice sounding but unenforceable platitudes.

In fact the HRA needs tightening, not watering down. It hasn't prevented control orders, restrictions on the right to protest and other attacks on civil liberties by New Labour (although the decision on the DNA database was a result). It wouldn't have prevented 42 days' detention. Given the occasion it would have been nice to see a more noble response from the government - a strong statement on the importance of human rights and a promise to uphold and strengthen the HRA. But we know by now that this is too much to hope for. What we have heard today only emphasizes the wisdom of those statesmen who wanted to try to use their eminence to bring attention to an issue that was under the radar of the media, many NGOs, and certainly most world leaders — the important domain of responsibility.

This concept was once so central to our philosophical and ethical discourse, but the leaders of that time made the point that it had been slipping—not in its importance, but in its visibility—and it was time to right that balance. If the Inter Action Council was right in the mid-1990s, how prescient they are and were when we look at the notion of responsibility today. Recent headlines speak of corporate leaders who have lied to their boards, auditors who have assisted in that lying, leaders who have deliberately or inadvertently misled their public on crucial decisions about whether to choose peace or go to war. Great organs of journalism such as the New York Times have had reporters totally fabricate stories, and there are church leaders who stand accused of sexual crimes.

The list goes on and on, in area after area—men and women in high places abusing their position, their privileges. And it's not just related to the political sphere or the international sphere. Today we could have also had a panel on corporate leadership, on religious leadership, on media leadership, where all the issues we've been talking of with regards to the terms of terrorism of the state we could have replicated in domain after domain. It is fair to say we are facing a crisis of responsibility in field after field. The interlocking set of institutions to police behavior and, more importantly, the internal clock of morality that we should possess have been turned back. The subject of how responsibility adheres to rights is an absolutely crucial one.

Historically we've spent a lot of time talking about the origins of rights—John Locke, the17th century and so on. In fact, ethical discourse goes back a thousand years before our discussions of rights. When we look at when democracy was first invented in 5th century Athens, the Athenians had a variety of discussions about the obligations of citizenship but not about rights. Socrates did not have rights when he was murdered by his fellow citizens. The essence of Confucian philosophy is how to have internal discipline so that we could discipline our emotions and have right behaviors beginning with ourselves, extending to our families, to our responsibilities to a broader society and eventually to our leadership. The Buddha talked about the necessity for internal transformation in order to discipline our human emotions. And why is that?

Theologian Reinhold Niebuhr in his book *Children of Light and the Children of the Darkness* argued that we all know as human beings that we can transcend toward love and sharing, but we have an almost equal determination to have our egos dominate our personalities, to have ambition control all else. Much of human life is a contending battle between those forces of light and forces of darkness. Therefore, our ethical and spiritual leaders have taught right from the start about implicating a personal sense of discipline and moral value to control the demons within. And we still continually need to control our demons within if we look at the *New York Times*, the Enrons and all the rest.

The emphasis here is on the internal discipline – the obligations to carry out a set of ethical norms beginning with ourselves as human beings – before looking at checks and balances and accountability and the rule of law. The first defense of civilization is the internal morality of each and every one of us. That is why when our great ethical thinkers and religious leaders began to develop their systems, they began with that sense of personal efficacy that we all should hold, and they were right; that's where it all starts.

With our discussion about rights we have to all understand that our societies would disappear if most of us didn't pay our taxes. Societies would disappear if most of us did not fulfill our contracts. Societies would disappear if no one voted. Society depends on trust and internal personal devotion to carrying out a set of obligations, and then when that internal morality fails we use the law to enforce it. But we could not do that in every case. Our societies all depend on that sense of personal responsibility for them to survive at all. Therefore, if we have a diminution in responsibility and particularly one among our leaders, as Prime Minister Malcolm Fraser talked about, that is a terrible sign and one which is worthy of the priority the InterAction Council has put on this subject.

The second main point that we have had several speakers allude to is that this has always been an issue since Jeremiah and Confucius and the Buddha up until today, in the first part of the 21st century. We've had speakers emphasizing why that concern is so critical today and that's because of a broad set of concerns around the responsibility to protect. Prime Minister Fraser talked about the responsibility to protect societies in an age of terrorism. Think back for a moment on the terrible picture that he painted of our Western societies so afraid of the forces of terrorism that we are even conniving at torture—torture, which was almost the first human abnormality that society wanted to outlaw. Yet we have voluntarily become torturers in our age. Think about what the prime minister said – what does it imply about the world we live in that we do not have outrage across the world against those who practice torture?

Instead, we have debates, but it hasn't been a central concern. What has happened to us in our fear is that we have had such derogation from a traditional adherence that if there was one thing we believed, it was that one should not torture. But we've begun to slip away from that, as the prime minister pointed out. In this tremendous debate about the responsibility of our leaders to protect us from outrages for our personal and physical security, the responsibility of how that protection function should be carried out has been lost. The internal clock of our leaders, the internal clock of the military, and the internal clock of the torturers themselves has been turned off.

And it's not just the Iraq War or Guantanamo Bay. In my own country, Canada, a Canadian of Syrian background, Mr. Qatar, suspected of terrorism was, with the connivance of our secret service along with the American authorities, instead of being sent back to Canada to be tried in a court of law on his suspected terrorism, there was a wink and a nudge and he was sent back to Syria to be tortured. Both our countries were implicated. Not wanting to do the torture themselves, they were only too happy to have the Syrians do it. What kind of countries and what kind of peoples are we that we would begin to connive in that kind of activity?

In our post-September 11 world, when we think how far we have derogated from our traditional adherence on things such as not having torture, just think back historically for a moment. If we go back to another age of worries about terrorism, immediately after World War I where in Canada fears of the Bolshevik Revolution, the Winnipeg General Strike, led to a host of illegal activities by our RCMP based on the fear of Bolshevik revolutionaries. Look how silly they now look years later, but they didn't look silly at the time. Think of the Palmer raids, Boston police, and the administration of Woodrow Wilson and the fears that the US would be undergoing a Red Revolution and the terrible abuses that occurred then, but to general acclaim with very little debate. And then look how silly and sick they look years later.

Japanese Americans and Japanese Canadians suspected of being terrorists from within—we all know what a shameful episode that was in this state and in the province of British Columbia. So, from time to time, bodies, peoples, democracies, go through fits, democratic distempers and that's when you really need that moral clock, responsibility, for people to say 'stop this.' And then behind that moral sense you then need courts and judges and Supreme Courts to prevent that distemper from spreading if it begins to occur. The prime minister put down an enormous challenge to us about whether we have been going off the deep end. We also, in some ways, have made the world worse by our tendency to intervene with words and our tendency not to intervene with resources in any meaningful way. When one goes to Sarajevo and Bosnia today, one is filled with attacks about the UN because hopes were raised so high that force might protect the Bosnian Muslims from the outrages of the Croats and Serbs.

Yet because the world did not want to put in sufficient resources and the Security Council did not want to give that force a robust ability to enhance, because there was not really a commitment to do anything about Bosnia but there was a fear to forthrightly tell our peoples that we would not do anything, everyone connived in a sham—a sham peacekeeping force that couldn't really protect and a whole series of sham resolutions that tumbled one upon the other. The result was that the people who saw that sham the quickest learned the UN was not really there to protect the people; they were there to protect the reputations of Bill Clinton and various others but not to protect the Bosnians themselves. And so we do a worse job when we say we have a responsibility to protect and we say to our citizens we are being responsible when we know we're not. Even more people will be killed because of that.

The UN is under constant attack in large part because the leaders have made a series of obligations to the UN in the Charter, but they do not have the responsibility to fulfill them. Much of the problem with our international machinery is not the laws; it's the political will to carry them out. That means that our leaders, by in large, are not fulfilling the responsibilities which they have agreed to and which our countries have signed treaties on. Ultimately much of the failure of the international machinery is another example of the failure of responsibility. So, the IAC, men and women of power, have spent time now to reflect on what they would do differently using their experience, not just to have an academic exercise, but what would be useful to help diplomats and leaders today.

The leaders from the recent past have said what is missing

is a charter about responsibility. Of all the things they could have done (they've done a variety of very useful things on nuclear non-proliferation and small arms at their meeting here at Santa Clara) one of the major items of their reflection of what is required in the world architecture was not a new treaty, but a new moral force or a charter of responsibility. That was a very important ethical denouement that the IAC took. The point was raised about enforcement. Having a code which talks about ethical behavior and which puts a premium on truth—this is not law, this is not enforceable. This is moral norms, but it's the norms of responsibility so that the internal clocks of our leaders can be turned on again. The charter won't guarantee it, but it will help.

It is a modest contribution, but it is a real one. When one thinks about the Universal Declaration of Human Rights, it didn't begin as law; it began as a set of principles, and it turned into law. The charter on responsibility begins with a series of principles - principles as parents, principles as leaders, principles as citizens. We all need to be reminded of those principles. And that's what the IAC is calling for. This is why the worry among some in the human rights community about the charter of responsibility I find difficult to understand. It is reminding peoples of their internal responsibilities and the obligations they have undertaken. That is what responsibility is about: What do I undertake to fulfill? That itself is a basic orientation that is then reflected in a variety of other ethical norms. It means you are serious about your word.

That is what the IAC calling for—people to be serious about their obligations, the undertakings they have done. There is nothing, in my view, antithetical with human rights about this proposal, which is be serious about the human rights treaties you sign instead of words that would take away from human rights. If you do not intend to undertake your obligations, the pieces of paper on human rights are worthless. The precondition to human rights is to have a sense of responsibility to carry out your undertakings. The two are absolutely complementary and one is a precondition of the other.

Why this particular undertaking of responsibility at this time? Historical researchers can show that in the original Declaration of Human Rights, there were representatives of the then-Republic of China who where active in it and the work of John Humphrey went to legal norms around the country. But since that time, the Universal Declaration has been under attack by those who follow Asian values and other kinds of values on the basis that this is a Western device. The InterAction Council, at this time and place, with their necessity to restore some sense of responsibility and to bring some attention to having a code of responsibility, began by inviting people from a variety of faiths, who all have their own ethical codes and their own sense of responsibility codes. What the IAC has done is not new.

There are codes of responsibility for the media, codes of responsibility everywhere. But they took the convening function of taking people from a variety of faiths and said what is in common that we can all agree to. So in a time when we talk about clash of civilizations, when religions are so antithetical, when we need to look at connectors, think of this initiative at this time that it sought to find the commonality about a variety of faith traditions. Have we ever needed it more?

6

Violation of Women's Rights

Women form half of the human beings inhabiting planet Earth. Since human rights are the rights of all human beings, male and female alike, human rights are women's rights. By the same token, a society in which men are not willing to extend human rights to their mothers, the women who bore and nurtured them; their daughters, products of their own loins; and their wives, the women who bear and raise their treasured sons, is a society in which men are unwilling to extend human rights to men of another family, tribe, language, religion, race, ethnic tradition, or nation. If a society does not hold justice and equality for all women in the highest regard, neither will it hold justice and equality for the many varieties of men in high regard. In a very real sense, women's rights are the basis of all human rights.

Women's rights belong to women as members of the human family, and, as such, are not dependent either on a woman's marital status or on the number or sex of the children she has borne. From time to time, it behooves us to examine human rights in the special context of women's rights. Since the primary responsibility of any society is to bear and raise future generations of male and female human beings, women's roles in reproduction must be held in the highest esteem and must not be permitted to become the basis for discrimination against women as women. Further, the responsibility for raising and nurturing future generations must fall upon men and women equally. Parents, male and female alike, have the right to guide the upbringing of their children according to the dictates of their consciences.

Women are important and, often, unpaid contribution to the family and the community must be considered in the event of a divorce, the death of the family's primary wage earner, and a woman's own death. Since a husband and wife are equal partners in creating and maintaining a family, upon her husband's death, one-half of the family's property is to be considered the property of the widow, property which she helped to create by her labor in the interests of the family unit. Women, equal to men in the eyes of the law, shall be subjected to the same laws, no more and no less, as men. All laws that restrict women as women are null and void. Women have the right to the same access as men to food, clothing, shelter, medicine, an education, job training, and employment.

Women, like men, have the right to rest and leisure, including a reasonable limitation on working hours, a living wage for a reasonable number of hours worked, and periodic holidays. Women have the right to equal pay for the same work as men. Just as woman has the right to enter the place of public execution, woman has the right to enter the place of public acclaim for her accomplishments. Women, like men, have the right to freely participate in the cultural life of the community, to enjoy the arts and to share in scientific, economic, and cultural advancement and their benefits. Women, equal to men in the eyes of the law, shall be subjected to the same laws, no more and no less, as men. For the violation of any law, women shall be subject to the same punishment as men, no more and no less. Women have the same rights as men to life, liberty, property, security, and the pursuit of happiness and can be denied these things only by the due process of law.

Consequently, "Crimes of honor" are, indeed, crimes, violations of human rights, and must be prosecuted to the fullest extent of the law. Women have the right to be free from all forms of domestic violence. Women have the same right to bodily autonomy as men, especially as regards their reproductive organs. Surgical alteration of a woman's sexual organs for any reason other than her health is a violation of her human rights. Compelling women to bear unwanted children and forbidding women from bearing wanted children are violations of women's human rights. Any act of unwanted sex, including child molestation, forced prostitution, military sexual slavery, trafficking in women, forced participation in the creation of pornography, sex by extortion, marriage by rape, rape as an instrument of war, rape as a means of terror or torture, acquaintance rape, and marital rape, is a violation of girls' and women's human rights. Selective abortion based on the sex of the fetus, female infanticide, and sex selection of embryos is violations of women's and girls' human rights.

The laws of both marriage and divorce apply equally to men and women. Marriage shall be entered into only with the free and full informed consent of the intending spouses. Children are not capable of providing informed consent to such an important undertaking. Neither education nor any profession may be closed to any qualified woman. Women, like men, have the right to assemble peacefully, for whatever reason their conscience dictates including, but not limited to, teaching, learning, debating, discussing, worshipping, owning and operating businesses either as individuals or as groups, creating and maintaining local, state, national, and international non-governmental organizations, such as institutions to promote the arts, the humanities, and the sciences, professional societies, educational establishments, medical facilities, social services organizations, churches, synagogues, mosques, temples, and other religious organizations, sports clubs, legal and legal aide societies, self-help groups, co-operatives, and trade unions, and engaging in all group endeavors in both social and civic arenas of life.

Women have the same rights as men to equal access to service provided by her government, including, but not limited to, services in such areas as education, medicine, law, finance and banking, farm assistance, technical assistance, transportation, sanitation, electricity, communications, water, social support services, land redistribution, home building, and public sector employment. Women are entitled to engage in the same legal public and private activities as men, including the right to travel with only the same restrictions as imposed upon men. Women have the right to own and to control their own passports regardless of marital status. Women are entitled to a nationality, regardless of their martial status and regardless of the nationality or actions of their husbands, fathers, sons, or other family members.

The rights to consent to the form of government under which one resides and to consent to the laws which govern one's actions are widely recognized as human rights, the rights of men and women alike. As such, a constitution is null and void if the majority of individuals comprising the nation or their representatives have not cooperated in drafting it. The equal voice of women must be present in the drafting of a nation's constitution. The right of suffrage, the right to vote by secret ballot, for the people to represent them in all levels of government including village, city, county, state, and national offices applies to women, as well as, men.

All male and female citizens, equal in the eyes of the law, have the right to run for public office and to serve in those offices, if elected. As citizens, women have an obligation to the state to sit on juries to assist in determining the guilt or innocence of an accused man or woman. Women have the right to have other women sit on a jury to help determine their guilt or innocence when charged with a crime. Women have a right to interpret the laws of the land as legal scholars, court officials, and magistrates. Women have a right to help to enforce the laws of the land both as police officers and as other civil officials responsible for uncovering suspected criminals and bringing them to a court of law.

Women, as well as men, must be equally admitted to all honors, positions, and public employment according to their capacity and without other distinctions besides those of their virtues and talents. Women, as well as men, must participate in the formation and implementation of all public policies. Women, as well as men, have the right as public officials to represent their government agency to local, state, national, and international non-governmental organizations, to various levels of other government agencies of their own nation's political structure, to foreign governments, and to international political institutions. Women, like men, have the right to petition the government for a redress of their grievances. No woman shall be held in slavery or involuntary servitude, except as punishment for a crime. Sexual slavery and trafficking in women are human rights violations.

No man or woman shall be subjected to torture or to cruel, inhuman, or degrading treatment or punishment, including genital mutilation and rape. Men and women alike are entitled to the equal protection of the law. No one shall be subjected to detention, regardless of whether the place of detention is a public place like a prison or a jail, or a private place like a house, without due process of law. Women, like men, have the right to enter into contracts and to own and administer property. The free communication of ideas and opinions, through the spoken, written, and printed word, is one of the most precious human rights for women, as well as, for men.

As such, women have the right to speak the name of the man who raped her, the name of the father of her illegitimate child, the name of a man who beats her, learn to read and write, teach the history of the women who came before her, describe the myriad of ways in which government and social policies affect her, both positively and negatively, as a woman, participate in all aspects of her religious faith and religious traditions both in public, as from the pulpit, and in private, as in personal prayer with her family and friend, and contribute to the development of the arts, literature, humanities, religion, culture, and the sciences.

Women's rights are human rights. This notion is at once fundamental and revolutionary. In theory, women have never been overtly excluded from the concept of human rights. In 1945, the UN Charter afforded to women and men equal economic, social, cultural, political and civil rights. Nevertheless, because women traditionally have been relegated to the private sphere and to subordinate status in society, they have generally been excluded from recognized definitions and interpretations of human rights. As such, women and girls' experiences with human rights abuse have been virtually ignored. Most of the casualties of war are women and children; most of the world's refugees and displaced people are women and children; most of the world's poor are women and children. Still, because of persistent discrimination against women and women's virtual invisibility, these human rights violations continue with no clear sign of abatement.

VIOLATION OF WOMEN'S HUMAN RIGHTS

The ways in which women experience human rights-and human rights violations-are unique. While human rights are often understood as the rights that everyone has by virtue of their humanity, the assumption that all humans have the same experiences and needs is particularly problematic for women.

- Historically, states have assumed responsibility for human rights violations only when state agents or officials were the perpetrators. Indeed, certain forms of violence against women by state agents have been acknowledged as torture. However, women more often face abuse from non-state actors, such as their employers, partners, husbands, families and community members. When international law is applied without an understanding of the state's responsibility for abuses committed by private actors, women are denied an essential part of the protection that the human rights system is supposed to provide. When the state dismisses the majority of violence against women as private or domestic matters, thereby allowing this violence to continue, it sends a clear message that violence against women is condoned.

  Kajal Khidr was accused of adultery by her husband's family and held hostage by six family members in Iraqi Kurdistan. Kajal Khidr was tortured and mutilated; family members cut off part of her nose and told her she would be killed after the birth of her child. After fleeing to Syria, two of her abusers were arrested. However, they were both released within twenty-four hours because authorities determined they had acted to safeguard the honor of the family. No charges were ever brought against them.

- Human rights violations against women are often complicated by further discrimination on the grounds of race, ethnicity, sexual identity, caste, religion, class or age. The type and prevalence of violence and discrimination that women experience are often determined by how their gender interacts with these other factors.

  Bhanwari Devi was raped by five men of a higher caste in India. The gender-specific sexual abuse that she suffered was compounded by discrimination based on her social status. In the acquittal of her attackers two years later, the court noted that the incident could not possibly have happened because upper caste men would not rape a woman of a lower caste.

- Human rights have long been understood to apply universally-to all people, at all times, in all places. However, in the case of women's human rights, this principle continues to be challenged. Some justify violations of women's human rights by placing precedence on cultural values and traditions. This view, however, fails to understand that some practices and beliefs termed "culture" or "tradition" often shape women's lives in a way that subordinates them and discriminates against them. By placing limitations of the universality of the human rights of women, cultural values rooted in unequal power relations between women and men become justification for the systematic denial of civil, cultural, economic, political and social rights.

  Hannah Koroma (Sierra Leone) was genitally mutilated against her will at the age of ten, as a rite of passage signifying her entrance into womanhood eligibility for marriage. The ritual was performed with a blunt penknife and Hanna Koroma was denied any anesthetic or antibiotics during or after the procedure. When the operation left her hemorrhaged and anemic, her community attributed her pain to witchcraft.

- Violence against women is rooted in a global culture that discriminates against women and denies them their equal rights with men. Women today earn less than men, own less property than men, and have less access to education, employment, housing and health care. This global culture of discrimination against women denies women their fundamental human rights and legitimizes the violent appropriation of women's bodies for individual gratification or political ends.

STATE RESPONSIBILITY FOR WOMEN'S HUMAN RIGHTS

Each of the human rights treaties and the whole of the human rights framework are essential for the realization of women's full spectrum of rights. States have a responsibility whether abuses against women are committed by state or non-state actors, in the public or private spheres. Their obligations under international human rights law can be summarized under three categories: respect, protect and fulfill.

- The state has an obligation to respect women's human rights through its direct action, agents and structures of law. A state's constitution must recognize equality between women and men in all spheres; state or official actors must be held accountable when they perpetrate violence against women; private actors who perpetrate violence against women must be prosecuted.
- The state has an obligation to protect women's human rights. The state must take all necessary measures to prevent individuals or groups from violating the rights of each individual. As such, the state must take affirmative steps to prevent direct and indirect discrimination against women. Women must be fairly represented in government and have legal access to all forms of employment.
- The state is also required to fulfill the human rights of women by ensuring opportunities for individuals to obtain what they need and to provide that which cannot be secured by personal efforts. This obligation for women and men ranges from providing food, water, housing and education to ensuring the conditions necessary for women's organizations to form and function.
- International law has developed the standard of due diligence as a way to measure whether a state has acted

with sufficient effort to live up to its responsibilities to uphold human rights, i.e. to respect, protect and fulfill. As a standard that has been incorporated into UN documents, due diligence is a term used to describe the minimum effort which a state must demonstrate to fulfill its responsibility to protect individuals from human rights abuses.

Women's rights and human rights are indivisible. All governments are obliged to uphold the basic human rights of each individual on an equal basis. States must recognize the unique context in which women experience human rights and take all necessary steps to protect women from discrimination and abuse in both the private and public spheres.

WOMEN'S RIGHTS VIOLATION IN AFGHANISTAN

The government of Afghanistan is waging a war upon women. Since the Taliban took power in 1996, women have had to wear *burqua* and have been beaten and stoned in public for not having the proper attire, even if this means simply not having the mesh covering in front of their eyes. One woman was beaten to DEATH by an angry mob of fundamentalists for accidentally exposing her arm while she was driving. Another was stoned to death for trying to leave the country with a man that was not a relative.

Women are not allowed to work or even go out in public without a male relative; professional women such as professors, translators, doctors, lawyers, artists and writers have been forced from their jobs and stuffed into their homes, so that depression is becoming so widespread that it has reached emergency levels. There's no way in such an extreme Islamic society to know the suicide rate with certainty, but relief workers are estimating that the suicide rate among women, who cannot find proper medication and treatment for severe depression and would rather take their lives than live in such conditions, has increased significantly.

Homes where a woman is present must have their windows painted so that she can never be seen by outsiders.

They must wear silent shoes so that they are never heard. Women live in fear of their lives for the slightest misbehavior. Because they cannot work, those without male relatives or husbands are either starving to death or begging on the street, even if they hold Ph.D.'s. There are almost no medical facilities available for women and, relief workers in protest have mostly left the country, taking medicine and psychologists and other things necessary to treat the sky-rocketing level of depression among women.

At one of the rare hospitals for women, reporters found still, nearly lifeless bodies lying motionless on top of beds, wrapped in their burqua, unwilling to speak, eat, or do anything, but slowly wasting away. Others have gone mad and were seen crouched in corners, perpetually rocking or crying, most of them in fear. One doctor is considering, when what little medication that is left finally runs out, leaving these women in front of the president's residence as a form of peaceful protest.

It is at the point where the term 'human rights violations' has become an understatement. Husbands have the power of life and death over their women relatives, specially their wives, but an angry mob has just as much right to stone or beat a woman, often to death, for exposing an inch of flesh or offending them in the slightest way. Women enjoyed relative freedom, to work, dress generally as they wanted, and drive and appear in public alone until only 1996. The rapidity of this position is the main reason for the depression and suicide; women who were once educators or doctors or simply used to basic human freedoms are now severely restricted and treated as sub-human in the name of right-wing fundamentalist Islam. It is not their tradition or 'culture,' but is alien to them, and it is extreme even for those cultures where fundamentalism is the rule. Everyone has a right to a tolerable human existence, even if they are women in a Muslim country. If we can threaten military force in Kosovo in the name of human rights for the sake of ethnic Albanians, citizens of the world can certainly express peaceful outrage at the oppression, murder and injustice committed against women by the Taliban.

Statement

In signing this, we agree that the current treatment of women in Afghanistan is completely unacceptable and deserves support and action by the United Nations and that the current situation overseas will not be tolerated. Mens' Rights is not a small issue anywhere, and it is unacceptable for women in the millennium to be treated as sub-human and as so much property. Equality and human decency are rights- not freedoms- whether one lives in Afghanistan or elsewhere. If after reading this you cannot find it in your heart to take 2 minutes out of your life to forward this and add your name then I would hope you never find yourself in this situation and ask for help. If so, someone else just might not want to take the 2 minutes out of their life to possibly better your situation and give you that second chance at life, with all its liberties, freedoms and justices that we all deserve.

Human rights as an issue occupies centre stage in contemporary public debate. Part of the debate on Human rights is about the origin and significance of the notion itself. Changes in a society demand changes in the way of maintaining social order. The techniques of social control are also adjusted to changed situations, as no system of social control works perfectly. People often deviate from social and legal norms, although non-conformity varies greatly in form and frequency. Though deviation is perceived as a threat to social stability yet attitude towards deviants keeps on changing with change in beliefs in the causes of deviant behavior in general and crime in particular. Almost everyday there are chilling instances of violence, ethnic cleansing, heinous torture, child abuse, man slaughter and several other human rights violations. Despite the adoption of the Universal Declaration Human Rights (1948) and special covenants provided for the rights of children, women and disabled, crimes continue unhindered and unabated.

Subjugation of Women

Violence affects the lives of millions of women worldwide, in all socio-economic and educational classes. It cuts across cultural and religious barriers, impeding the right of women to participate fully in society. Violence against women takes a dismaying variety of forms, from domestic abuse and rape to child marriages and female circumcision. All are violations of the most fundamental human rights. In India women constitute nearly fifty percent of our population. Women are denied human rights from the cradle to the grave. Infanticide is rampant in certain parts of the country where the birth of a girl child is not welcome. Nearly forty-one percent of the women abroad play an active role in the production process. In India the situation leaves much to be desired. Sexual abuse and flesh trade are gnawing evils, which threaten the existence of women as independent entities.

KINDS OF VIOLENCE AGAINST WOMEN

DOMESTIC VIOLENCE

Violence against women in the family occurs in developed and developing countries alike. It has long been considered a private matter by bystanders – including neighbours, the community and government. But such private matters have a tendency to become public tragedies.

Traditional Practices

In many countries, women fall victim to traditional practices that violate their human rights. The persistence of the problem has much to do with the fact that most of these physically and psychologically harmful customs are deeply rooted in the tradition and culture of society.

Female Genital Mutilation

According to the World Health Organization, 85 million to 115 million girls and women in the population have undergone some form of female genital mutilation and suffer from its adverse health effects.

Son Preference

Son preference affects women in many countries, particularly in Asia. Its consequences can be anything from foetal or female infanticide to neglect of the girl child over her brother in terms of such essential needs as nutrition, basic health care and education. In India, some women choose to terminate their pregnancies when expecting daughters but carry their pregnancies to term when expecting sons.

According to reports from India, genetic testing for sex selection has become a booming business, especially in the country's northern regions. Indian gender-detection clinics drew protests from women's groups after the appearance of advertisements suggesting that it was better to spend $38 now to terminate a female foetus than $3,800 later on her dowry. A study of amniocentesis procedures conducted in a large Bombay hospital found that 95.5 per cent of foetuses identified as female were aborted compared with a far smaller percentage of male foetuses.

Dowry-related Violence and Early Marriage

Dowry is the greatest crime against women. Are our daughters and sisters for sale? Women are virtually sold into the marriage market. Huge dowries are still demanded even when the girl can supplement the man's income. In such a milieu, a woman enjoys no rights because she is a woman. In some countries, weddings are preceded by the payment of an agreed-upon dowry by the bride's family. Failure to pay the dowry can lead to violence. In India, an average of five women a day is burned in dowry-related disputes – and many more cases are never reported. Early marriage, especially without the consent of the girl, is another form of human rights violation. Early marriage followed by multiple pregnancies can affect the health of women for life.

VIOLENCE IN THE COMMUNITY

Rape

Rape is a weapon to subjugate women. The woman is safe nowhere. Justice prides herself on being blind to everything but the truth - yet as far as rape is concerned; the facts paint a different picture. Rape can occur anywhere, even in the family, where it can take the form of marital rape or incest. It occurs in the community, where a woman can fall prey to any abuser. It also occurs in situations of armed conflict and in refugee camps.

Sexual assault within Marriage

In many countries sexual assault by a husband on his wife is not considered to be a crime: a wife is expected to submit. It is thus very difficult in practice for a woman to prove that sexual assault has occurred unless she can demonstrate serious injury.

Sexual Harassment

Sexual harassment in the workplace is a growing concern for women. Employers abuse their authority to seek sexual favours from their female co-workers or subordinates, sometimes promising promotions or other forms of career advancement or simply creating an untenable and hostile work environment. Women who refuse to give in to such unwanted sexual advances often run the risk of anything from demotion to dismissal. But in recent years more women have been coming forward to report such practices and some taking their cases to court. In a significant judgment of Vishaka vs State of Rajasthan, the Supreme Court laid down exhaustive guidelines for preventing sexual harassment of working women in their place of work until legislation is enacted for this purpose.

Prostitution and Trafficking

Many women are forced into prostitution either by their parents, husbands or boyfriends — or as a result of the difficult economic and social conditions in which they find themselves. They are also lured into prostitution, sometimes by mail-order bride agencies that promise to find them a husband or a job in a foreign country. As a result, they very often find themselves illegally confined in brothels in slavery-like conditions where they are physically abused and their passports withheld.

Most women initially victimized by sexual traffickers have little inkling of what awaits them. They generally get a very small percentage of what the customer pays to the pimp or the brothel owner. Once they are caught up in the system there is practically no way out, and they find themselves in a very vulnerable situation. Since prostitution is illegal in many countries, it is difficult for prostitutes to come forward and ask for protection if they become victims of rape or want to escape from brothels. Customers, on the other hand, are rarely the object of penal laws.

VIOLENCE AGAINST WOMEN MIGRANT WORKERS

Female migrant workers typically leave their countries for better living conditions and better pay -but the real benefits accrue to both the host countries and the countries of origin. For home countries, money sent home by migrant workers is an important source of hard currency, while receiving countries are able to find workers for low-paying jobs that might otherwise go unfilled. But migrant workers themselves fare badly, and sometimes tragically. Many become virtual slaves, subject to abuse and rape by their employers.

Pornography

Another concern highlighted is pornography, which represents a form of violence against women that glamorizes the degradation and maltreatment of women and asserts their subordinate function as mere receptacles for male lust.

VIOLENCE PERPETRATED OR CONDONED BY STATES

Custodial Violence against Women

Violence against women by the very people who are supposed to protect them — members of the law enforcement and criminal justice systems — is widespread. Women are physically or verbally abused; they also suffer sexual and physical torture. According to Amnesty International, thousands of women held in custody are routinely raped in police detention centre worldwide. In the Tuka Ram vs State of Maharashtra - The judgment did not distinguish between consent and forcible submission. Correspondingly the judgments in Bhanwari Devi and a few other cases were unjust and in favor of the accused.

Governments agreed to adopt and implement national legislation to end violence against women and to work actively to ratify all international agreements that relate to violence against women. They agreed that there should be shelters, legal aid and other services for girls and women at risk, and counselling and rehabilitation for perpetrators. Governments also pledged to adopt appropriate measures in the field of education to modify the social and cultural patterns of conduct of men and women. And the Platform called on media professionals to develop self-regulatory guidelines to address violent, degrading and pornographic materials while encouraging non-stereotyped, balanced and diverse images of women.

The meaning of gender and sexuality and the balance of power between women and men at all levels of society must be reviewed. Combating violence against women requires challenging the way that gender roles and power relations are articulated in society. In many countries women have a low status. They are considered as inferior and there is a strong belief that men are superior to them and even own them. Changing peoples attitude and mentality towards women will take a long time- at least a generation, many believe, and perhaps longer. Nevertheless, raising awareness of the issue of violence against women, and educating boys and men to view women as valuable partners in life, in the development of a society and in the attainment of peace are just as important as taking legal steps to protect women's human rights.

Violence against Women, a Severe Violation of Women's Human Rights Civil society organizations based in the border city of Juarez have registered and denounced, since 1993, the discriminatory treatment, the negligence and the acquiescence of local and federal authorities related to the forced disappearance and murder of hundreds of women. The call for justice has crossed Ciudad Juárez's boarders.

In the following days, Mexico will be standing trial at the Inter-American Human Rights Court for violating the right of women to live free from violence, specifically for the disappearance, torture and assassination of three women, two of them adolescents. The bodies of Esmeralda Herrera Monreal, Claudia Ivette González and Laura Berenice Ramos Monárrez, were found with the bodies of five other women in a cotton field in Ciudad Juárez. Eight years have passed since these crimes were committed, yet they still remain unpunished.

At last, the mothers of Esmeralda Herrera, Claudia Ivette and Laura Berenice will be heard by an impartial court in Santiago de Chile, where the public hearing of the Case of Campo Algodonero will take place. During all these years, the mothers of Irma, Josefina and Claudia, as well as their defenders, have been harassed, threatened and targeted in smear campaigns directed by Mexican authorities. The Inter-American Court is at a crucial moment, facing the challenge of hearing a case that entails serious and continued violations to women's human rights committed by the Mexican State. The time has come for the Court to clearly define State responsibilities regarding violence against women, which is sustained on historically unequal power relationships between women and men, and affects a broader group of women, as well as all of them as a gender.

Knowing what happened and accessing justice in these cases are essential requirements for social reconstruction. While being a woman represents a mortal danger, none of us will be able to exercise our rights and liberties. We express our concern for the physical integrity of women's human rights defenders whose life and families have been in danger as a consequence of their declarations in the media, the legal representation of specific cases in local, federal and international Courts, as well as their demands for real, categorical and effective public policies and governmental actions to stop violence against women in Ciudad Juárez. These women fear that the risk will increase as a result of the case being heard at the Inter-American Court.

We urge the Inter-American Court to categorically pronounce itself on the severe and permanent violations to women's human rights perpetrated by the Mexican State, and to point out clear mechanisms for the reparation of the damage inflicted to the families of Esmeralda Herrera, Claudia Ivette and Laura Berenice. Religion and Women's Human Rights The European Women's Lobby (EWL) is a non-governmental umbrella organisation (NGO) bringing together women's NGOs from 25 Member States of the European Union and accession countries, as well as from 18 European-wide and international organisations. EWL's mission is to work together to achieve equality between women and men, to eliminate all forms of discrimination against women, to ensure respect for women's human rights and to eradicate violence against women.

Hence EWL documents ways in which the achievement of these goals is impeded by any trends and calls for changes that will remove barriers to their achievement. In particular, concerns expressed by EWL members about a perceived stronger influence on governments of religious argumentation with respect to women's role and gender equality have led to this position paper. Our task is to continue to name, expose and condemn those practices that violate women's rights and silence women's voices wherever they may be. EWL refers to those areas in which cultural and religious practices and in some instances, legal practices, continue systematically to discriminate against women and the girl child either directly or indirectly, excluding them from public and political life, denying them equal rights to economic independence, including in marriage, divorce and inheritance and denying women's rights to autonomy in matters of sexual and reproductive choice and health.

All of these practices should be named for what they are, i.e. violations of women's human rights and should never be placed within a cultural context that at the end of the day conceals the reality under a cultural mask. In the face of this, the challenge is great but not insurmountable. Growing importance of religious power in Europe EWL observes that a more conservative political climate over the past decade in Europe and globally has led to a growth in the influence of religion - all religions - in Europe. EWL recognises the threat religions play in refusing to question patriarchal cultures which hold up the role of wife, mother and housewife as the ideal and refuse to adopt positive measures in favour of women, for example in parliamentary elections. This is particularly marked however, in relation to two of the major religions - Christianity, particularly the Roman Catholic Church, but also more fundamentalist, protestant strands, and Islam.

EWL is not concerned with the faith to which any one may adhere and regards religious freedom as well as the freedom not to believe in any divine being as essential human rights. EWL acknowledges that many women find comfort and wisdom in their faith and would not wish to undermine this positive experience. EWL also recognises that religious influences may be progressive, for example when tolerance and equality are part of the teaching. And EWL is fully aware that traditions or cultural practices that are harmful or violate human rights have developed that are closely associated with religious commands but may not directly be attributable to them.

None the less, EWL is concerned that religion is impacting on European and national level policies in ways which undermine equality between women and men, and curtails women's access to and enjoyment of their basic human rights. Religion - used as justification for infringements of women's human rights The argument is frequently made by religious authorities and by adherents that discriminatory actions are not to be found within the faith - that is, in the revered books, such as the Bible or the Koran. None the less religion is used to justify commandments directed only at women such as dress codes that render them invisible, that require the shaving of the head, that restrict the movement of women outside and inside the home, the holding of positions of authority within the churches as ministers or priests and outside in places of work and organisations and to deny them access to education or to work outside the home and to fulfill their potential in all walks of life.

The most painful violations occur often in relation to marriage and the family - especially a woman's rights to choose her own partner or not to choose at all, to bear or not bear children and to choose the number and spacing of them, to divorce or not, and on divorce, to enjoy the same rights and privileges as her husband. One example of the latter is the withholding of the certificate of religious divorce for women in Orthodox Judaism. The divorcing husband is free to live his life while his wife remains tied to him and he may bargain for payments to be made to him before he will release her under Jewish law. Indeed religions worldwide seek to control female sexuality and condemn women's expression and enjoyment of their sexuality routinely with much greater harshness than that of men.

Most religions also condemn all sexual relationships except those between a woman and her husband - women in some societies may still be stoned for adultery and/or killed for so-called "honour crimes". And only heterosexuality is condoned. Furthermore, doctrine in almost all religions is developed only by men so that: "….half of Europe's population (the female half) has scant or no opportunity to influence religious doctrine. Hence the more religious influence we allow to seep back into our societies and our political decision-making processes, the less representative and the less respectful of women's rights the resulting policies and practices will tend to be."

The Framework of Human Rights Instruments EWL holds governments to the commitments made by all European and States Parties of the United Nations, in the Beijing Platform for Action, in Human Rights instruments globally and in the ECE region and especially in the Convention on the Elimination of All forms of Discrimination Against Women (CEDAW). At no time will EWL accept cultural relativism when the argument may be made that a violation of women's rights is decreed by faith and culture and is therefore exempt from human rights concerns. In particular, EWL insists on a woman's right to bodily integrity and freedom from violence and on her right to reproductive choice, health care and services. Her right to form partnerships and marry, to choose the timing and number of her children and to take steps to meet these goals may not be impeded.

Actions needed to support the values and principles of the European Union for equality between women and men and global human rights including among NGOs EWL and its members have become alarmed by the presence of certain ultra-conservative religious lobby groups, who may be identified as fundamentalists, seeking to exercise influence, for example within the EU and at the United Nations, especially targeting the annual Commission on the Status of Women, against rights won with great difficulty over time that enable women's equality and empowerment. Both moderate religious organisations and women's organisations seek to safeguard, not to undermine, policies and practice globally and within the EU that carry forward the mandate and implement intrinsic values of the Union for equality between women and men as well as enabling access to human rights.

In particular, EWL strongly supports the statement: "Freedom of religion cannot be accepted as a pretext to justify violations of women's rights, be they open, subtle, legal or illegal, practiced with or without the nominal consent of the victims - women." EWL Demands EWL consequently calls on EU Member States to:

1. Implement the Council of Europe Resolution immediately.
2. Promote an inter-religious dialogue on all levels in order to create a common ethical platform honouring the basic principle of equality between women and men.
3. Condemn any form of religious practice that results in the violation of women's human rights.
4. Identify and implement measures to assist and protect women who are victims of religious practice that violates their rights.
5. Inform women who are victims of religious practice that violates their rights about these rights and put preventative measures in place.
6. Prohibit and punish practices for which justification is claimed on religious grounds and which damage a woman's physical integrity and basic human rights, whether this practice takes place within the borders of the EU or in third countries.

7. Condemn and punish genital mutilation, honour crimes and any form of violence, in particular domestic violence, carried out in the name of religion and enact legislation to prohibit and criminalize these practices.
8. Within religious schools and where religious education is permitted in schools, ensure that this teaching is in conformity with gender equality principles.
9. Guarantee, maintain and promote the sexual and reproductive rights of all women without religious or cultural distinctions; provide information about the risks of sexual diseases such as AIDS and detail every woman's right to the integrity of her own body.
10. Ensure women are recognised as entitled to rights in their own capacity and not indirectly through their father, husband, other relative or any other person(s) - i.e. recognise the individualisation of women's rights in all areas.
11. Guarantee and facilitate political asylum in the European Union Member States for all women who are victims of or who are threatened with persecution linked to religious practice in their country.
12. Guarantee strong support for Women's NGOs fighting against religious oppression.
13. Consider demonstrable respect for women's rights as a condition for aid in partner countries at international level and within EU foreign and development aid policies.
14. Seek to guarantee the supremacy of basic freedoms and rights by ensuring a clear separation between Church and State.

WOMEN'S LAND AND PROPERTY RIGHTS ARE HUMAN RIGHTS

The Sub-Commission on the Prevention of Discrimination and Protection of Minorities, a human rights body at the United Nations, adopted its second resolution on Women's Right to Land, Property and Adequate Housing on 20 August 1998. This resolution follows from last year's on the same topic. This resolution is most important for recognising that women's rights to land and property are human rights. It states "that the discrimination faced by women with respect to acquiring and securing land, property and housing, as well as financing for land, property and housing constitutes a violation of women's human rights to equality, protection against discrimination and to equal enjoyment of the right to an adequate standard of living, including adequate housing."

There are a number of effective ways in which the Sub-Commission resolutions can be used to promote, protect and enforce human rights. Here are three suggestions:

a. If you or your organisation uses litigation as a strategy for change, the opening paragraphs of the resolutions can be used/cited to support legal arguments regarding women's right to adequate housing and to land and property. It should be noted, however, that resolutions of this sort do not have the force of law and therefore should only be used to support or uphold rights that are already recognised and codified in legally binding instruments.
b. The resolutions can also be sent directly to government officials in your region/country to inform them that the United Nations has clearly identified women's right to land, property and housing as human rights and to pressure them to take this resolution (and the documents on which it relies) into consideration.
c. The resolutions may also be used as an educational tool to raise awareness. In its current form it can be used with some lawyers, judges, governmental officials, non-governmental organisations (NGOs) and academics to assist them in understanding the issues related to women and housing, land and property and some of the essential linkages as found in the resolution. If the resolution were transformed into an easier-to-read format, it could also be used as a popular educational tool.

The following is the full text of the latest resolution:

- Women and the Right to Land, Property and Adequate Housing.

- The Sub-Commission on Prevention of Discrimination and Protection of Minorities,
- Recalling Commission on Human Rights resolution 1998/51 of 17 April 1998 calling for the integration of the human rights of women throughout the United Nations system,
- Recalling also Sub-Commission resolutions 1997/19 of 27 August 1997 entitled "Women and the Right to Adequate Housing and to Land and Property," and 1997/9 of 22 August 1997 entitled "Implementation of the Human Rights of Women and the Girl Child,"
- Recalling further, the recognition and legal foundations of the right to adequate housing contained in, inter alia, articles 7, 12, 17 and 25, paragraph 1, of the Universal Declaration of Human Rights; article 2 paragraph 2, and article 11 paragraph 1, of the International Covenant on Economic, Social and Cultural Rights; article 2 paragraph 1, and articles 17 and 26 of the International Covenant on Civil and Political Rights; the Optional Protocol to the International Covenant on Civil and Political Rights; article 5 (e) (iii) of the International Convention on the Elimination of All Forms of Racial Discrimination; articles 4 and 27 of the Convention on the Rights of the Child and article 14 paragraph 2 (g) and (h) and article 16 (h) of the Convention on the Elimination of All Forms of Discrimination Against Women,
- Reaffirming the right to be free from discrimination based on sex and the equal right of men and women to the enjoyment of all civil, cultural, economic, political and social rights as stipulated in, inter alia, the International Bill of Human Rights,
- Bearing in mind the Habitat Agenda (A/CONF.165/14) adopted by the United Nations Conference on Human Settlements (Habitat II) and the Platform for Action (A/CONF.177/20) adopted by the Fourth World Conference on Women,
- Concerned that as a result of the discrimination faced by women with respect to acquiring and securing land, property and housing, the number of women living in

poverty is increasing disproportionately to the number of men and that women's experiences of poverty are particularly severe and prohibit women from escaping the poverty trap,

- Recognising that the existence and perpetuation of gender-biased laws, policies and traditions which deny women credit and loans and keep women from owning and inheriting land, property and housing and which exclude women from fully participating in development processes discriminate against women and create insecure and inadequate housing and living conditions,
- Deeply concerned that inadequate and insecure housing and living conditions give rise to serious mental and physical health problems for women and contribute to cause and are often the result of violence against women,

  Stressing that the impact of discrimination and violence against women on women's ability to access and secure land, property and housing is particularly acute for women who are internally displaced as a result of armed conflict situations and development projects.
- Concerned that international and regional trade, finance and investment policies often increase gender inequality in terms of access to land, property, housing and other productive resources and undermine women's capacity to gain and retain these resources.
- Mindful that women's inequality will not always be remedied by the identical treatment of men and women and that adequate remedies may require that women be treated differently from men based on a consideration of women's specific socio-economic context.
- Affirms that the discrimination faced by women with respect to acquiring and securing land, property and housing as well as financing for lan d, property and housing, constitutes a violation of women's human rights to equality, protection against discrimination and to equal enjoyment of the right to an adequate standard of living, including adequate housing;
- Strongly urges governments to comply fully with all of their international and regional obligations and

commitments concerning the legally recognised rights of women to land, property, inheritance, adequate housing including security of tenure, and an adequate standard of living;

- Urges governments to review their laws, policies, customs and traditions pertaining to land, property and housing rights, to amend and repeal laws and policies and to encourage the transformation of customs and traditions which deny women security of tenure and equal access and rights to land, property and housing, and to adopt and enforce legislation which protects and promotes women's rights to own, inherit, lease or rent land, property and housing;
- Encourages governments, international agencies and non-governmental organisations to provide judges, lawyers, political and other public officials, community leaders and other concerned persons with information and human rights education concerning women's rights to land, property and housing;
- Recommends that governments, international financial institutions, local lending agents, housing finance institutions and other credit facilities review their policies and eliminate those which discriminate against women and keep women from securing financial resources necessary to access and secure land, property and housing and, in this regard, that special consideration be given to single women and households headed by women;
- Suggests that the international trade, investment and financial institutions, in particular the World Bank, the International Monetary Fund, the World Trade Organisation and the Organisation for Economic Cooperation and Development, take fully into account the human rights implications for women of their policies;
- Invites governments, the United Nations Development Programme, the Office of the United Nations High Commissioner for Human Rights, the Office of the United Nations High Commissioner for Refugees, the United Nations Centre for Human Settlements and the United

Nations Development Fund for Women to allocate resources for further documentation of the impact of internal displacement as a result of armed conflict situations and development projects on women, particularly with respect to women's access to land, property and housing;

- Invites the United Nations High Commissioner for Human Rights, in pursuance of her mandate, to undertake initiatives that promote women's rights to land, property and to an adequate standard of living, including adequate housing;
- Requests the Secretary-General to propose to the Committee on the Elimination of Discrimination Against Women to pay special attention to women's rights to land, property and an adequate standard of living, including adequate housing, when examining States parties reports and to explore the possibility of adopting a general recommendation on this theme as it relates, inter alia, to the provisions of article 14 of the Convention on the Elimination of All Forms of Discrimination Against Women, with a view to clarifying the obligations of States parties to this Convention in this respect;
- Suggests to the Committee on Economic, Social and Cultural Rights to undertake a thorough discussion of the critical issue of the relationship between women's rights to land and property and the International Covenant on Economic, Social and Cultural Rights to include the results of this discussion in its general comment on women.

7

Violation of Child Rights

India has the largest child population in the world, with about 40% of the total population below the age of 15 years and 51.5% of these between the ages of 0 to 6 years. Right through the ages, care for children has been one of the causes to which Indian policy has remained committed. In the independent India, this commitment was enshrined in our Constitutional provisions. The Constitution of India in its Directive Principles of State Policy pledges that "the State shall, in particular, direct its policy towards securing... that the health and strength of workers, men and women, and the tender age of children, are not abused and that citizens are not forced by economic necessity to enter avocations unsuited to their age or strength; that children are given opportunities and facilities to develop in a healthy manner and in conditions of freedom and dignity and that childhood and youth are protected against exploitation and against moral and material abandonment".

As a follow up to this commitment, Government of India adopted a National Policy for Children in 1974 which reaffirmed the Constitutional provisions and declared that "it shall be the policy of the State to provide adequate services to children, both before and after birth and through the period of growth, to ensure their full physical, mental and social development. It further stresses that the State shall progressively increase the scope of such services so that, within a reasonable time, all children in the country enjoy optimum conditions for their balanced growth".

National Policy and Charter for Children, 2001 reads that, "Whereas the Constitution of India enshrines both in Chapter 3 and 4 of the Constitution of India, the cause and the best interest of children, in so far that:

- The State can make special provisions for children [Art 15 (3)]
- No child below the age of 14 years shall be employed to work in a factory, mine or any other hazardous employment (Art. 24).
- The tender age of children is not abused and that citizens are not forced by economic necessity to enter avocations unsuited to their age or strength (Art. 39 e).
- Children are given opportunities and facilities to develop in a healthy manner and in conditions of freedom and dignity and that youth are protected against exploitation and against moral and material abandonment (Art. 39 f).
- Whereas through the National Policy for Children, 1974, we are committed to provide for adequate services to children, both before and after birth and throughout the period of growth, to ensure their full physical, mental and social development.
- Whereas we affirm that children's rights - economic, social, cultural and civil, are fundamental, human rights and must be protected through combined action of the State, civil society, communities and families in their obligations in fulfilling children's rights.
- Whereas we also affirm that children's rights must be exercised in the context of intrinsic and attendant duties directed towards preserving and strengthening the family, society and the Nation, and by inculcating a sense of values directed towards the same end.
- Whereas India has acceded to the United Nations Convention on Rights of the Child in 1992, wherein it has committed itself to realize the best interests of the child through the maximum extent of its available resources.
- And whereas we believe that by respecting the child, society is respecting itself.

Recently the Government of India has decided to constitute a National Commission for Children that would be a statutory body setup by an Act of Parliament to give further protection to children and act as an ombudsman for them. The commission will have certain judicial powers, will guide policy on children related subjects and take effective steps for review and better implementation of laws and programs meant for the survival, development and protection of children. It would also oversee the overall and proper implementation of the laws and programs relating to children in the country.

However, destruction of unborn and new-born infants, stringent measures including physical torture at home and in teaching institutions to introduce discipline and teaching program, child labor system, etc. all extending up to cruelty on children are still there. The incidents of cruelty may not remain limited to assault and injury only, providing the child insufficient food, inadequate care, protection and education, child slavery (though banned is reported in this part of the world), kidnapping or seducing a girl child for immoral traffic and sexual assault on young girls and boys are the other examples of atrocities on children. The present study attempts to examine the extent to which violation of children's rights can be brought to light by the specialty of forensic medicine.

MATERIAL AND METHODS

155 cases of alleged child abuse referred to Government Medical College Hospital Chandigarh, for medico-legal examination/autopsy from January 2000 to Dec. 2004 were retrospectively reviewed. The case records from the Medical Records Department of the hospital as well as the Investigating Agencies were analyzed with regards to the profile of the victims of abuse. The data pertaining to crimes against the children, published by National Crime Records Bureau from 2001 to 2003 was also analyzed to present the national scenario. Observation During period under study, a total of 155 children below 16 years were referred to the hospital for medico-legal examination, of which 9 (6%) were brought for medico-legal autopsy. Of the different cases of abuse, physical abuse

accounted for 108 (70%) victims while sexual abuse accounted for 47 (30%) victims.

Again, 89 (61%) cases were brought by police, while 57 (39%) were brought by their parents, either for treatment of injury/ pain etc., but who, on examination, were found to be either physically or sexually abused. Boys, 64 (60%), were more at risk in cases of physical abuse, while girls, 39 (83%), were at risk in cases of sexual abuse. Children, of the age group, 14-16 years, were the most common victims of both physical abuse [35 (32%) cases] and sexual abuse [43 (28%) cases]. Their oppression decreased with the decrease in their age. An appreciable percentage of boys were also sexually abused, 11 (23%) cases, of which those belonging to the age group 8-10 years, constituted the most victims, 4 (36%) cases.

Maximum cases of physical abuse occurred among the school dropouts / doing nothing 'at home', 36 (33%) cases, followed by those working at auto repair shops or small-scale factories, 23 (21%) and 22 (20%) cases, respectively whereas majority of sexual abuse also took place among the 'at home' category, (45%). Data published by National Crime Records Bureau, Ministry of Home Affairs, and Government of India, showing crimes against children in the country and percentage variation in 2003 over 2002 reveals the extent of reported cases.

According to the State of Children report, there are over 35 million girls in India, who are out of school, are neglected or involved in one or the other work. Juveniles engaged in prostitution and children of sex-workers; children abused sexually or physically; underfed children; abandoned children; slum children; street children; refugee children; and juvenile servitude constitute the pool of neglected and destitute juveniles. Within the family, children are forcibly engaged in domestic servitude and used as first choice to assist parents on the field by the small farm families. Outside the family, they are engaged as indented servitude in workshops, hotels, small industries, footpath vending, fire-works, carpet weaving etc.

For the employers, child workers are advantageous as they cannot form unions, could be exploited for longer hours for meager wages and could be even used in hazardous and unhygienic work environment. Child labor is not a new phenomenon, what is, however, new is its perception as a social problem. In the recent past, there has been a distinct change in the value orientation and attitudinal ethos of the legitimizing groups of society vis-à-vis child labor. In the pre-industrial agricultural society in India, children worked as helpers and learners in 'hereditarily determined' family occupations under the benign supervision of adult family members.

The work place was an extension of the home and the work was characterized by personal and informal relationship. The tasks of technology and the work involved were simple and non-hazardous, which the child could learn smoothly, almost unconsciously over the years through imitation and association. With the advent of industrialization and urbanization, the social scenario changed. The family members no longer work as a team and in caste-sanctioned occupations. The child has to work as an individual person, either under an employer or independently, without enjoying the benevolent protection of his guardian. His work exposes him to various kinds of health hazards emanating from the excessive use of chemicals and poisonous substances in industries and the pollutants discharged by them and here arises the problem of child labor.

United Nations Convention on the rights of children sets out basic rights and standards for judging the welfare of children. It encompasses both the maltreatment of children within family settings and that occurring through group processes and social forces. In the United States, if any professional entertains any suspicion as to the maltreatment of the child, he is required by law to report the things to the local child welfare agency (mandatory reporting). In India, any doctor who has reason to suspect about the maltreatment of a child is required to report the matter to the police.

However, despite the Juvenile Justice Act 2000 providing for taking special measures towards the care and protection of children, many types of abuse are frequently reported in media as is evident from the National crime records Bureau data. The term child abuse refers to any act or failure to act that violates the rights of the child that endangers his or her optimum health, survival or development. A recent WHO estimate shows that 40 million children aged 0-14 around the world suffer form abuse and neglect and require health and social care. Child abuse or maltreatment is commonly divided into five categories: physical abuse, emotional abuse, sexual abuse, neglect and exploitation.

Although any of these forms may be found separately, they often occur together but the cases of abuse frequently seen by healthcare workers include physical abuse, sexual abuse and neglect. Physical abuse has been explained as physical assault of a child by any person having custody, care, or charge of that child. Methods may include hitting, throwing inducing burns or scalds, biting, poisoning etc. Physical abuse occurs at all ages, although biological squeal are more severe in infancy, becoming weaker throughout the childhood and disappearing by adolescence.

There is a strong association with low socioeconomic status. To some extent, the problem of physical abuse was unveiled by Silverman (1953) and Wooley and Evans (1955) in its exact shape, magnitude and significance, who established the deliberate trauma character of certain specific types of pathological lesions, earlier detected by J. Caffey (1946) a pediatric radiologist. Sexual abuse has been explained as sexual activities that involve a child and an adult, or a significantly older child. The abuse may be in the form of: 1) contact sexual activities that include - penile or digital penetration or acts like kissing or touching of genitalia or making the child touch or fondle genitalia of the perpetrator and 2) non contact sexual activities that may include exhibitionism or encouraging the children to have sex together.

Neglect refers to the under-provision of the child's basic needs, both physical and psychological that may occur through parents or through institutions like orphanages, nurseries, educational establishments etc. However, this perspective is limited and may not afford adequate protection to children since societal factors (e.g., poverty) that compromise the abilities of parents to care for their children also impair children's health and development and as such 'neglect' must be evaluated within a societal context. The present study also revealed that the problem was more prevalent in lower socio-economic group as majority of the victims 42% of physical abuse were working at auto repair shops or small factories or as roadside vendors.

This necessitates the need for interaction among various agencies concerned with the welfare of children. However, implementation of legislation, policy and programs for children is extremely inter-sectoral, and is dispersed across eight departments both at the center and in the states - mainly the departments of Family welfare, Education, Labor, Social Justice and Empowerment, Water and Sanitation, Youth Affairs, Woman and Child Development, Information and Broadcasting and encompasses jurisdiction of the Center and States/Union Territories, often with the participation of the non-governmental sector. Here the question arises that if any welfare program to be implemented is to be routed through so many channels what will actually reach the needy in general, and in the present scenario of "BANDAR-BAANT" prevalent in India, in particular.

It is too often reported that rural and urban India has pervasive practices of child labor, juvenile servitude, domestic juvenile servitude and trafficking of juvenile girls. Despite enactment of the Juvenile Justice Act 1986 and 2000, and in spite of several positive provisions embodied into the Indian Constitution and the Universal Human Rights Declaration aimed at safeguarding the rights of children - leisure, learning and play - the social reality continues to be grim. We find a large segment of children outside the school portals and equally a large number engaged either in work or in delinquent activities. There is a need to identify potential risk factors for baby battering, child labor, child sexual abuse etc., so as to better understand the problem, improve the treatment of the victim as well as perpetrator and take preventive steps to restrict the incidence of child abuse.

Announcements of new legislation, commissions or programs by the respective governments in the absence of the will to implement the same have nothing more than politically motivated ornamental values. A societal awareness to boldly report the cases of child abuse, honest and scientific investigation by the Investigating Agencies and speedy delivery of justice by the Courts is all that is required in addition to a change in the attitude of the community towards the children. It must be remembered that rights and duties are two sides of being human. A child can achieve his rights only if others perform their duties. Proper performance of duties by the parents, teachers, and government officials of the various departments associated with child welfare and community at large is necessary for fulfilling the rights of children and here comes the role of forensic medicine also.

There is no way to thoroughly enumerate the various ways in which children around the world are economically exploited and physically mistreated. But the numbers are great and the suffering widespread. Behind the hideous imagery of children beaten or sexually abused by parents; ravaged beyond their years by hard living and drug abuse on the streets; maimed by landmines or turned into killers by war; stricken with AIDS - are the all-too-common struggles against disease, hardship, and family or social traditions that compromise children's humanity or subject them to physical and emotional suffering.

While victims of injustice and poverty have always had trouble being heard, none have had more trouble, historically, than children. Whether exploited as child labourers or prostitutes, drafted as young teenagers into armed forces, forced as young girls into a lonely life as domestic workers, deprived of an education to work on the family farm, or denied adequate nutrition and health care, children need help and protection from an adult world that perpetrates most of the abuse.

THE SPECIAL RAPPORTEUR'S ROLE

To highlight the existence of the most egregious violations of international human rights law and encourage Governments to investigate particular cases, the United Nations Commission on Human Rights has appointed a Special Rapporteur on the sale of children, child prostitution and child pornography. The Special Rapporteur, an expert in the field, works to gather and analyse facts for the Commission. The condition most common to children who suffer, or are deprived of, opportunity is the poverty resulting from economic injustice. "The most perverse form of denial of child rights is poverty, because poverty makes it impossible to satisfy those needs that are basic rights", says Tereza Albenez, Special Advisor to the United Nations Children's Fund (UNICEF) on the Convention on the Rights of the Child.

According to figures compiled by UNICEF- the United Nations organization most directly concerned with children's issues- there are now well over a dozen countries in which conditions for children are far below the norms to be expected for their levels of economic development. This includes such gauges as malnutrition levels; under-five mortality rates; percentage of children reaching the fifth grade of primary school; and low literacy rates for women. In many poor countries, children work to supplement meagre family income or otherwise to help the family business. Although they may not always work under the most desirable conditions, most are not being intentionally exploited by their families. The real issue in such cases is not whether the children work or not, but whether the conditions under which they work are just, and whether they are being denied other basic rights because of their work — such as the right to education, to freedom from abuse, and to proper health care.

SOLVING A COMPLEX DILEMMA

A number of those working on behalf of child rights have come to realize that in many of the poorer countries, if children are to stop working, some form of financial compensation must be found for their families. One creative response to this kind of complex dilemma has come from Bangladesh. In reaction to United States Congressional legislation mandating a boycott of companies in the garment industry that use child labour, companies in the garment industry in Bangladesh began ousting children from their jobs — as many as 50,000 in a four-month period. The result was that many of the children were worse off than they had been when they were working, having taken other, less desirable jobs or living in the street — but not going to school.

In July 1995, after negotiations with non-governmental organizations (NGOs), as well as UNICEF and the International Labour Organization (ILO), the Bangladesh Garment Manufacturers and Exporters Association (BGMEA) signed a Memorandum of Understanding stipulating that BGMEA would ask "that no under aged worker will be terminated until the appropriate school programmes for the workers can be put in place". UNICEF has committed itself to supporting the education of the children, and the ILO has pledged to contribute money and technical assistance to the establishment of a labour inspection system to monitor implementation of the Memorandum of Understanding. Under the agreement, stipends will be provided to child workers attending the school programmes. All parties also agreed to take steps "to create positive public awareness" with respect to issues of child labour and education.

INJUSTICES PERPETRATED BY ADULTS

But the more direct injustices perpetrated largely by adults — and manifested in the large numbers of children exploited as labourers and prostitutes or maimed by war — require further public exposure and protective laws that are actually enforced. In the last decade, an estimated two million children have been killed in armed conflict, many of them by some of the 100 million landmines thought to be concealed in 62 countries. A total of perhaps four to five million more have been disabled as a result of their experience in war, and more than 12 million have been made homeless.

As for child labour, while experts agree that there are few accurate statistics available, the best estimates from the ILO are that there are nearly 80 million children under 15 working as labourers. It is also estimated that the number of children under 18 involved in prostitution exceeds two million, one million of whom are in Asia and 300,000 in the United States.

"Poverty cannot be accepted as a pretext and justification for the exploitation of children," wrote Vitit Muntarbhorn, until 1995 the Special Rapporteur on the sale of children, child prostitution and child pornography. "It does not explain the huge global demand with, in many instances, customers from rich countries circumventing their national laws to exploit children in other countries. Sex tourism has spread its illicit wings wide, and paedophiles search for their victims in all parts of the globe. The problem is compounded by the criminal networks which benefit from the trade in children, and by collusion and corruption in many national settings".

VICTIMIZING THE MARGINALIZED

"It has become increasingly obvious that many children used for labour and sexual exploitation are lured from particular racial or social groups, rather than from the well-endowed groups in power," the Special Rapporteur went on, in a January 1994 report to the United Nations Commission on Human Rights. "In South Asia, it is the children of the 'untouchables' who are most often victimized in child labour situations". The Special Rapporteur said a field visit to Nepal showed that "it is primarily girls from hill-tribe groups in that country who are tricked and sold into prostitution, both local and transnational. The pattern is repeated in other parts of the world, where the children of minorities, migrant workers and/or indigenous peoples, who are already marginalized, are often the main victims of such exploitation".

The Special Rapporteur- Mr. Muntarbhorn was succeeded by Mrs. O. Calcetas-Santos- has often had difficulty obtaining information from Governments in response to queries about such matters as the sale and abduction of children; bonded labour; child prostitution; or sale of child organs. But in certain cases the Rapporteur's inquiries have added an international level of accountability in otherwise domestic cases.

ABUSES AGAINST STREET CHILDREN

In August 1993, to cite one example, the Special Rapporteur communicated with the Brazilian Government concerning allegations of the exploitation and abuse of street children by law-enforcement officials. The officials were alleged to have killed eight street children and injured others in Rio de Janeiro in July 1993. The allegation followed a long list of others noted in the Special Rapporteur's report on Brazil submitted to the Commission on Human Rights in 1992. The Brazilian Government responded by acknowledging the charge. "As pointed out in your communication, this incident is not an isolated case", the Government said in its response. "The Brazilian Government is well aware that the killings of street children are not a new phenomenon and that certain elements of the policy may be implicated in the actions of 'death' squads".

Three policemen and a fourth man were in prison awaiting trial for murder, and the commander of the Fifth Police Corps in Rio de Janeiro, to whom the three policemen were subordinated, was dismissed from his post. Non-governmental organizations have played an important role in pressuring Governments to respect both international law and in many cases similar laws in their own countries, particularly when it is clear that they have been partly or largely responsible for violations of those laws. Human Rights Watch, a non-governmental human rights organization with offices in Europe and the United States, has investigated numerous allegations. These include trafficking of women and girls from Nepal into India for use as prostitutes; the conditions of bonded labourers in Pakistan, many of whom are children; and the improper detention of juveniles by the criminal-justice system in Jamaica. Human Rights Watch recently released reports on India and Pakistan in mid-1995 that were highly critical of Government complicity.

In the United States, new tools for fighting sexual abuse of children overseas and international child pornography have been incorporated into the Mann Act, a 1910 Act of Congress originally aimed at prohibiting the interstate transportation of women "for immoral purposes". The amendments, approved after several years of lobbying by voluntary agencies, make it illegal for American citizens and resident aliens to travel abroad to engage in sexual acts with minors. The measures would bring the law into line with US domestic policy. The law — part of the Violent Crime Control and Law Enforcement Act of 1994, which was signed into law by President Clinton – also pertains to those who conspire to commit such acts, such as sex-tour operators. A 1986 amendment to the Mann Act made it a crime to transport a person under 18 between states or abroad with the intention of having the young person engage in sexual activity.

HALTING UNLAWFUL JAILING

In response to an earlier report on conditions in Jamaica, where juvenile offenders were being unlawfully locked up with adults, some of the children were released. Local Government agencies and organizations began to explore alternatives to imprisonment for juvenile offenders, and training programmes on the rights of juveniles was begun for guards. "If you get people out of custody or get Governments to change their policy", says Lois Whitman, Director of the Children's Rights Project at Human Rights Watch, "that is progress". It was not until recently that children have become a constituency in their own right, on whose behalf a number of international organizations, Government laws and human rights decrees have been created to advocate more equitable treatment for children under existing laws and for a more equitable share of resources and opportunities.

Prior to the 20th century, children were for the most part regarded as inferior and subordinate to adults, and childhood was a period of life that was often brief and regarded as a stage of passage to adulthood. Now, in the latter half of the century, childhood is regarded as a relatively sacred part of life among many of the more affluent. But it is still a period of great struggle and deprivation for children in most of the rest of the world. Children have been included, either directly or indirectly, in most of the nearly 80 treaties and decrees on human rights in this century. The first major step on behalf of children taken by the United Nations was UNICEF's creation in December 1946.

Two years later, the Universal Declaration of Human Rights was adopted by the General Assembly. The provisions of that Declaration and its two International Covenants on human rights, adopted in 1966, recognized that child rights need protection. The 1959 Declaration on the Rights of the Child was the first United Nations statement devoted exclusively to the rights of children, but served more as a moral rather than legally binding framework. The special plight of girls was addressed in part by the Convention on the Elimination of All Forms of Discrimination Against Women, adopted in 1979. The Working Group on Contemporary Forms of Slavery annually addresses such issues as child labour and debt bondage.

A GLOBAL PACT ON CHILDREN'S RIGHTS

It took until the 1990s, however, for all of the pieces to come together in the form of the Convention on the Rights of the Child, which was adopted by the General Assembly in 1989. The Convention's 54 articles cover everything from a child's right to be free from sexual and economic exploitation, to the right to his or her own opinion, and to the right to education, health care, and economic opportunity. By September 1995, 178 countries had ratified the Convention. A dozen more, some of which had been created since the Convention was adopted six years earlier, were considering it. As a result of this growing support, according to Ms Albenez of UNICEF, childhood is coming to be widely seen not as "some kind of probation period before becoming an adult". Instead, she said, "the child emerges as an individual with dignity who has all the rights of a full human being."

The initiative for the Convention came from the Government of Poland, which submitted a Draft Convention to the Commission on Human Rights in 1978, prior to celebration of the 20th anniversary of the Declaration on the Rights of the Child during the International Year of the Child in 1979. That led to a decade of collaboration between a small group of non-governmental organizations, including Radda Barnen of Sweden, the International Child Catholic Bureau, and Defense for Children International, and United Nations human rights experts. After a lengthy period of careful negotiations, the Convention on the Rights of the Child was adopted in November 1989 by a vote of the General Assembly. By September of the following year, the Convention had obtained the 20 ratifications required for its entry into force as international law. Its importance as a foundation of modern human rights law was later underscored at the 1993 World Conference on Human Rights in Vienna.

HUMAN RIGHTS AND DEVELOPMENT

By the late 1980s, progress in attracting support for the Convention had drawn the attention of UNICEF. While the organization has always devoted itself to the improvement of social and economic conditions for children, primarily in the fields of health and education, it was not until then that it saw the potential for integrating human rights objectives with more traditional development programmes. While UNICEF originally included the Convention as one of a number of its programme and advocacy concerns, by late 1994 UNICEF's Executive Director, James P. Grant, announced that the Convention would become the framework for all of UNICEF's programming.

In May 1995, UNICEF announced a new procurement policy on child labour, pledging to purchase materials and supplies only from companies that do not exploit child labour. The UNICEF Representative in each country is required to assess the local situation and evaluate the child labour practices of local companies. Historically there had been a conceptual divide between those who acted as advocates on behalf of human rights and those who pursued the development of economic and social policies and social welfare programmes. Because the Convention on the Rights of the Child covers so much ground, it has provided a conceptual and legislative umbrella for both traditions. The child-protection issues normally associated with human rights are included – among them those of sexual and economic exploitation, of refugee status, and of juvenile justice.

MAKING NEEDS A MATTER OF RIGHTS

Advocacy for many things that had previously been considered as needs and dealt with by Government programmes, the success of which often depended upon political considerations – such as food, shelter, and access to education and health care – can now be fortified by their inclusion as one of a larger number of human rights. "Needs you can't claim," says Ms Albenez of UNICEF. "Rights you can claim. Now you have claims for each of those needs."

Social reformers and human rights lawyers have defended individual children's rights or pursued political or policy objectives deemed advantageous to children for many years. But with the Convention the concern can now be regarded as universal. The ratification of the Convention by so many countries means that its articles and principles are now being adapted to, and becoming part of, national laws. The World Conference on Human Rights called for universal ratification of the Child Convention by 1995. While the recent intensification of interest and concentration of resources devoted to child rights following adoption of the Convention has not yet yielded particularly dramatic or even measurable results directly affecting the daily lives of most of the world's children, it has spawned efforts at legislative reform in countries around the world – particularly in Latin America and Southeast Asia.

A CATALYST FOR NATIONAL ACTION

"The Convention is our essential framework," says Mrs. Raadi-Azarakhchi of the Centre for Human Rights who serve as the Secretary of the Committee on the Rights of the Child, a United Nations body. "It's really a catalyst for action at national level. It provides universal standards – but there are ways it can be interpreted that can be suited to various cultural situations." The Committee on the Rights of the Child was established by the Convention as a means of monitoring and aiding Governments in bringing their national laws and practices into conformity with the treaty. By late 1995, the Committee, which consists of 10 international members with backgrounds in law, education and social work, had reviewed some 40 reports on implementation plans since 1993 from countries that had ratified the Convention. Reports are required within two years of ratification, and are used as a means of opening a dialogue between members of the Committee, the Government of a ratifying state, and the public in that country.

Non-governmental organizations are invited to contribute information or comment, and in over 20 countries have published alternative reports that either add to or take issue with the Government reports. The Committee reviews the reports and releases its recommendations, which the Government is subsequently obligated to make public. A follow-up report from each Government is required five years later. It has provided one way of measuring just how serious a Government is about honouring the Convention with legislative or social policy reform.

A LAG IN NATIONAL REPORTS

According to UNICEF's 1995 Progress of Nations, by the end of February 1995 there were 35 countries that were more than two years late in submitting their reports, and 21 that were more than a year overdue. About one-third of the 174 countries that had ratified the Convention by April 1995 had done so while lodging reservations about certain provisions with the Secretary- General of the United Nations. In some cases countries have felt the Convention doesn't go far enough. Several countries have stated that it would be better for the Convention to stipulate 18 rather than 15 as the minimum age for participation in armed conflict.

Other countries have expressed reservations about matters such as the precise definition of a child and freedom of conscience and religion. Still others have more sweeping and potentially problematic reservations, such as those of several Islamic countries that reserve the right not to apply articles in the Convention that are incompatible with shariah law. In some cases, Government reports have been challenged as insufficient. In the Philippines, the Government report was challenged by both the National Coalition of NGOs for Monitoring the Convention on the Rights of the Child and the Committee on the Rights of the Child.

The Committee noted "a lack of reliable qualitative and quantitative data, a shortcoming of means for programs of implementation, and a lack of indicators and mechanisms to evaluate the progress and impact of policies adopted." The Committee ultimately encouraged the Government to support wider participation of governmental agencies and non-governmental organizations in the process of bringing their national laws into line with the provisions of the Convention.

THE POWER OF MORAL SUASION

Much of the power of the Convention comes from mutual example and pressure from the public and from donor countries rather than any real enforcement power. Those that fail to take action or do not take it seriously enough can be admonished by Governments that have taken steps to abide by the Convention. But more persuasive pressure may come from those countries that ratify the Convention and, in turn, receive donor funding for various national initiatives, or assistance with the drafting of laws or establishment of child-advocacy bureaus.

"We have seen enough in five years to know that this approach works," writes Hoda Badra, Chairperson of the International Committee on the Rights of the Child in 1995, in UNICEF's Progress of Nations. "When the Government of Vietnam, for example, accepted that we were more interested in helping than criticizing, they submitted an open and self-critical report. Subsequently, Viet Nam acted: laws covering the protection, care and education of children have all been passed."

Others countries have done the same. The Government of Tunisia has made an unusual effort. The Council of Ministers adopted a Code for the Protection of the Child on 17 May 1995, and a delegate for child protection has been appointed in each of the 23 governorates to oversee implementation of the Convention at the sub-national level. Since July 1991, education has been mandatory for children from 6 to 16 years old, and legal action can be taken against parents who do not comply.

PROGRESS IN NATIONAL PROGRAMMES

The Indonesian Government has increased budget allocations for health services to mothers and children during a period of austerity, developed manuals for law enforcement training on the Convention, and established a Child Protection Institute. In Costa Rica, a new Legal Code for Minors is being developed using the Convention as the framework. In response to comments from the Committee on the Rights of the Child on the great number of national and international child adoptions in Costa Rica, the Legislature has started reviewing the Hague Convention on international adoption.

In Jamaica, the Government has started a legislative review and, despite heavy debt payments, is increasing its expenditures for children. In Nicaragua, the Government report to the Committee has been made public, a basis is being established for a Child and Adolescent legal code, and a public policy for children is being considered. And in 1991, the Government of Colombia created the State Information Agency for Child Rights.

LISTENING TO CHILDREN'S VOICES

In the best spirit of the Convention, the Government of Nepal is seeking input from children as part of its preparation for reporting to the Committee. In April 1995, 29 children participated in a four-day workshop on the Convention sponsored by a consortium of NGOs and UNICEF. Included were working children, a street boy, a disabled girl, children from refugee communities and those from both urban English-language schools and Nepali schools. Ultimately, they took discussion of the Convention back to their communities and met with the Prime Minister.

Even in countries where both the legality and morality of human rights covenants have been abandoned or repeatedly violated, efforts are being made in the name of the Convention. In Sudan, UNICEF and Operation Lifeline Sudan (OLS) partners have solicited support for the Convention from the Sudan Peoples' Liberation Movement (SPLM) and the South Sudan Independence Movement (SSIM), the rebel movements in control of much of southern Sudan. This is happening in an area where there are no national laws, and where military rule prevails. Relations between OLS and political authorities are governed by ground rules which OLS recently rewrote to include a statement of humanitarian principles. These principles include a statement of support both for the Convention and the Geneva Convention, according to the Report from Sudan.

"Both rebel movements have signed the ground rules", the Report said. "This is an important step forward since it is the first time the movements have made such pledges toward child rights and will provide UNICEF/OLS with a much better opportunity to address breaches and violations." But the realities in much of the world are that despite national laws that conform to a United Nations Convention, enforcement will be the determining factor in whether or not children's rights are protected. Even in countries with sophisticated legal systems the lack of enforcement is a problem. "In India," according to the Special Rapporteur, "despite laws prohibiting children under 14 from working in hazardous industries, violations is widespread. They include transgressions in industries such as those producing matches, fireworks, glass and bricks, in diamond cutting and lock making, and in stone quarries."

The hope is that the Convention will continue to stimulate the kind of debate that often leads to attitudinal change. Child rights need to be actively respected rather than simply acknowledged, and advocates admit that more than the passage of laws and publicizing of the Convention will be required. "It really is a matter of a change of mentality," says Mrs. Raadi-Azarakhchi of the International Committee on the Rights of the Child. "We believe the Convention is a wonderful instrument," says Ricardo Domenici, secretary-general of the NGO group Defense of Children International and an advocate of the Convention for more than a decade. "But unless there are really socially conscious policies in the country, the Convention won't make that much of a difference. It is still true that things are not very good for children."

The Concept of equality of all human beings, as embodied in the Universal Declaration of Human Rights of 1948 stipulates under Article 25 Para two that childhood is entitled to special care and assistance. The above principle along with other principles of the Universal Declaration concerning child were incorporated in the Declaration of the Rights of the Child of 1959.The International Covenant on Civil and Political rights under Articles 23 and 24 and the International Covenant on Economic, Social and Cultural Rights under Article 10 made provisions for the care of the child.

The position of India in terms of child labour is not an appreciable one; with a credible estimates ranging from 60 to 115 million, India has the largest number of working children in the world. Whether they are sweating in the heat of stone quarries, working in the fields 16 hours a day, picking rags in the city streets, or hidden away as domestic servants, these children endure miserable and difficult lives. They earn little and are made to work more. They struggle to make enough to eat and perhaps to help feed their families as well. They do not go to school. Many of them have been working since the age of four or five, and by the time they attain adulthood they may be irrevocably sick and deformed they will certainly be exhausted, and in this way they are debarred from enjoying the basic human rights, which are essential for the advancement of one's personality.

The International Convention and other international instruments, which deal with the subject of child labour are as follows:

- Convention on the Rights of the Child, 1989;
- Worst form of Child labour Convention 1999; and
- Worst form of Child Labour Recommendation.

The supreme law of the country, the Constitution of India, too provides certain rights to children and prohibits child labour. Such provisions are as follows:

- Article 24 provides that no child below the age of 14 years shall be employed in any factory or mine or engaged in any other hazardous work.
- Article 39 (f) says that state, in particular, shall direct its policy towards securing that the health and strength of workers, men and women and the tender age of the

children are not abused and that citizens are not forced by economic necessity to enter vocations unsuited to their age or strength.

- Article 39 (f) provides that children are given opportunities and facilities to develop in a healthy manner and in conditions of freedom and dignity and that childhood and youth are protected against exploitations and against moral and material abandonment.
- Article 45 declares that the state shall endeavour to provide, within the period of 10 years from the commencement of the Constitution, free and compulsory education for all children until they complete the age of 14 years.
- Article 21A (added by the 86th Amendment Act 2002) provides that the state shall provide free and compulsory education to all children between the ages of six to 14 years in such a manner as the state may by law determine.
- Article 51A (k) (added by the 86th Amendment Act 2002) provides who is parent or guardian to provide opportunities for education to his child or the case may be, ward between the age of six and 14 years.

The attention in respect of employment of child labour and the violation of fundamental rights has been brought before the Apex Court in several cases. The Apex Court has issued detailed directions to eradicate the practice of employing children in hazardous industries, mines, or other works. Prevention of child labour is a Herculean task. It has to be seen that the tender age of children is not abused and the children are given opportunities and facilities to develop in a healthy manner and in conditions of freedom and dignity. It cannot be achieved by merely enacting laws; mere legislations cannot be used for the massive task of social engineering.

As long as the social attitude and thinking remains deep rooted in the prevailing society and the law enforcement agencies remain silent, justice cannot be promoted by paper enactments. The laws enacted for the benefit and development of child labour should be supported and backed by public opinion. If progressive legislation lacks the support of public opinion it just becomes a dead law. It should be asserted that a social reform be done in consonant with social thinking, behaviour and after creation of strong public opinion as laws could be effective only if they are backed by a major selection of society. The law can be effective if two conditions are to be satisfied; one, supportive public opinion in its favour.

Apart from this, public awareness through education, media and other means, political will and commitment combined with efficient administrative support are needed to tackle the problem of children. Special government machinery should be set up for eradication of the problems related to child labour and protection of their rights so that we can give them better deal in life by providing them basic amenities of life so as to make them better citizens of our nation.

It is an undisputable fact that the child of today is the future of our country. So the investment made on children is an asset for the future of our country. As a child is not a vase to be filled, but a fire to be lit, they should not be exploited by engaging them in employment in tender age but they should be given all necessary amenities and support so that they become responsible citizens of the nation and make the world a happier place to live in.

CONVENTION ON THE RIGHTS OF THE CHILD

UNICEF's mission is to advocate for the protection of children's rights, to help meet their basic needs and to expand their opportunities to reach their full potential. UNICEF is guided in doing this by the provisions and principles of the Convention on the Rights of the Child. Built on varied legal systems and cultural traditions, the Convention is a universally agreed set of non-negotiable standards and obligations.

These basic standards—also called human rights—set minimum entitlements and freedoms that should be respected by governments. They are founded on respect for the dignity and worth of each individual, regardless of race, colour, gender, language, religion, opinions, origins, wealth, birth status or ability and therefore apply to every human being everywhere. With these rights comes the obligation on both governments and individuals not to infringe on the parallel rights of others. These standards are both interdependent and indivisible; we cannot ensure some rights without—or at the expense of—other rights.

A LEGALLY BINDING INSTRUMENT

The Convention on the Rights of the Child is the first legally binding international instrument to incorporate the full range of human rights—civil, cultural, economic, political and social rights. In 1989, world leaders decided that children needed a special convention just for them because people under 18 years old often need special care and protection that adults do not. The leaders also wanted to make sure that the world recognized that children have human rights too. The Convention sets out these rights in 54 articles and two Optional Protocols. It spells out the basic human rights that children everywhere have: the right to survival; to develop to the fullest; to protection from harmful influences, abuse and exploitation; and to participate fully in family, cultural and social life.

The four core principles of the Convention are non-discrimination; devotion to the best interests of the child; the right to life, survival and development; and respect for the views of the child. Every right spelled out in the Convention is inherent to the human dignity and harmonious development of every child. The Convention protects children's rights by setting standards in health care; education; and legal, civil and social services. By agreeing to undertake the obligations of the Convention (by ratifying or acceding to it), national governments have committed themselves to protecting and ensuring children's rights and they have agreed to hold themselves accountable for this commitment before the international community. States parties to the Convention are obliged to develop and undertake all actions and policies in the light of the best interests of the child.

The United Nations Convention on the Rights of the Child, often referred to as CRC or UNCRC, is an international convention setting out the civil, political, economic, social and cultural rights of children. Nations that ratify this international convention are bound to it by international law. Compliance is monitored by the United Nations Committee on the Rights of the Child which is composed of members from countries around the world. Once a year, the Committee submits a report to the Third Committee of the United Nations General Assembly, which also hears a statement from the CRC Chair, and the Assembly adopts a Resolution on the Rights of the Child.

Governments of countries that have ratified the Convention are required to report to, and appear before, the United Nations Committee on the Rights of the Child periodically to be examined on their progress with regards to the advancement of the implementation of the Convention and the status of child rights in their country. Their reports and the committee's written views and concerns are available on the committee's website. The United Nations General Assembly adopted the Convention and opened it for signature on 20 November 1989 (the 30th anniversary of its Declaration of the Rights of the Child). It came into force on 2 September 1990, after it was ratified by the required number of nations. As of December 2008, 193 countries have ratified it, including every member of the United Nations except the United States and Somalia.

Two optional protocols were adopted on 25 May 2000. The first one restricts the involvement of children in military conflicts, and the second one prohibits the sale of children, child prostitution and child pornography. Both protocols have been ratified by more than 120 states. The Convention generally defines a child as any person under the age of 18, unless an earlier age of majority is recognized by a country's law.

CONTENTS

The Convention deals with the child-specific needs and rights. It requires that states act in the best interests of the child. This approach is different from the common law approach found in many countries that had previously treated children and wives as possessions or chattels, ownership of which was often argued over in family disputes. In many jurisdictions, properly implementing the Convention requires an overhaul of child custody and guardianship laws, or, at the very least, a creative approach within the existing laws.

The Convention acknowledges that every child has certain basic rights, including the right to life, his or her own name and identity, to be raised by his or her parents within a family or cultural grouping and have a relationship with both parents, even if they are separated. The Convention obliges states to allow parents to exercise their parental responsibilities. The Convention also acknowledges that children have the right to express their opinions and to have those opinions heard and acted upon when appropriate, to be protected from abuse or exploitation, to have their privacy protected and requires that their lives not be subject to excessive interference.

The Convention also obliges signatory states to provide separate legal representation for a child in any judicial dispute concerning their care and asks that the child's viewpoint be heard in such cases. The Convention forbids capital punishment for children. Contrary to what is often claimed, it does not forbid corporal punishment, which is not mentioned at all in the text.

STATE PARTIES AND SIGNATORIES

As of December 2008, 193 countries have ratified it, including every member of the United Nations except the United States and Somalia.

Canada

Canada has ratified the Convention but has not fully implemented the Convention in Canadian domestic laws. A nonprofit organization called the Canadian Children's Rights Council promotes awareness of the CRC in Canadian media, and provides resources on their website pertaining to the Convention. Youth criminal laws in Canada underwent major changes resulting in the Youth Criminal Justice Act (YCJA) which went into effect on 1 April 2003. In 1989, the Canadian House of Commons voted unanimously to pass a non-binding resolution to end child poverty by the year 2000. However, the child poverty rate did not change between 1989 and 2000; 16% of Canadian children still live in poverty.

India

In India, there is no outright ban on child labor, and the practice is generally permitted in most industries except those deemed "hazardous". Although a law in October 2006 banned child labor in hotels, restaurants, and as domestic servants, there continues to be high demand for children as hired help in the home.

Current estimates as to the number of child laborers in the country range from the government's conservative estimate of 12 million children fewer than 14 years of age to the much higher estimates of children's rights activists, which hover around 60 million. Little is being done to address the problem since the economy is booming and the nuclear family is spreading, thereby increasing demand for child laborers. Under the auspices of the Unicef financed Udisha initiative the Government of India is specifying the outline of a means of change and improvement in child care.

Iran

Although the Islamic Republic of Iran is a state party to the Convention on the Rights of the Child, international human rights organisations and foreign governments routinely denounce executions of Iranian child offenders as a violation of the treaty.

Ireland

The Republic of Ireland signed the Convention on the Rights of the Child on 30 September 1990 and ratified it, without reservation, on 21 September 1992. In response to criticisms expressed in the 1998 review by the UN Committee on the Rights of the Child in Geneva, the Irish government established the office of Ombudsman for Children and drew up a national children's strategy. In 2006, following concerns expressed by the committee that the wording of the Irish Constitution does not allow the State to intervene in cases of abuse other than in very exceptional cases, the Irish government undertook to amend the constitution to make a more explicit commitment to children's rights.

New Zealand

New Zealand ratified the Convention 6 April 1993 with reservations concerning the right to distinguish between persons according to the nature of their authority to be in New Zealand, the need for legislative action on economic exploitation - which it argued was adequately protected by existing law, and the provisions for the separation of juvenile offenders from adult offenders.

In 1994, the Court of Appeal dismissed the suggestion that the Minister for Immigration and his department were at liberty to ignore the convention, arguing that this would imply that the country's adherence was 'at least partly window-dressing'.

Saudi Arabia

Saudi Arabia ratified the Convention in 1996, with a reservation 'with respect to all such articles as are in conflict with the provisions of Islamic law' and considers it to be a valid source of domestic law. The Committee on the Rights of the Child, which reviewed Saudi Arabia's treatment of children under the Convention in January 2005, strongly condemned the government for its practice of imposing the death penalty on juveniles, calling it "a serious violation of the fundamental rights".

The committee said it was "deeply alarmed" over the discretionary power judges hold to treat juveniles as adults: In its 2004 report the Saudi Arabia government had stated that it "never imposes capital punishment on persons... below the age of 18". However the government delegation later acknowledged that a judge could impose the death penalty whenever he decided that the convicted person had reached his or her majority, regardless of the person's actual age at the time of the crime or at the time of the scheduled execution.

United Kingdom

The United Kingdom ratified the Convention on 16 December 1991, with several declarations and reservations, and made its first report to the Committee on the Rights of the Child in January 1995. Concerns raised by the Committee included the growth in child poverty and inequality, the extent of violence towards children, the use of custody for young offenders, the low age of criminal responsibility, and the lack of opportunities for children and young people to express views.

The 2002 report of the Committee expressed similar concerns, including the welfare of children in custody, unequal treatment of asylum seekers, and the negative impact of poverty on children's rights. There was much attention in the media to the criticism of UK parent's rights to hit their children as 'a serious violation of the dignity of the child. In September 2008 the UK government decided to give up its reservations and agree to the Convention in full.

United States

The United States government played an active role in the drafting of the Convention and signed it on 16 February 1995, but has not ratified it. Opposition to the Convention is in part due to what are seen as potential conflicts with the Constitution and because of opposition by some political and religious conservatives. The Heritage Foundation sees the conflict as an issue of national control over domestic policy. President Barack Obama has described the failure to ratify the Convention as 'embarrassing' and has promised to review this. The US has signed and ratified both of the optional protocols to the Convention.

The United States government played an active role in the drafting of the Convention. It commented on nearly all of the articles, and proposed the original text of seven of them. Three of these come direct from the US constitution and were proposed by the administration of President Ronald Reagan.

On 16 February 1995, Madeleine Albright, at the time the U.S. Ambassador to the United Nations, signed the Convention. It has not so far been ratified; the United States historically has employed a cautious approach to ratification of treaties: for example, the Convention on the Elimination of All Forms of Racial Discrimination was only ratified 28 years after being signed by President Lyndon B. Johnson.

Though generally supportive of the Convention, President Bill Clinton did not submit it to the Senate for its advice and consent. President Barack Obama has described the failure to ratify the Convention as 'embarrassing' and has promised to review this. The failure to ratify the treaty so far is in part due to potential conflicts with the constitution and because of opposition by some political and religious conservatives to the treaty. The administration of President George W. Bush explicitly stated its opposition to the treaty:

"The Convention on the Rights of the Child may be a positive tool for promoting child welfare for those countries that have adopted it. But we believe the text goes too far when it asserts entitlements based on economic, social and cultural rights. ... The human rights-based approach ... poses significant problems as used in this text."

Active opposition to the Convention in the United States has been concentrated in politically conservative groups. Senator Jesse Helms, the former chairman of the Senate Foreign Relations Committee, described it as a "bag of worms," an effort to "chip away at the U.S. Constitution."

Legal concerns over ratification have mostly focused on issues of sovereignty and federalism. The United States generally does not sign treaties that it believes would impair its sovereignty. American laws for the protection of children are at the state, rather than the federal level, and the Tenth Amendment to the United States Constitution restricts the authority of the federal government to pass legislation or ratify treaties that will protect children. The U.S. Constitution not only limits federal jurisdiction over children, the U.S. Supreme Court has held that to some significant degree, no government—federal, state, or local—may interfere with the parent-child relationship.

The USA and Somalia are the only countries which have failed to ratify that agreement. Most often Americans dismiss the CRC with the reasoning that the nation already has in place everything the treaty espouses, and that it would make no practical difference. The two reasons often given for the US Senate not ratifying the convention were:

- Some states allowed children to be given the death penalty, which the Convention would not allow. The Supreme Court decision in *Roper v. Simmons* has since held execution of juveniles to be unconstitutional, citing the Convention as one of several indications that "the United States now stands alone in a world that has turned its face against the juvenile death penalty".
- The claim by conservatives that "this Treaty would virtually undermine parents' rights as we know it in the United States."

Ratification of the UNCRC by the United States would require the U.S. governments to appear before the U.N. Committee on the Rights of the Child, a panel of child rights experts from around the world, every 5 years to explain their implementation of such issues as universal health insurance for all American children, currently a human right in all other western industrialized nations. In 2006, 11.7% of children in the U.S. did not have health insurance.

The Heritage Foundation sees the conflict as an issue of national control over domestic policy: "Although not originally promoted as an entity that would become involved in actively seeking to shape member states' domestic policies, the U.N. has become increasingly intrusive in these arenas." They express concern about "sovereign jurisdiction over domes-tic policymaking and preserving the freedom of American civil society", and argue that the actual practice of some UN Committees has been to review national policies that are unrelated, or are marginally related to the actual language of the Convention. Some supporters of home schooling have expressed concern that the Convention will subvert the authority of parents.

David Smolin argues that the objections from the religious and political conservatives stem from their view that the U.N. is an elitist institution, which they do not trust to properly handle sensitive decisions regarding family issues. He suggests that legitimate concerns of critics could be met with appropriate reservations by the U.S.

One of the most controversial tenets of the Convention is the participatory rights granted to children. The Convention champions youth voice in new ways. Article 12 states:

"Parties shall assure to the child who is capable of forming his or her own views the right to express those views freely in all matters affecting the child, the views of the child being given due weight in accordance with the age and maturity of the child ... the child shall in particular be provided the opportunity to be heard in any judicial and administrative proceedings affecting the child..."

David Smolin, otherwise a proponent who urges U.S. reservations, argues that Article 5, which includes a provision stating that parents "provide, in a manner consistent with the evolving capacities of the child, appropriate direction and guidance in the exercise by the child of the rights recognized in the present Convention", "is couched in language which seems to reduce the parental role to that of giving advice". The Campaign for U.S. Ratification of the Convention on the Rights of the Child argues that the Convention protects parental responsibility from government interference.

The Campaign for U.S. Ratification of the Convention on the Rights of the Child argues that criticisms mentioned by opponents of the convention "are the result of misconceptions, erroneous information, and a lack of understanding about how international human rights treaties are implemented in the United States", and that ratification "would establish a useful framework from which our leaders could create cost-effective and comprehensive policies and programs that address the specific needs of children and families."

World Vision, which is a large evangelical Christian relief NGO, has supported ratification of the Convention. Smolin states that this support is probably more typical of worldwide evangelical Christian opinion because, globally, Christians who seek to help the "vulnerable, poor, needy, and oppressed...apparently find more inspiration than fear in the words of the CRC." Other organisations which have supported ratification include Church World Service, the National Spiritual Assembly of the Bahá'ís of the United States, Church Women United, and the National Council of Churches. David Smolin argues that Article 29 limits the fundamental right of parents and others to educate children in private school by requiring that all such schools support the principles contained in the United Nations Charter and a list of specific values and ideals.

He argues that "Supreme Court case law has provided that a combination of parental rights and religious liberties provide a broader right of parents and private schools to control the values and curriculum of private education free from State interference. Article 37 of the Convention prohibits sentencing of juveniles to life imprisonment with no opportunity for parole. Laws in approximately 20 U.S. states appear to conflict with this article. The 2005 U.S. Supreme Court decision Roper v. Simmons found juvenile execution unconstitutional as cruel and unusual punishment, but does not cover the question of life without possibility of parole.

OPTIONAL PROTOCOLS

Two optional protocols were adopted by the UN General Assembly on 25 May 2000. The Optional Protocol on the Involvement of Children in Armed Conflict requires governments to ensure that children under the age of eighteen are not recruited compulsorily into their armed forces, and calls on governments to do everything feasible to ensure that members of their armed forces who are under eighteen years of age do not take part in hostilities. This protocol entered into force on 12 July 2002; as of March 2009, 127 states are party to the protocol and another 28 states have signed but not yet ratified it. The Optional Protocol on the Sale of Children, Child Prostitution and Child Pornography requires states to prohibit the sale of children, child prostitution and child pornography. It entered into force on 18 January 2002; as of March 2009, 131 states are party to the protocol and another 31 states have signed but not yet ratified it.

8

Communal Violence in India

Communal riots have become the fate of India, thanks to our politicians and their selfish interests. And ironically most of the riots are engineered by those politicians who claim to be most patriotic. Their patriotism is designed to win power by propagating hate politics against minority communities. The year 2003, too, like previous years, saw its own quota of communal violence in which numerous lives were lost and hundreds were injured and properties worth crores of rupees were damaged. Most of the major states both in north and south were affected by communal violence. It is in smaller states with small Muslim population like Haryana, Punjab, Himachal Pradesh, etc., which did not witness incidents of violence.

Assam and other North Eastern states generally experience ethnic violence but not so much communal violence. Last year there were hardly any incidents of communal violence in this zone. Also, West Bengal was free of major communal incidents. Since the Left Front government has taken over West Bengal has been free of communal violence, though not of communalism. Bihar too, since Laloo Prasad Yadav has been in command has not seen major riots. Thus it is clear that if governments are determined to curb communal violence it can be effectively checked. The communal violence began in Gujarat as the New Year began. Gujarat is ruled by Narendra Modi, a hard core RSS man who was responsible for Gujarat carnage of 2002. It witnessed a series of communal clashes on 2nd January 2003. Most of these incidents occurred in Central

Gujarat, the region from where the BJP won maximum number of seats. And no wonder most of the victims were from minority community.

On 2nd January, Darbhanga, Bihar, witnessed communal riot in Lalbagh area in which eight persons were injured including two policemen and police had to impose curfew. And on the same day communal violence took place in Ahmad Nagar, Maharashtra, in which five persons were injured including one 70 year old woman. The hate propagandists have created such polarisation between Hindus and Muslims that any small incident like scooterists knocking down a member of another community or cricket game involving two communities' results in communal clashes. In Vidarbha towns of Akot and Risod cricket resulted in communal clashes on 9th January in which one person was stabbed and six injured and in Risod 150 shops were gutted resulting in loss of crores of rupees. Risod is a sleepy town in Washim district.

On 14th January violence erupted in Ganjbasoda town in Vidisha district of M.P. due to alleged case of cow slaughter. Cow slaughter is another issue on which violence erupts time and again. On hearing about cow slaughter the mob went on rampage setting 60 shops belonging to Muslims were on fire. Members of Bajrang Dal are alleged to be behind these communal disturbances. These Bajrang Dals were encouraged by the success of BJP in Gujarat. Some houses and vehicles were also set on fire. Twenty two persons were arrested.

Bhivandi is another communally sensitive town where communal situation worsened two days before Eidul Azha on February 9 when some Bajrang Dal men attacked cows being brought by Muslims. The police took nine cows in custody and police-Muslim clashes flared up in which 34 persons were injured including 26 policemen. The Rapid Action Force was immediately brought to control the situation. The communal cauldron in Bhivandi was first stirred by Bajrang Dals and incitement by some Muslims leaders added to the gravity of the situation. For Gujarat, communal violence has become so common that if it does not take place it is news.

Communal violence took place in Mehsana district on the occasion of Eidul Azha on 12th February in which at least eight persons including a police constable received stab and sword injuries in Takodi village of Mehsana district. It all started with some Muslims allegedly bringing calves for slaughter. When the police tried to stop it, they were greeted by volley of stones. It is interesting to note as some sources said that the real cause of trouble was *Panchayat* election in which a Hindu was elected *Sarpanch* with the help of some Muslims and the other group of Muslims opposing the Hindu *Sarpanch* did not allow these Muslims to enter the mosque. On 19th February there was trouble in Dhar, M.P. when some Bajrang Dal members tried to enter the Kamalmoula mosque forcibly. When the police did not allow them there was call for bandh and violence erupted.

There were incidents of violence and some one threw petrol bomb on police and police fired back in which two persons were injured. Another police station was *gheraoed* and some motor vehicles were set afire. One police van was also set on fire. On 26th February clashes broke out between Hindus and Muslims in Bangalore while a Hindu religious procession was passing from near a mosque. There was stone throwing from both sides in Vedika and Ashok Nagar areas. Many shops and vehicles were damaged. Ahmedabad and Baroda also witnessed communal clashes on 2nd March after Indo-Pak cricket match.

The police fired in which one Muslim youth was killed in Shahpur area. Same day stray incidents were also reported from Baroda and a group of Hindus celebrating India's victory over Pakistan clashed with a group of Muslims also celebrating India's victory. The next round of communal flare up was reported from Gorakhpur in U.P. on 20th March. It is a highly sensitive town where Gorakhnath temple is situated and Mahant Adityanath of BJP contests election from there. Adityanath is known for his militancy and extremism. He is a BJP M.P. from this area. The clashes took place on the occasion of Holi when a procession of Holi revellers led by Mahant Aditynath was going through Zafra locality. An argument broke out with some members of a minority community and the Holi revellers in a fit of anger broke down the 'wall of Kerbala'. The two groups began to throw brickbats at each other and some people started firing.

The Imam of Ghazi Rauza mosque was hit in the cross - fire and died. More than a dozen scooters and vehicles were burnt and shops looted. Two more persons were killed and thus in all three persons died during the disturbances. Mayawati, the then Chief Minister removed Director General of Police for his failure to control communal violence. Though Kerala is comparatively free from communal clashes but for last two years there have been clashes between Muslims and RSS activists. In January 2002, some five persons were killed when the Hindus attacked Muslim fishermen. The Muslims retaliated this time and on May 2, seven persons were killed in Marad beach area under Beypore police station in Kerala.

In 2002, RSS had killed Muslims and in 2003 a brother of one of the deceased took revenge by killing seven persons. The Muslims had used a nearby mosque for hiding weapons and the mosque was later taken over by the state authorities. The Muslims fled from the village in fear and Sangh Parivar did not allow them to return. They could return only after a few months when the chief minister intervened. Normally Jammu and Kashmir has been free from communal violence despite repeated attempts by militants to cause communal violence. However, a small communal incident occurred on 1st July between Hindus and Muslims and shops were burnt and looted in Jammu.

The trouble started when 150 Hindus who had fled from Kullar area due to threats from militants were sitting on dharna. They started pelting stones on the shops belonging to Muslims as they objected to blocking the road. The authorities rushed to the trouble spot. Sub-divisional magistrate of Kishtwar was roughed up by the demonstrators. Four shops and three small structures were set ablaze. Police fired to disperse the mob. Four civilians and seven policemen were injured. There was serious communal trouble in Kodinar town of Junagarh district in Gujarat.

The VHP and Bajrang Dal people looted and burnt 26 shops belonging to Muslims. The police arrested 53 persons, which included one Bajrang Dal leader. The police seized one car, one tractor, swords, gas cutter, and tins of kerosene and gas cylinders from the rioters. According to the police there was short circuit in one Hindu shop and it was burnt. But the VHP and Bajrang Dal leaders without verifying set rumour afloat that Muslims have burnt the shop. The VHP organised *bandh* in protest against the arrest of 53 persons. Bihar experiences not much communal violence thanks to Laloo Prasad's efforts. But that does not mean there is no communalism and RSS is inactive. RSS-VHP is quite active in spreading communal hatred. In Ara, Bihar, communal violence broke out on 5th October on the occasion of Durga Puja. The RSS controls some puja samitis.

According to eye -witnesses there were a garbage dump near the pooja pandal and people used it as open urinal also. On that day a Muslim youth was urinating when members of pooja samiti tried to stop him and there was harsh argument. The RSS gave it a communal colour. Some RSS youth went round on motor cycles spreading the rumour that the Muslim youth not only urinated on the Durga idol but broke the *kalash* also. Some miscreants gathered and started burning and looting Muslim shops. When the situation became out of control the police opened fire killing two Hindu youths. Some 70 shops were burnt and 48 cars set ablaze.

It is obvious that it was conspiracy by the RSS to spread communal violence in Bihar and try to seize power from Laloo Prasad Yadav. Laloo knows this well and he not only took immediate step to curb the violence but also denounced it as a RSS conspiracy. On October 15 Kurla, an eastern suburb of Mumbai went up in flames when a Muslim girl was teased by some Hindu youths at night. There was argument between members of the two communities and then violence erupted. Kurla has large Muslim population and is highly communally sensitive. Police was rushed and Jt. Commissioner of Police Javed Ahmed also visited the area.

The situation calmed down but erupted next morning again. Some miscreants pelted stones at Jama Masjid on New

Mill road. In retaliation petrol bombs and soda water bottles were thrown at Hanuman Mandir. Several persons were injured grievously. State Reserve police, Rapid Action Force and Riot Police were rushed. Gujarat cauldron continues to boil since the post-Godhra carnage and communal incidents occur every few days. Such violence revisited on 2nd November leaving three persons dead and 45 injured. This time it occurred in Viramgam, 65 kms. from Ahmedabad. There was heavy stone pelting, arson and firing.

One person was killed when police fired 15 rounds and two persons fell to bullets from private arms. Trouble broke out when a cricket ball landed in the nearby temple. This was enough provocation for communal violence. Marauding began and at least 30 shops were looted and burnt. Curfew was imposed at 12.40 p.m. In all twenty five persons were arrested including the BJP councillor Puroshottambhai Vasrambhai Jadav who fired from his gun killing one person. His gun was also seized. Those killed were identified as Zakir Allah Rakkha Multani (30), Zakir Yousuf Multani (35) and Sharif Shafibhai (25). On 17th November violence broke out in Vai in Satara district of Maharashtra. Vai is a sacred town for Hindus. The violence broke out when some members of Pratabgadh Utsav Samiti forcibly tried to stop a truck taking some cattle. More than 500 persons collected near a place of worship and stone pelting and arson began. The Hindutvawadis spread rumour in the town which intensified violence.

On 21st November violence broke out in Parbhani in Marathwada area when a bomb exploded near Jama Masjid after last Juma prayer of Ramadan in which 35 Muslims were injured and curfew was imposed in Parbhani district. According to the police two motorcycle riders threw the bomb when a prayer was going on in Rahmatnagar mosque. It is said that Shiv Sena-BJP workers are involved in the explosion. The writer is an Indian scholar and chairman, Centre for Study of Society and Secularism, Mumbai.

Even before the last cinder could burn out in the badlands of Gujarat, myths were circulated, accusations were leveled explanations and counter-explanations were advanced about the manner in which members of the minority community had 'started' the riot in the first place by sending the train up in flames. The subsequent murder and mayhem was then categorized by the Gujarat government (and the central government as well with their silence on the pogrom) as an 'equal and opposite reaction' to the train-burning incident at Godhra.

Various fears were expressed by the BJP government and its Sangh affiliates about the 'lesson' that needed to be taught to the Muslims failing which they would have taken over the state, both in numbers as well as power. Further the 'Pakistani agents' who thronged the streets of Ahmedabad and Vadodara had to be shown their place. The politico- religious reasons given by those belonging to the governmental machinery in the state and the countrywide network of the Sangh Parivar failed to convince anyone. After all, they smacked of a lack of logic and compounded obduracy.

The carnage, however, would lead a number of scholars, both young and old, to re-examine the existing explanations of the various causative factors of religious conflagrations. Paul Brass terms these explications as 'unsatisfactory' and 'mystifying' in his work on Hindu-Muslim violence in contemporary India. Naturalizing accounts of riots have invariably portrayed them as inevitable eruptions of anger and violence between communities divided by deep, incommensurable and often historical differences. The paper would in the next few pages attempt to take a broad but detailed account of these explanations and the theorists who are credited with having advanced them.

A study of the major authoritative work done by Paul Brass, Ashutosh Varshney, Imtiaz Ahmad and Steven Wilkinson would lead to a most varied and differentiated mass of thought and scholarship which could go a long way in putting the issue of Hindu-Muslim violence in perspective. The veracity with which the Gujarat state government pushed for early elections in the aftermath of the worst communal violence since Independence (notwithstanding the state) startled both scholars as well as media-watchers who had been witness, even though distant and mute to the horrors that unfolded on the streets of Ahmedabad and Vadodara to name only a fraction of the total area of the extent of the violence.

The dissolving of the state assembly only confirmed what purists had feared- the violence was a result of the insecurity of the BJP after weighed down by defeat at the municipal and *panchayat* elections. Steven Wilkinson, in the seminal ' Putting Gujarat in Perspective' deconstructs the entire debate on state complicity by delineating a wider shift in Indian politics. The state governments delay in calling in the Army established beyond doubt that the anti-minority pogrom was being carried out with the involvement of not only the politicians but the state machinery as well. As in most riots in the country before and after Independence, minorities suffered disproportionately in Gujarat from February 27, 2002 to the beginning of April, 2002.

Minorities Commission figures on the communal riots that took place from 1985-87 stand testimony to the fact that in almost every bout of communal violence, the minorities are taken to the butcher. Given the fact that the state governments are responsible for law and order in India, the question why some state governments are successful in controlling riot situations and preventing one from occurring and others are not is not only relevant but also vexing. Wilkinson argues that ethnic riots are far from being spontaneous eruptions of anger. Instead they are often planned by politicians for a clear electoral purpose. Subsequently, it then follows that these very politicians will also prevent riots if and when it is in their interest to do so.

These violent conflagrations are, therefore caused by political elites who play on existing communal tensions to advance a political agenda. Instrumental political explanations for violence have been labeled 'unsatisfactory' not only by Wilkinson but also by other theorists. The Duke University professor lends credence to his criticism of instrumental explanations by invoking the actions of certain state governments. The first point of refutation that he makes is that scholars who look at political elites and their reasons for inciting violence offer little insight into why some politicians tend to do exactly the opposite and use their political capital and control of the state to prevent ethnic conflict. The second major problem identified by Wilkinson, with many political explanations for ethnic violence is that they fail to account for the variation in patterns of violence within states.

In order to clear any confusion arising out of the criticism made against the existing theories, Wilkinson posits three 'possible' explanations for the differences in state performance, which will be elaborated upon in the course of the paper. First, decades of corruption, criminalization, politicization and a general lack of state capacity have left Indian state governments too weak to prevent riots. Second, Indian state governments are unable or unwilling to protect minorities because they systematically under-represent them within their governments, police forces and local administrations. Lastly and most importantly, the degree of party competition affects the value governments place on attracting 'Muslim swing voters', which effects whether or not the government will order the respective administrations to protect the minorities.

Since Wilkinson's scholarship primarily deals with the actions of the state in fomenting or preventing ethnic violence between Hindus and Muslims in accordance with their electoral incentives, it is imperative to take a detailed account of the arguments that he posits in this regard. He focuses on state and town level electoral incentives which remain important even if we assume various other factors, socio-economic and otherwise, to be constant and controlled. At the local level, the politicians would try to ensure that the identity that favors their party is the one that is most salient in the minds of a majority of voters. Those parties that represent elites within ethnic groups will invariably use polarizing anti-minority events in order to encourage the members of their ethnic category to identify with their party and the 'majority' identity.

The most effective method, according to Wilkinson, for elite dominated ethnic parties to mobilize those target voters who are at risk of voting for the main rival parties will be to use 'ethnic wedge issues'. This is summarily accomplished by highlighting the 'Muslim threat' especially in urban areas where the party hopes to win over the pivotal Hindu voters. The form of anti-minority mobilization taken recourse to depends on both the identity which the party wants to make salient and also the fact that the Indian state, similar to other states, privileges some form of public ritual or procession which culminates in immense mobilization.

In fact, C. A Bayly shows that riots occurred because of, or in the wake of, religious processions in the late eighteenth century and early nineteenth centuries. Scholars like Tambiah have also noted that processions often degenerate into rioting as a result of the manipulation by leaders who wish to bring about some form of mobilization in their favour. Defensive counter- mobilization by the minorities is portrayed as 'anti-national' and the myth of the 'foreign hand' is often invoked. When large crowds face each other and the threat of the situation deteriorating increases which is then construed to be the handiwork of the Muslims alone.

Conditions such as these produces 'community consciousness' that translates into a wave for or against the party which further leads to a swing that either reaps rewards or brickbats. Wilkinson argues that to win an election it is not necessary to appeal to each and every voter but to the pivotal swing voters who generally are those undecided voters who fear the consequences of not taking a defensive stand against the members of the other community. Statistical evidence suggests that proximity to an election sharply increases the likelihood of a riot. Factors such as economic competition, Muslim population and percentage of refugees from Pakistan are not numerically significant in explaining the occurrence of a Hindu-Muslim riot even though computation shows that as the Hindu-Muslim balance of a town reaches 50-50, the possibility of a riot goes up a few notches.

Three kinds of situations may develop which prove that as electoral competition increases, the level of riots goes down. First, the existence of three or more parties provides a security blanket to the minorities as the importance of swing votes increases provided the majoritarian party is not trying to attract the fringe Hindu votes. A bi-polar state party system creates a potentially dangerous situation for the minorities, especially when the majoritarian party, which owns the anti-minority issues, tries to foment violence. The third situation can be exemplified by Gujarat and the events that unfolded in that state in the year 2002. Disaster awaits the minority community, however, when the anti-minority, majoritarian party is in power. The anti- minority government will prevent violence only when the destruction threatens to wean away the loyal voters.

Any potential advantage to the government will not be sacrificed in order to protect the minorities. The number of elections that are preceded by communal killings has taken an upswing over the years, especially since the Hindu nationalist BJP gained political prominence. If the L.K Advani led *rath yatra* (chariot procession) that traversed most parts of the country left a trail of blood in its wake, the mammoth saffron wave that swept the India in election after election proves beyond doubt the fact that Hindu-Muslim riots increases the likelihood of the BJP improving its electoral performance.

The above argument refutes the claim made by Ashutosh Varshney in his work on ethnic violence in which he almost absolves politicians, the strategic roles played by them in fomenting violence and the Sangh Parivar that has been associated with most post-Independence Hindu-Muslim conflict by stressing on the existence or absence of civic ties between members of the two communities as the major factor that either leads to violence or to peace. Electoral incentives are the prime movers of an ethnic riot. Wilkinson, however, further investigates the reaction of a state government and its administrative machinery to communal violence, whether in controlling the conflagration or letting the fires burn.

The two major indices that are used for this purpose are-state autonomy and state capacity Wilkinson's central argument is that state weakness does not account for state level differences in the level of Hindu-Muslim violence. He finds that the relationship between state autonomy (the lack of political interference or otherwise) and state capacity is inversely proportional to variations in occurrence of Hindu-

Muslim riots. States that are said to be the lowest on the autonomy and capacity barometer have done remarkably well to prevent riots. Even the weakest state governments, like Bihar and Uttar Pradesh, still seem to possess the minimal state capacity necessary to prevent Hindu-Muslim riots if this is prioritized by the state's political leaders.

The mere fact that there are sharp state level variations in the occurrence as well as the prevention and control of riots suggest that the problem is not so much state capacity as the instructions given by politicians to state officials telling them whether to protect or not to protect minorities. Certain specific aspects however are linked to state capacity and poor performance in preventing riots. The financial weakness of some state governments can be a cause for concern. Interestingly enough, the Gujarat state government was hardly cash-strapped when the pogrom took place in the state.

Secondly, the police and judicial systems in many states are understaffed and overloaded, which reduces the perceived risk rioters face of arrest, prosecution and conviction. Punitive transfers also have an independent negative effect on riot preparedness, because frequent transfers reduce officers' knowledge about their districts, the potential trouble spots and the one best way to prevent a riot. Political interference with state autonomy is alleged to increase Hindu-Muslim violence in different ways. Instructions from the political bosses to either drop or go slow in investigating cases of mob brutality and murder by certain influential members of the citizenry or political retribution that they delay in taking stern action especially against groups that enjoy state protection are the common ways in which state autonomy is eroded and in some cases demolished.

Obviously enough the central thrust of the work done by Steven Wilkinson traces the linkages between party competition and ethnic violence but at the same time he finds that high levels of electoral competition can reduce as well as precipitate ethnic violence. The existence or otherwise of civic ties between Hindus and Muslims at the town level is the primary cause of conflict or the lack of it between the two is the central assertion made by Ashutosh Varshney in his recent work on the subject. Where such networks of civic engagement exist, tensions and conflicts are regulated and managed; where they are missing, communal identities lead to endemic and ghastly violence. These networks can be broken down into: associational forms of engagement and everyday forms of engagement. Both forms of civic engagement if intercommunal promote peace.

The capacity, however, of the associational forms to withstand national level exogenous shocks is substantially higher. Varshney argues that associational forms turn out to be sturdier in the face of politicians trying to foment communal trouble. Vigorous associational life acts as a serious constraint on the polarizing strategies of political elites. The mechanisms that connect civil society (non-state domain) and ethnic conflict can be broadly classified into two categories. By promoting communication between members of different religious communities, civic networks often make neighborhood peace possible. People come together routinely to form temporary organizations in the face of tensions.

These can be highly effective, and are known as 'peace committees'. Such organized bodies are difficult in those urban concentrations where civic engagement between Hindus and Muslims does not exist. The second mechanism describes why associational forms of engagement are sturdier than everyday forms in dealing with ethnic and communal tensions. Vibrant organizations serving the economic, cultural and social needs of the two communities can promote communal peace, which can be solidly expressed. Varshney, however, presents a profound paradox. Everyday engagement is so complete in the village level in India that associational forms of engagement are few and far between. Yet rural India has experienced fewer riots since independence.

In contrast, even though associational life flourishes in the cities, even petty rumors can cause deadly bouts of communal violence. The argument fails to stand its ground once the 'anonymity' argument is put forward. Cities tend to be less interconnected and more anonymous. Size, can reduce the extent and effectiveness of everyday interaction. This explanation leads us to the two other major findings that make its appearance in the work done by Varshney. First, the share of villages in communal rioting is remarkably small. According to Varshney, Hindu-Muslim violence is primarily an urban phenomenon. The violence in Gujarat can be termed unique in several ways including the occurrence of large-scale communal violence in the rural areas. The tribal infested Dangs and Sabarkantha district saw the largest number of killings in the rural belt, however, much lesser that those killed in urban centers like Ahmedabad and Vadodara.

The second argument that the political scientist makes as far as town-level variation is concerned is a little more problematic than the first one. He differentiates between 'riot-prone cities' and others where he identifies eight cities- Ahmedabad, Bombay, Aligarh, Hyderabad, Meerut, Baroda, Calcutta and Delhi- to be particularly high on the riot scale. Eighty two percent of the urban population therefore, is not riot-prone. India's Hindu-Muslim violence therefore, is city specific. State and national level politics provides the context within which the local mechanisms linked with violence are activated. Cities are also the sites for large-scale civic engagement, which constrains local politicians in their strategic behavior. These riot prone cities lack such forms of engagement that leads to the political elites taking advantage of the volatility of the situation. In peaceful cities, an institutionalized peace system exists, where organizations are communally integrated.

These civic organizations, for all practical purposes become the ears and arms of the local administration. It then follows that, if the civic edifice is interethnic and associational, it can take 'ethnic earthquakes' such as a partition and desecration of a holy place. If the form of civic engagement is intraethnic in everyday life, earthquakes of smaller intensity can bring the edifice down. Varshney, thus states that a multiethnic society with few interconnections across ethnic boundaries is very vulnerable to ethnic disorders and violence. In Hyderabad city, for instance, most Hindus and Muslims do not meet in a civic setting where mutual relations can be formed.

Lacking these networks even competent police officers and administrators, watch a riot unfolding helplessly. The emphasis on civic engagement as the mechanism that either foments or controls communal violence tends to displace focus from the role played by the Hindu nationalist Sangh Parivar in engineering riots and pogroms since independence. Paul Brass is critical of Varshney's 'blame displacing' theorization and the fact that he identifies the Gujarat violence as the first of its kind in India. III "Most of his work gives a clean chit to the Sangh Parivar," commented Prof. Brass in the course of his lecture.

Varshney, according to the celebrated theorist, refuses to recognize that many riots in the post-independence period have been outright pogroms. He indulges in a kind of 'apologetics' to the Sangh Parivar. The phrase 'ethnic earthquake' is, in the words of Prof. Brass, a myth about spontaneous outbreaks of communal violence. What is not a myth however is that communal riots are 'organized' and 'produced' by a network of known persons in the city or town. Most of these known persons are members of the Sangh Parivar who are devoted to the cult of violence for the protection of Hinduism. Despite the fact that there are 'waves' or 'chains' in the occurrence patterns of communal rioting, there has been no notable period when such violence has been absent.

Paul Brass, in the many enlightening pages that follow his introduction, develops and demonstrates the argument as to why communal tensions are maintained, accompanied from time to time by lethal rioting, and how it is essential for the development of militant Hindu nationalism and for other organizations and individuals. Communal riots, according to the renowned scholar are endemic in India. The phenomenon of certain sites that are prone to violence or otherwise, entering and disappearing from the list of riot-hit cities is therefore, somewhat flummoxing. While investigating the spatial variation in the incidence of Hindu-Muslim riots, he tries to classify the various issues that continue to surprise in categories of persistence, differential incidence/timing, classification/meaning and power.

The struggle over meaning, explanations and power relations requires attention to a communal discourse that has entrenched itself rather deep in the body politic of the country. Brass uses the term 'hegemonic' to explain the communal discourse that pervades Indian politics. This discourse, fiercely Hindu nationalistic, has been successful in corrupting history as well as memory. He identifies three elements inherent in the spread of this hegemonic communal discourse. Historisation leads to the distortion of history and the division of history into periods where Muslims are seen as conquerors. The fundamental antagonism is over-emphasized. The aspect of memorialisation includes greater attention given to the dead heroes of one particular faith.

The dramatizing and exaggerating nuances used to glorify what the Sangh Parivar calls 'the struggle for the birthplace of Lord Rama', is essential to memorialization. Evidence exists to show that memorialization leads to demonization of the 'other'. The Muslims, the 'others' in the Indian case, are portrayed in literature, cinema and other forms of human expression as 'racially different inferior beings who invaded our country and cultural space'. Myths, lending credence to this process of demonization, are taken recourse to in the form of the spoken word as well as the written letter. Muslims are seen as violent and a danger to Hindu women.

Some utterly preposterous myths that have made their presence felt in the last two decades or so are the invariably higher rates of population growth among the Muslims through which they are trying to take over power both at the local and the national level and the fact that most of them are 'Pakistani agents'. Another feature of the communal discourse is 'body symbolism'. Muslim rule is portrayed as 'slavery' of the Hindus. The politics of body symbolism depicts the partition in visceral terms i.e. tearing apart of the Hindu body. The Muslims thus are dangerous to the Hindu body and need to be removed before the danger can actually present itself.

This explains why most post-independence riots have been outright pogroms against the Muslims. Prof. Brass delineates three phases in the production process of riots. He compares a riot to a 'staged drama'. Dipankar Gupta uses the term 'picnic rioting' to describe the manner in which Hindu mobs actually celebrate the killing of Muslims. The Gujarat riots exemplified the herding of saffron clad mobs into trucks and the subsequent journey into specially marked colonies of Muslim concentration. The first phase therefore, is one of preparation (rehearsal) in which tensions are kept alive. Killing of a cow and the kidnap of a Hindu girl are the common methods. The following phase is one of activation (enactment). The political circumstance must be right for a riot to be precipitated. An election could be such an occasion.

The last phase of riot production is explanation or interpretation where blame displacement comes into play. Prof. Brass further argues that there exists a division of labour in the production of riots. Riot systems are institutionalized. Specific roles are assigned to persons like that of scouts or informants, rumormongers and propagandists. Vernacular journalists enact their parts admirably by coming out with wild and inciting stories. The recruiters are those who collect people to form mobs. Special duties are assigned to, whom Prof. Brass calls, 'fire tenders' who go around scouting for rumours that could help in fomenting a riot. These men invariably are members of either the VHP or the Bajrang Dal. 'Conversion specialists' ultimately decide whether to begin a riot or not.

Causal questions about the spatial spread of riots are of utmost importance. Why exactly are they produced in certain cities or towns and why not in others? Steven Wilkinson's answer to this question has already been looked at. Brass asserts that the contexts are primarily political as mass mobilizations usually precede elections. A sizeable number of Muslims in a particular town or city is essential for the production of riots. The demise of the Congress system has created a space that is normally filled by the other political formation, which also benefits from riots and their production. The BJP has emerged as such a formation that benefits disproportionally through riots.

The Gujarat situation is self-evident in this regard. Brass in his new book takes Aligarh as his case for study and periodises the history of riot production in that city. The early period belonged to the Congress, which dominated till the late 1950s. This domination began to be contested between the 1960s and the 1980s. The last period, which is also the current phase, is a contest between the BJP and the Janta Dal- Samajwadi Party combine. He is critical of Varshney for ignoring the 1990-91 communal pogroms, which was solely the handiwork of the Sangh Parivar. Such scholarship, he further clarifies, distorts all analytical social studies.

Brass and Wilkinson agree therefore that, riots and electoral politics are closely connected to each other. They proclaim in their respective works that there exists an absence of political will to control riots and these cuts across political parties. Both further argue that the Sangh Parivar are the primary sources of most communal conflict in the country since independence. Sociologists have a penchant for examining social conflict and Imtiaz Ahmad is no different in his approach. He, being one of the first scholars to propound the socio-economic theories for communal conflict, views Hindu- Muslim conflict as an extension of the wider social conflict that includes inter as well as intra communal riots, caste violence and other forms of sectional upheavals.

The emphasis placed on Hindu-Muslim conflict in case of social and communal violence comes but naturally considering the huge impact the various riots between the two communities have had on the Indian polity and society. Ahmad argues that economic prosperity of the Muslims is a factor that precipitates endemic anger on the part of the Hindus who fear being swamped, both socially and economically by the nouveau riche Muslims. This antagonism results in riots, which spreads to other parts of the state. An argument that has been advanced by numerous scholars following Imtiaz Ahmad, the above brings to the fore the social contradictions that have given rise to many communal conflagrations in the past and are likely to do so in future.

The ghosts of Gujarat cannot be invoked here as the violence there was 'produced' by the government of the day. The tensions that prevail, in the rural plains of the north-western state, are somewhat akin to the argument made by Prof. Ahmad. Frequent riots in the diamond city of Surat prove his point beyond any doubt. The democratic process therefore, is responsible for communal conflict and the lack of it. The scholars discussed above have advanced conclusive arguments about the role of democracy and the electoral system.

The kind of electoral system that gets institutionalized over time determines the frequency of communal riots. Further, the arguments made above prove that riots are produced by specialists who could be politicians or members of the majoritarian formation. The paper, thus puts the whole issue of 'causal factors' of communal riots into perspective and provides us with a number of theories, most of them interconnected to explain a riot, especially when a Gujarat occurs in the history of mankind!

The 2002 Gujarat pogrom describes a series of communal riots between the communities of Hindus and Muslims that took place in the Indian State of Gujarat between February and May 2002. The riots occurred at the Godhra train burning. The train had left Godhra Station and it was forcibly stopped and attacked by a 500 strong weapon carrying Muslim men that targeted one of the coaches containing the Hindu religious pilgrims and burnt them alive. 58 Hindu pilgrims, 23 men, 15 women and 20 children perished. This incident was the flashpoint that started the communal Gujarat violence.

In September 2008 the Godhra Commission confirmed that there was an attack, by a Muslim mob. Going further, the report claims that one Hassan Lalu had thrown burning objects into the train and 140 litres of petrol had been used to set the train on fire, adding that stones were thrown at passengers to stop them from fleeing. According to official figures tabled in the parliament, more than a thousand people were killed (790 Muslims and 254 Hindus) in the violence after the train incident. More than one hundred and fifty thousand people were displaced (about 100,000 Muslims and 40,000 Hindus).

Organisations such as Human Rights Watch criticized the Indian government for failure to address the resulting humanitarian condition of people, "overwhelming majority of them Muslim," who fled their homes for relief camps in the aftermath of the events. Many of the investigations and prosecution of those accused of violence during the riots have been opened for reinvestigation and prosecution. According to an official estimate, 1044 people were killed in the violence - 790 Muslims and 254 Hindus including those killed in the Godhra train fire. Another 223 people were reported missing, 2,548 injured, 919 women widowed and 606 children orphaned. About 100,000 Muslims and 40,000 Hindus were in relief camps.

The large-scale, collective violence has been generally been described as riots or inter-communal clashes. The perpetrators of the violence as well as Sangh parivar leaders and the Gujarat government maintain that the violence was a spontaneous, uncontrollable reaction to the Godhra train burning. Going by the numbers, the vested interests have termed it a massacre and an attempted pogrom or genocide of the Muslim population, emphasizing that the violence was largely directed against defenceless people, indiscriminate with regard to age or sex and alleging that it was pre-planned, organised and aided by the local authorities and political leaders.

GODHRA TRAIN BURNING

On February 27, 2002, 58 Hindus, including 25 women and 15 children were burnt alive in a railway coach by a Muslim mob in the town of Godhra following an altercation between local Muslims and activists of the Vishva Hindu Parishad (Kar Sevaks) returning by the Sabarmathi express train from Ayodhya. Initial media reports blamed the local Muslims for setting the coach on fire, in what Gujarat chief minister Narendra Modi and the VHP leader Giriraj Kishore alleged was a "pre-planned" attack. The New Nanavati Report states that the Attack on the "Kar Sevaks" on the train from Ayodhya was pre-planned and exonerates Chief Minister Narendra Modi. A previous report on the Godhra train burning, filed by Justice Banerjee, a more recent report filed by Justice Nanavati states that it was "pre-planned" by the mob.

The Gujarat High Court ruling, as of 2006, has declared as illegal and unconstitutional, setting up of the Umesh Chandra Banerjee committee, which had concluded the fire started by accident. Gujarat High Court quashed the conclusions of the Banerjee Committee and declared its formation as a "colourful exercise," "illegal, unconstitutional, null and void," and its argument of accidental fire "opposed to the prima facie accepted facts on record." The bodies of those killed in the train were brought to Ahmedabad, where a procession was held, a move seen as a major provocation for the ensuing communal violence. The VHP issued a call for a state-wide strike on February 28, 2002, which was supported by the BJP.

POST-GODHRA VIOLENCE

Almost 151 towns and 993 villages in fifteen to sixteen of the state's 25 districts were affected by the post-Godhra violence, which was particularly severe in about five or six districts. The violence raged largely between February 28 and March 3, and after a drop, restarted on March 15, continuing till mid June. Northern and central Gujarat, as well as the north-eastern tribal belt where Hindutva mobilisation efforts were strong, were the worst affected while Saurashtra and Kutch remained largely peaceful. Attacks by large mobs began in the districts of Ahmedabad, Vadodara, Saberkantha and, for the first time in its history, Gandhinagar on February 28. Violence spread to the largely rural districts of Panchmahals, Mehsana, Kheda, Junagadh, Banaskantha, Patan, Anand and Narmada the next day. Over the next two days, Bharuch and Rajkot and later Surat were hit.

The first incidents of attacks on the minority Muslim community started at Ahmedabad, where Hindus began throwing stones at and later burned a Muslim housing complex known as Gulburg Society, and then spread elsewhere. The initial violence was believed to be instigated by unsubstantiated rumours, endorsed by a senior VHP leader, of Muslims having kidnapped three Hindu girls during the Godhra train attack. In Ahmedabad, the dargah of the Sufi saint-poet Wali Gujarati in Shahibaug and the 16th century Gumte Masjid mosque in Isanpur were destroyed. The

Muhafiz Khan Masjid at Gheekanta was ransacked. Police records list 298 dargahs, 205 mosques, 17 temples and three churches as damaged in the months of March and April.

ATTACKS ON MUSLIMS

In Naroda, according to Human Rights Watch, at least 65 Muslims were killed, many of them women who were sexually assaulted by violent mobs. One of the witnesses testified before the Nanavati commission that that BJP leader Maya Kodnani, Bajrang Dal leader Babu Bajrangi and others led mobs on February 28 in the Naroda-Patia area. However, on 13 April 2009 a Special Investigation Team (SIT) submitted before the Supreme Court of India that many of these allegations, including those of Naroda-Patia, were highly dubious; many of the affidavits by the witnesses were identical and appeared to have been "tutored" by a vested NGO.

A high profile case involved an Ex-Congress MP Ehsan Jafri who was surrounded by Hindu mobs (including Congress workers) while many other Muslim residents in the area took shelter in his compound. Jafri was believed to have contacted the local police stations, MPs of the area as well as the Chief Minister Modi to save the people from the ever increasing mob. However, no police reinforcement had reached his place and the few policemen present were ineffective and unwilling to control the violent mob." Eventually he was burnt to death, along with fifty others.

According to HRW in its widely-quoted report, mobs of thousands, dressed in saffron scarves and khaki shorts - and armed with swords, sophisticated explosives, and gas cylinders, were guided by voter lists and printouts of addresses of Muslim-owned properties, information obtained from the local municipal administration. Muslims in Ahmedabad alleged that there were elements of planning in the violence. Fourteen people, including women and children, were killed by a mob at the Best Bakery in the town of Vadodara on the night of 1 March. On March 3, fourteen members of Bilkis Bano's family including her two-month old daughter were killed in a mob attack near Chapparwad village in Dahod district. Seven women including Bilkis Bano, then five months pregnant, were raped.

ATTACKS ON HINDUS

Attacks on Hindus by Muslim mobs in Danilimda, Modasa, Himmatnagar, Bharuch, Sindhi Market, Bhanderi Pole, and other localities in the city of Ahmedabad in Gujarat were perpetrated by Muslim mobs. There was a significant loss of property. Late in March, more than one thousand Hindus in Dariyapur and Kalupur, including 550 dalits, fled their homes to stay in makeshift shelters after being attacked by Muslims mobs. According to the HRW report, over ten thousand Hindus were made homeless. Several Hindu residential areas, including Mahajan No Vaado, a fortified enclave in Muslim dominated Jamalpur, were targeted following calls for retaliation.

In the morning the mosques began announcing that Islam was in danger, that there was poison in the milk. This is their code word. We are the only Hindus here, poison here means us. The rioting lasted between 2:15 p.m. and 5:30 p.m. Residents were unable go to work, fearing attacks. A Hindu temple in the area was destroyed. In Himmatnagar, a young man was killed when he went to a Muslim enclave on business.

TOLL

According to an official estimate, 1044 people were killed in the violence - 790 Muslims and 254 Hindus including those killed in the Godhra train fire. Another 223 people were reported missing, 2,548 injured, 919 women widowed and 606 children orphaned. Unofficial estimates put the death toll closer to 2000, with Muslims forming a high proportion of those killed. When missing people were declared dead after 7 years, total deaths went up from 952 to 1,180.

ECONOMIC BOYCOTT OF MUSLIMS

The People's Union for Civil Liberties alleges that pamphlets were circulated by the Sangh Parivar to incite violence against and call for an economic boycott of the Muslim community. Shortly after the riots, when most Muslims were still in relief camps, a leaflet campaign "urging Hindus to boycott Muslim-owned shops and other establishments" was widely reported. The leaflets urged the Hindu reader not to frequent Muslim-owned restaurants, work in Muslim-run offices, hire Muslims or see films starring Muslim actors; they further assured the reader that the boycott would "throttle these elements.

It will break their backbone. Then it will be difficult for them to live in any corner of this country." The economic boycott and "pressure from Hindu radicals" caused fewer employers to re-hire returning Muslims. No group claimed direct responsibility for the leaflets but a senior official of Vishva Hindu Parishad (VHP) was quoted as saying he was "in complete agreement with whatever is propagated through them." As a consequence of the leaflet campaign, observers claimed that year and even two and half years later, the economic boycott of Muslims was severe in Pavagadh district. As a consequence of the boycott and continued threats, relief organisations lamented that they were having to build "ghettoes" for the displaced.. However, many Muslims have welcomed the post-riots stability, which has allowed for economic prosperity for Muslims in some areas, as well as being a catalyst for encouraging education among the Muslim populace.

SECURITY MEASURES

By the evening of February 28, curfews were imposed in twenty seven towns and cities. By March 25, thirty five towns were under curfew. Police records show 21,563 preventive arrests were made by the end of April (17,947 of the arrested were listed as Hindus and 3,616 as Muslims) as well as 13,989 substantive arrests (9,954 Hindus and 4,035 Muslims). New York Times' Celia Dugger reported that witnesses were "dismayed by the lack of intervention from local police", who often "watched the events taking place and took no action against the attacks on Muslims and their property".

Human Rights Watch reported that in some cases members of the state police force led rioting mobs, "aiming and firing at every Muslim who got in the way", or instead of offering assistance "led the victims directly into the hands of their killers." Calls for assistance to the police, fire brigades, and even ambulance services generally proved futile. By the end of April, police recorded 170 people as killed in police firing, of whom 93 were Muslims and 77 were Hindus.

Hindu residents of Mahajan No Vaado, part of the Muslim dominated area of Jamalpur, told HRW that on March 1, the police ignored phone calls and left them fend for themselves when a Muslim mob attacked. Numerous calls by Hindus throughout the riots were reportedly ignored by the police. One thousand army troops were flown in by the evening of March 1 to restore order. Intelligence officials alleged that the deployment was deliberately delayed by the state and central governments. On May 3, former Punjab police chief K P S Gill was appointed as security adviser to the Chief Minister.

The Gujarat government transferred several senior police officers who had taken active measures to contain and investigate violent attacks to administrative positions. R B Sreekumar, who served as Gujarat's intelligence chief during the riots, alleged that the state government issued "unconstitutional directives", with officials asking him to kill Muslims involved in rioting or disrupting a Hindu religious event. The Gujarat government denied the allegations, calling them "baseless" and instigated out of malice because Mr. Sreekumar was not promoted.

Defending the Modi administration in the Rajya Sabha against charges of genocide, BJP spokesman V K Malhotra said that the official toll of 254 Hindus, killed mostly in police firing, indicates how the state authorities took effective steps to curb the violence. BJP MP and journalist Balbir Punj disputed allegations of bias against Muslims by the BJP-run state government, pointing out that the majority of those arrested during and after the riots were Hindus. An unidentified pamphlet circulated to journalists in Gujarat in 2007 labelled Modi's government as anti-Hindu for arresting VHP workers and Hindu activists involved in the riots.

ROLE OF GOVERNMENT AND POLICE

The Narendra Modi led state government was reprimanded immediately for failing to prevent the riots, but then increasingly for actively fomenting and participating in it, which was a far more serious charge. Crtiques came repeatedly from the Supreme Court, and the upper house of the Indian parliament unanimously passed a resolution calling for federal intervention in Gujarat; a similar censure motion in the lower house was defeated by about 100 votes.

The United States Department of State in its International Religious Freedom Report 2003 commented on the episode, based on this report by USCIRF:

"India's National Human Rights Commission (NHRC), an official body, found evidence in the killings of premeditation by members of Hindu extremist groups; complicity by Gujarat state government officials; and police inaction in the midst of attacks on Muslims. The NHRC also noted "widespread reports and allegations of well-organized persons, armed with mobile telephones and addresses, singling out certain homes and properties for death and destruction in certain districts-sometimes within view of police stations and personnel," suggesting the attacks may have been planned in advance. Christians were also victims in Gujarat, and many churches were destroyed."

In April 2002, retired Supreme Court justices V. R. Krishna Iyer and P. B. Sawant headed a citizen's panel to investigate the riots. Their report includes testimony of the then Gujarat BJP minister Haren Pandya (since murdered), who testified about an evening meeting convened by Narendra Modi the evening of the Godhra train burning. At this meeting, officials were instructed not to obstruct the Hindu rage following the incident. The report also highlighted a second meeting, held in Lunawada village of Panchmahal district, and attended by state ministers Ashok Bhatt, and Prabhatsinh Chauhan, and other BJP and RSS leaders, where "detailed plans were made on the use of kerosene and petrol for arson and other methods of killing."

In 2003, a comment by G.T. Nanavati, who leads the official commission investigating the riots, that part of the evidence collected and reviewed till then did not indicate any serious lapse on the part of the government or police in Gujarat was criticised as inappropriate by aid and reconciliation activists and other jurists. In response to allegations of state involvement, Gujarat government spokesman, Bharat Pandya, told the BBC that the rioting was a spontaneous Hindu backlash fuelled by widespread anger against Muslims. He said "Hindus are frustrated over the role of Muslims in the on-going violence in Indian-administered Kashmir and other parts of India."

The US Ambassador at Large for International Religious Freedom, John Hanford, expressing concern over religious intolerance in Indian politics, said that while the rioters may have been aided by state and local officials, he did not believe that the BJP-led central government was involved in inciting the riots. At the same time, about two hundred policemen lost their lives trying to control the violence in Gujarat.

CRIMINAL PROSECUTIONS

The Indian Supreme Court has been strongly critical of the state government's investigation and prosecution of those accused of violence during the riots, directing police to review about 2,000 of the 4,000 riot related cases that had been closed citing lack of evidence or leads. Following this direction, police identified nearly 1,600 cases for reinvestigation, arrested 640 accused and launched investigations against 40 police officers for their failures. Human Rights Watch alleges that state and law enforcement officials harass and intimidate key witnesses, NGOs, social activists and lawyers who are fighting to seek justice for riot victims.

In its 2003 annual report, Amnesty International says, "the same police force that was accused of colluding with the attackers was put in charge of the investigations into the massacres, undermining the process of delivery of justice to the victims." The Best Bakery murder trial received wide attention after witnesses retracted testimony in court and all accused were acquitted. The Indian Supreme Court, acting on a petition by social activist Teesta Setalvad, ordered a retrial outside Gujarat in which nine accused were found guilty in 2006. A key witness, Zaheera Sheikh, who repeatedly changed her testimony during the trials and the petition, was found guilty of perjury.

After a local court dismissed the case against her assailants, Bilkis Bano approached the National Human Rights Commission and petitioned the Supreme Court seeking a retrial. The Supreme Court granted the motion, directing the Central Bureau of Investigation to take over the investigation, transferring the case out of Gujarat and directing the central government to appoint the public prosecutor. Charges were filed in a Mumbai court against nineteen people as well as six police officials and a government doctor over their role in the initial investigations. In January 2008, eleven men were sentenced to life imprisonment for the rape and murders and a policeman was convicted of falsifying evidence.

In 2005, the Vadodara fast track court acquitted 108 people accused of murdering two youths, during a mob attack on a group of displaced Muslims returning under police escort to their homes in Avdhootnagar. The court passed strictures against the police for failing to protect the people under their escort and failing to identify the attackers they had witnessed. Nine people were convicted of killing a Hindu man and injuring another during group clashes in Danilimda, Ahmedabad on April 12, while 25 others were acquitted. Eight people, including a VHP leader and a member of the BJP, were convicted for the murder of seven members of a family and the rape of two minor girls in the village of Eral in Panchmahal district.

Fifty two people from Pavagadh and Dhikva villages in Panchmahal district were acquitted of rioting charges for lack of evidence. A stringent anti-terror law, the POTA, was used by the Gujarat government to charge 131 people in connection to the Godhra train fire, but not invoked in prosecuting any of the accused in the post-Godhra riots. In 2005 the POTA Review Committee set up by central government to review the application of the law opined that the Godhra accused should not be tried under the provisions of POTA.

PUBLIC ENQUIRIES

Shah-Nanavati Commission

On March 6, the Gujarat government set up a commission of enquiry headed by retired High Court judge K.G. Shah to enquire into the Godhra train burning and the subsequent violence and submit a report in three months. Following criticism from victims' organisations, activists and political parties over Shah's alleged proximity to the BJP, on May 22, the government reconstituted the commission, appointing retired Supreme Court Justice G.T. Nanavati to lead the commission. In 2008, the Nanavati commission came out largely in favour of he Gujarat government's aspect. Nanavati's evidence hinged on the acquisition of 140 liters of petrol hours before the arrival of the train and the storage of the said petrol at the alleged key conspirator's, Razzak Kurkur, guest house.

This was further corroborated by forensic evidence showing fuel was poured on the train compartment before being burnt. The alleged mastermind was said to be the cleric Maulvi Husain Haji Ibrahim Umarji and a dismissed CRPF officer by the name of Nanumiyan, from Assam, who had instigated the Muslim crowds. Furthermore, two Kashmiris, Gulamnabi and Ali Mohammed, were in the same guesthouse for a fortnight prior to the event speaking about the Kashmir liberation movement.

The CPM and the Congress party both came out railing against the exoneration of the Gujarat government by the commission citing the timing of the report (with general elections months away) as evident of unfairness. Congress spokesperson Veerappa Moily commented at the strange absolvement of the Gujarat government for complacency for the carnage. He also said the report reinforced communal prejudices.

NATIONAL HUMAN RIGHTS COMMISSION

In its Proceedings of 1 April 2002, the Commission had set out its Preliminary Comments and Recommendations on the situation and sent a Confidential Report of the team of the Commission that visited Gujarat from 19 March-22 March 2002 to Gujarat government and Central Home Ministry. The Gujarat government in its reply did not provide its response to the confidential report. Therefore, the Commission was compelled to release the confidential report in its entirety and observed that nothing in the reports received in response "rebuts the presumption that the Modi administration failed in its duty to protect the rights of the people of Gujarat" by not exercising its jurisdiction over non-state players that may cause or facilitate the violation of human rights.

It further observed that "the violence in the State, which was initially claimed to have been brought under control in seventy two hours, persisted in varying degree for over two months, the toll in death and destruction rising with the passage of time despite the measures reportedly taken by the State Government". The report claims failure of intelligence, failure to take appropriate action, patterns of arrests, uneven handling of major cases, and "Distorted FIRs: 'extraneous influences', issue of transparency and integrity" as key factors in the incident(s).

Banerjee Committee

In September 2004, a panel appointed by the central government and headed by former Supreme Court judge UC Banerjee to probe the Godhra train fire concluded that the fire was accidental. Its findings were challenged by the BJP and the Gujarat inspector-general of police. In October 2006, the Gujarat High Court ruled that the panel was set up illegally, in violation of the Commissions of Inquiry Act, 1952 which prohibits the setting up of separate commissions by state and central governments to probe a matter of public importance.

Concerned Citizens Tribunal

The citizen tribunal headed by retired Supreme Court justice Krishna Iyer collected evidence and testimony from more than 2000 riot victims, witnesses and others. In its report, the tribunal accuses the state government and chief minister Modi of complicity in the violence. While Krishna Iyer was nominally part of this tribunal, he made it clear in the preface of the report that his involvement was very limited.

Aftermath

Opposition parties as well as three coalition partners of the BJP-led central government demanded the dismissal of Gujarat Chief Minister Narendra Modi for failing to contain the violence, with some calling for the removal of Union Home Minister L K Advani as well. On July 18, Chief Minister Narendra Modi asked the Governor of Gujarat to dissolve the state assembly and call fresh elections. The Indian Election Commission ruled out early elections, citing the prevailing law and order situation, a decision the union government unsuccessfully appealed against in the Supreme Court.

In August 2002 a plot by Lashkar-e-Toiba to assassinate Narendra Modi, Praveen Togadia, and other Sangh Parivar leaders was unearthed by Indian police. Delhi Police Special Commissioner K. K. Paul noted their motive was to avenge the "injustices caused to the Muslims in Gujarat". In September 2002, at least 29 people were killed when Islamic fundamentalist gunmen engaged in the Akshardham Temple attack in the city of Gandhinagar in Gujarat. The Pakistani ISI and Islamic terrorist group Lashkar-e-Toiba were accused of supporting the terrorists, but they have denied this accusation

Elections were held in December and Modi was returned to power in a landslide victory. Emails made public by the perpetrators of a series of bombings in western India in July 2008 indicated that those attacks were "the revenge of Gujarat".

RELIEF EFFORTS

Amnesty International's annual report on India in 2003 claimed the "Gujarat government did not actively fulfill its duty to provide appropriate relief and rehabilitation to the survivors". The state government initially offered compensation payments of 200,000 rupees to the families of those who died in the Godhra train fire and 100,000 rupees to the families of those who died in the subsequent riots, which local Muslims described as discriminatory. Subsequently, the government set the compensation amount at 150,000 rupees.

By March 27, nearly 100,000 displaced people moved into 101 relief camps. This swelled to over 150,000 in 104 camps the next two weeks. The camps were run by community groups and NGOs, with the government committing to provide amenities and supplementary services. Drinking water, medical help, clothing and blankets were in short supply at the camps. At least another 100 camps were denied government support, according to a camp organiser and relief supplies were prevented from reaching the camps over fears that they may be carrying arms.

Relief camp organisers alleged that the state government was coercing refugees to leave relief camps, with 25,000 people made to leave eighteen camps that were shut down. Following government assurances that camps would not be shut down, the Gujarat High Court bench ordered that camp organisers be given a supervisory role to ensure that the assurances were met. On the 23rd of May 2008, the Union Government announced a 320 crore rupee (US $ 80 million) relief package for the victims of the riots.

MEDIA COVERAGE

Covering the first major communal riots following in the advent of satellite television to India, television news channels set a precedent by identifying the community of those involved in the violence, breaking a long-standing practice. Critical reporting on the Gujarat government's handling of the situation helped bring about the Indian government's intervention in controlling the violence. The Gujarat government banned television news channels critical of the government's response. STAR News, Zee News, Aaj Tak, CNN as well as local stations were blocked.

The Editorial Guild of India rejected the charge that graphic news coverage aggravated the situation, saying that the coverage exposed the "horrors" of the riots as well as the "supine if not complicit" attitude of the state, helping propel remedial action. The team also faulted Gujarati language papers Gujarat Samachar and the pro-Hindutva Sandesh of distorted and provocative reporting. The Godhra fire received extensive news coverage until it was overtaken by the subsequent violence and the presentation of the Union budget. Television and newspaper reports, particularly local Gujarati language media, carried graphic and at times sensationalised images and accounts of the Godhra train fire. S Gurumurthy, Arvind Lavakare and columnist Rajeev Srinivasan argue that news reports emphasized the provocative behaviour of the kar sevaks on the Sabarmathi Express in an effort to rationalise the subsequent mob attack at Godhra and displace blame from the mob on to the *kar sevaks*.

Rajeev Srinivasan questions the veracity of several newspaper accounts of the violence, alleging that they diminish or justify violence against Hindus or play up violence against Muslims. He disputes the view, which he attributes to "the intelligentsia", that the Ram janmabhoomi agitation and Hindu fundamentalism are the proximate causes of the Gujarat violence, arguing instead that a "general Hindu frustration" over allegedly discriminatory government policies and Islamic fundamentalism led to the riots.

BJP MP Balbir Punj has criticised an Arundhati Roy essay, pointing out a factual error in it, and accusing a "secular pack" in the media of hyperbole and sensationalising the riots as part of an agenda of what he calls 'defamation' and 'left wing anti-India propaganda'. Punj writes "She (Roy) terms Gujarat the 'petri dish' of the Sangh Parivar. The fact is that Godhra has been used as a crucible by the secular fundamentalists." Punj later continues, "Loss of 900-odd innocent lives (both Hindus and Muslims) is definitely not'genocide' of any one community". Punj also says, "The secular pack is not only guilty of parading half-truths but also of condoning and inciting violence".

In 2004, the weekly newspaper Tehelka published a hidden camera exposé alleging that a BJP legislator Madhu Srivastava bribed Zaheera Sheikh, a witness in the Best Bakery killings trial. Srivatsava denied the allegation, and an inquiry committee appointed by the Indian Supreme Court drew an "adverse inference" from the video footage, though it failed to uncover evidence that money was actually paid. In a 2007 expose, the newspaper released hidden camera footage of several members of the BJP, VHP and the Bajrang Dal admitting their role in the riots. Among those featured in the tapes was the special counsel representing the Gujarat government before the Nanavati-Shah Commission, Arvind Pandya, who resigned from his post after they were made public? While the report was criticized by some as being politically motivated, some newspapers said the revelations simply reinforced what was common knowledge.

The Gujarat government blocked telecast of cable news channels broadcasting the expose, a move strongly condemned by the Editors Guild of India. The riots were also the subject of a 2004 documentary film by Rakesh Sharma (filmmaker), called Final Solution (Gujarat Riots). The film was denied entry to Mumbai International Film Festival in 2004 due to objections by Censor Board of India, but won two awards at the 54th Berlin International Film Festival (2004).

CONTROVERSIES ON THE RIOTS

Atrocities against Women

There was widespread public outrage regarding atrocities against women during the riots. These included acts of rape against women and female children, and mutilations. In some cases, crime reports to the Police (First Information Reports or FIRs) were neither promptly nor accurately recorded and the victims harassed and intimidated. An international fact finding committee formed of experts from US, UK, France, Germany and Sri Lanka reported, "Sexual violence was being used as a strategy for terrorising women belonging to minority community in the state."

Taking a stand decried by the media and other rights groups, Nafisa Hussain, a member of the National Commission for Women accused organisations and the media of needlessly exaggerating the plight of women victims of the riots which was strongly disputed as Gujarat did not have a State Commission for Women to act on the ground. The newspaper Tribune reported that "The National Commission for Women has reluctantly agreed to the complicity of Gujarat Government in the communal violence in the state." The tone of their most recent report was reported by the Tribune as "lenient".

Controversy over Contrived Cases

On April 14, 2009, a report in Times of India alleged that the report of the Special Investigation Team (SIT) set up by the Supreme Court of India to investigate and expedite the Gujarat riot cases had accused Teesta Setalvad of "cooking up macabre tales of killings". Teesta Setalvad denied any spicing up of riot incidents and said that the Times of India report was not based on SIT report, but based on the allegations made by Gujarat Government counsel in the Supreme Court.

9

Human Rights Scenario in Jammu and Kashmir

The human rights record of the Indian security forces in Kashmir has been characterized by arbitrary arrests, torture, rape and extrajudicial killings. These have been extensively documented by human rights organizations such as Human Rights Watch and the PUCL (People's Union for Civil Liberties) and others. Most of these violations routinely go unchecked and unpunished, "justified" as unavoidable in a proxy war managed by Pakistan; only a handful cases have been brought to justice by due process. Often, New Delhi's response to the reports by various human rights organizations has been evasive.

2477 civilians had been killed by the Indian forces in the period 1990-1998 (PTI release, 13 September 1998), according to conservative estimates by official sources which mostly exclude thousands of custodial killings. In April 1997, the Minister of State for Home Affairs admitted that 454 persons were missing since 1990.

CIVILIAN KILLINGS IN FIRINGS

The insurgency that began in 1989 in the Valley involved hundreds of thousands of Kashmiris marching on the streets of Srinagar between January and May 1990. Under Jagmohan's regime, India's response to the protests was brutal with indiscriminate firings at unarmed protesters; the atrocities committed by Indian forces has been acknowledged by senior

Indian officials including the Prime Ministers Rajiv Gandhi, Chandrashekhar and P.V. Narasimha Rao during their tenure and the State Governor Girish Saxena.

- On 20 January 1990, an estimated 100 people were killed when a large group of unarmed protesters were fired upon by the Indian troops at the Gawakadal Bridge.
- On March 1 1990, an estimated one million took to the streets and more than forty people were killed in police firing.
- In May 1990, an estimated 200,000 Kashmiris took to the streets in a funeral procession of the martyred leader Mirwaiz Maulvi Farooq; over 100 were killed in police firing.
- In January 1993, 40 people were killed in Sopore by security forces that burnt down a section of the town after two of their men were killed.
- In March 2000, nine civilians were killed in police firing in a large demonstration at Brakpora protesting killing of civilians at Panchalthan.
- In August 2000, 35 civilians were killed including 23 Amarnath pilgrims in Pahalgam; it has come to light that most of the people were killed in fact by the panic-stricken CRPF jawans who continued firing for another 20 minutes after the two suspected militants were killed; a commission under Lt.Gen. Mukherjee found 17 police officers responsible.
    - Kamal Mitra Chenoy, Report On human rights violations in Kashmir.
- Indian forces also have severely beaten 17 journalists in May 2001.
    - Human Rights Watch, India/Pakistan Summit: Call to Address Human Rights in Kashmir, 2001.
- In January 2002, Indian troops killed a civilian and wounded another in a firing at a demonstration at Sodal, protesting civilian beatings in search operations.

TORTURE AND CUSTODIAL KILLINGS

Civilians suspected of having information about militants, many of them innocent, are routinely detained, tortured and killed in custody, besides militants. Methods of torture include severe beatings, electric shock, crushing the leg muscles with a wooden roller, and burning with heated objects. In 1995, Amnesty International documented 706 cases of custodial killings in the period 1990-1994, nearly all after gruesome torture; In its response to Amnesty, the Government of India (GOI) responded to 519 out of 706 cases in an evasive manner, dismissing half of them as "encounter killings" without supporting evidence despite eye-witness reports to the contrary; The government indicated that there was *prima facie* evidence of human rights violations in 85 other cases which were said to be under investigation, however no one has been brought to justice till date.

- Amnesty International, Torture and Deaths in Custody in Jammu and Kashmir, 1995.
- Amnesty International, Analysis of the Government of India's response to Amnesty International's report on torture and deaths in custody in Jammu and Kashmir, 1995.

On 26 April 1993, The Kashmir Times run by Ved Bhasin carried a report of police records listing 132 persons to have been killed in custody in the preceding 33 days alone. The Kashmir Monitor, a human rights group, has reported around 220 custodial deaths for the period June'94-April'95 which represent the bare minimum. Estimate of the number of custodial killings since 1990 by human rights organizations runs in several thousands, many of them are civilians.

- Pankaj Mishra, Death in Kashmir
- Human Rights Watch,India's Secret Army In Kashmir

Disappearances

In August 2000, Amnesty International reported that the fates of up to 1,000 persons reported missing in Jammu and Kashmir since 1990 remain unexplained by authorities. Few of the hundreds of habeas corpus petitions filed by families of the "disappeared" before the judiciary in Jammu and Kashmir have been brought to a resolution. The Kashmir Monitor has also documented around 300 cases of disappearance during 1989-95.

- Amnesty International, India (Jammu and Kashmir): Day of the "Disappeared", 2000.

Rapes

Hundreds of women have been raped with impunity and most of them go unreported given the social stigma and fear of retribution by the State; The GOI has been quick to deny and cover-up most of those cases which do get reported; The reported gang-rape of nine women at Shopian in October 1992 by an army unit was dismissed off-handedly after investigation by army and police, the very units charged with the crime, despite solid medical evidence to the contrary; no independent investigation by an impartial agency was carried out. The reported mass rape of over 20 women at Konan Poshpura in February 1991 was also handled in a similar evasive manner; the complaint was not investigated in a timely manner by an impartial agency and the medical evidence was dismissed without good cause; one of the victims who was nine months pregnant during the incident delivered a baby with a fractured left arm; Governor Girish Saxena who denied the incident admitted to mass rapes in the past by the Indian forces however. Rapes continue to be reported, an example from this year being the April 17 gang-rape of a 17-year old girl in Pahalgam.

- Amnesty International, Torture and Deaths in Custody in Jammu and Kashmir, 1995.
- Asia Watch and Physicians for Human Rights, The Human Rights Crisis in Kashmir: A Pattern of Impunity, 1993, pp.98-107.
- Tavleen Singh, Kashmir: A Tragedy of Errors, New Delhi 1995, p.177
- BBC News, Kashmir troops held after rape, April 19, 2002.

Pro-India Renegade Militants

The phenomenon of renegade militants has been extensively documented by Human Rights Watch. Renegades are former militants who have surrendered and changed sides to the Indian forces. Since the 1989 insurgency in Kashmir, renegades have been used for extrajudicial executions of militants (besides human right activists, journalists and other civilians) and later conveniently dismissed as "intergroup rivalries". Many of these groups have been responsible for grave human rights abuses, including summary executions, torture, and illegal detention as well as election-related intimidation of voters. They are never arrested or prosecuted and go scot-free.

- Human Rights Watch, India's Secret Army In Kashmir

In 1997, the Director General of Police Gurbachan Jagat acknowledged that the continued services of the renegades had become counter-productive in view of their excesses; an estimated 5000 renegades were reportedly 'rehabilitated' as Special Police Officers (SPO) in the State police and many others were absorbed in the security forces. The present number of renegade militants continues to be significant and the estimates vary; in 1999, Gurbachan Jagat acknowledged that there were 1,200 renegades in the payroll of New Delhi; According to a renegade representative Javed Shah, the number of renegades exceeded 2,000; Renegades remain a dreaded group.

- Amnesty International, Disappearances in Jammu and Kashmir, 1999.
- Indian Express, J&K's friendly ultras say pay more, or else..., 4 May, 1999.

The Chattisinghpora cover-up

In March 2000, around the time of US President Clinton's visit to India, unidentified gunmen gunned down 35 Sikhs at Chittisinghpora; India blamed foreign militants; Kashmiris blamed renegade militants employed by Indian security forces; A few days after the massacre, security forces killed five persons in an "encounter" at Panchalthan village and claimed they are "foreign militants" responsible for the Sikh massacre. Later, in July 2002, DNA testing of the corpses proved that the five persons killed were civilians.

The relatives of the five murdered villagers held a series of demonstrations for public exhuming of the bodies; A crowd of five thousand unarmed civilians at Brakpora was fired upon by the police; Nine more men died; When the bodies were finally exhumed, they were discovered to have been burnt and defaced, but curiously dressed in brand new army fatigues. They were identified by the relatives as the local villagers who went missing. Initial attempts in DNA testing of the exhumed bodies were compromised by fudging of the DNA samples in a cover-up attempt by the authorities; Later results indicated that the five persons killed by the Indian forces were indeed civilians and that Indian forces engaged in a deliberate subterfuge to portray them as "foreign" militants responsible for the Sikh massacre.

The Pandian Commission investigated the firing at Brakpora and pronounced that three police officers be tried for murder, however no action has been taken against them till date; No judicial inquiry into the Sikh massacre itself has been conducted till date despite repeated announcements. While some argue that the Chattisinghpora massacre may very well have been engineered by the Indian forces for political gains during Clinton's visit, the least that can be said is that confirmed, unpunished atrocities of the security forces most certainly do not inspire confidence in the people, and fuel resentment instead.

The Army-renegade Nexus

- Jalil Andrabi, the human right activist was abducted by the paramilitary and renegades in March 1996 in the presence of eye-witnesses and tortured to death in custody. Despite the GOI's initial denials of the army's involvement, the Special Investigation Team identified an army Major in April 1997 as the person responsible for the death; however the accused major was released with no punishment.

- H.N. Wanchoo, the noted human rights activist had documented and filed writ petitions for hundreds of custodial deaths in 1992; Being a Pandit, his petitions were an embarrassment to the Central and State governments. He was assassinated by unidentified gunmen in December 1992; although the government claimed that the persons responsible belonged to the militant outfit Jamiat-ul Mujahidin, human rights activists who investigated the case have alleged that the militants of that group were released from jail on condition that they kill Wanchoo. Following his death, none of the custodial death cases were heard in the court and lawyers attempting to get the cases listed have reportedly found that many of the files of these cases were now missing from the High Court premises.
- Dr. Farooq Ahmad Ashai, chief of orthopaedics and a human rights activist who had spoken against the GOI was killed by gunshots from a CRPF bunker while travelling in a car clearly marked with a red cross. The government stated that he had been killed in 'crossfire', despite evidence to the contrary. Dr. Abdul Ahad Guru, a surgeon who had treated torture victims was killed by unidentified gunmen. A government source alleged to Human Rights Watch that Zulkar Nan, a militant, had been released specifically to carry out the murder. Shortly afterwards, Indian security forces shot and killed Zulkar Nan.
- Mirwaiz Maulvi Farooq and Abdul Ghani Lone, two Kashmiri activists were killed by unidentified gunmen on 21 May 1990 and 2002 respectively. In both cases, the governments blamed militants while some Kashmiris blamed Indian sponsored renegades.

ACCOUNTABILITY

The National Human Rights Commission's (NHRC) presence has not been effective in improving the human rights record; For instance, the NHRC lacks the jurisdiction to investigate complaints of violations by the army and paramilitary forces. New Delhi continues to deny permission for various human rights organizations such as Human Rights Watch, UN Special Rapporteur of Torture and others, to visit Jammu and Kashmir and investigate the violations.

Chief Secretary Ashok Jaitley acknowledged that while disciplinary action was taken against security personnel involved in large massacres in the mid-1990s, no prosecutions take place as no witness will dare step forward. What action is taken is not made public. In the past, the GOI has made public a number of prosecutions of members of security forces for rape. However, even these amount to no more than a handful; many other incidents of rape have never been prosecuted. In its 1999 report, Human Rights Watch stated that was not aware of a single prosecution in a case of the torture or summary execution of a detainee in the ten years since the conflict began.

The fact that the officer indicted in the 1996 murder of a human rights lawyer Jalil Andrabi, has not yet been arrested, contrasts sharply with the GOI's claim that it has ensured greater accountability from its forces in Kashmir.

- Human Rights Watch, The Ongoing Problem of Impunity, 1999.
- Amnesty International, Torture and Deaths in Custody in Jammu and Kashmir, 1995.
- Amnesty International, Impunity must end in Jammu and Kashmir, 2001.

FULL FORCE OF THE LAW

The Armed Forces Special Powers Act of 1958 and the Disturbed Areas Act of 1976 give police extraordinary powers of search and arrest without warrants and detention. The Special Powers Act provides that unless approval is obtained from the Central Government, no "prosecution, suit, or other legal proceeding shall be instituted...against any person in respect of anything done or purported to be done in exercise of the powers of the act." To human rights groups, it is such provisions that allow security forces to operate with virtual impunity.

According to one NGO, there were 1,300 writs of *habeas corpus* pending in the Jammu and Kashmir High Court in 1999 in such detention cases. The government is also known to abuse such powers, an example being the case of Yasin Malik, chairman of the JKLF, a separatist group. He was arrested under POTA on 23 March on charges of accepting illegal money, a charge which he refuted as a frame-up. Intriguingly the prosecution failed to present the mandatory *challan* within ninety days of his detention under POTA despite repeated directions by the court and the judge ordered his release on bail; subsequently he was rearrested under the Public Safety Act (PSA). The events clearly show that the POTA case was indeed a frame-up.

A charge which the GOI did not deny in a response to Amnesty was that it had issued secret orders to the Police to disregard complaints of human rights violations against the security forces in FIRs. This leads to the conclusion that the number of registered complaints is probably fewer than the number of excesses actually committed.

- Amnesty International, Analysis of the Government of India's response to Amnesty International's report on torture and deaths in custody in Jammu and Kashmir, 1995.

In October 1996, a Union Home Ministry report for 1995-96 stated that 272 J&K security personnel including 153 BSF, 80 CRPF, and 39 army personnel, had been "sacked, jailed or disciplined" for abuses committed in the past five years; a number hardly proportional to the number of violators, by most accounts. Human rights situation in Kashmir is as bleak as it has been during the last two decades. The gross violation of basic human rights is continuing unabated, says Ghulam Nabi Khayal, who presented this paper at the National Seminar on Kashmir organised by Jamia Millia University, Delhi last week.

The track record of human rights situation in Jammu & Kashmir, particularly during the last two decades, does not merit any praise or appreciation. It is quite heart rending that the human rights charter adopted by the United Nations has been thrown to winds in this strife torn border state by all those who hold a gun in their hands. The worst and most horrific period of gross violation of the human rights across Kashmir Valley has been during early nineties when only a few incidents of indiscriminate gunfire opened by the forces on unarmed civilians resulted in the killing of about three hundred people including old men, women and children.

The excessive use of force was wantonly witnessed when the funeral procession of Mirwaiz Molvi Farooq, who had been gunned down on 21 May 1990 allegedly by the militants, was fired upon by the forces killing about 40 persons on spot. The forces did not spare even the coffin of the late Mirwaiz and several bullets were found having been pumped into his dead body. This gory incident was so shocking that the former prime minister, Chander Shekhar said in the Parliament, "we must hang our heads in shame." The required action followed quickly by shifting of Jagmohan, the most controversial Governor of the State, during whose tenure Kashmir was seen bathing only in blood.

According to a conservative survey conducted by a few local groups, there are as many as ten thousand widows spending their days of life in penury, misery and prolonged agony. Their husbands, whether militants or otherwise, are no more and this is not their fault that they have been left at the mercy of Allah. Several so called organisations, NGOs, numbering about five thousand, claim to be the saviors of this miserable lot of the fair sex but they have failed to help out even a small number of them though these fake organisations have been receiving huge funds of money for this very purpose both from Delhi and Islamabad.

This criminal negligence towards a suffering community has obviously given rise to social evils in the Valley where the hapless widows are naturally forced to be exploited in different immoral ways to earn their two square meals. The irony of the fate is that the widows of slain militants are categorically denied permission to perform Hajj pilgrimage which they could do after managing the required money. Also, a valid passport is not issued to them under instructions from the Central government. Their fault, depriving them of a very pious religious performance, is yet to be defined. Why should they be punished for a sin they never committed?

The present scenario across Kashmir is a little brighter for, the militants are not seen indulging in anti social and objectionable activities, also due to the fact that a majority of them has been physically eliminated by the forces during the last two decades of unprecedented armed uprising. At the same time, and unfortunately, a number of surrendered militants, locally nicknamed as Ikhwanis or renegades, are still at large to harass people by way of arson, kidnappings for ransom, molestation of women and even brutal killing of common people. These heinous crimes mostly take place in far off villages in the Valley and are hushed up as not reported due to the social taboos of the Kashmiri Muslim society.

These renegades function directly under the Rashtriya Rifles of the army and the official patronage is available to them so acrimoniously that they are neither hauled up nor are they brought to justice for crimes they are committing unabated. The Universal Declaration of Human Rights adopted by the United Nations General Assembly on 10 December 1948, says among other things in its Article Number three that "every one has the right to life, liberty and security of person." These basic guarantees offered to the human being by Almighty God and by the UNO are to a large extent, not available to a common man in Kashmir despite the horrifying fact that about 100,000 people in the State have already been done to untimely death in this turmoil.

As far as the conditions prevailing in various prisons, where Kashmiri suspects or hardcore militants re lodged, are concerned, they can be described as inhuman and nothing else. Even today, scores of detenues are languishing in jails all over the country, from Jammu up to Koimbatore, without being tried in a court of law for the crime they have allegedly committed. Some of these prisoners are there behind the bars for more than 15 years now and no legal procedure has been adopted to facilitate for them a fair trial in an impartial court of law.

The UN human rights declaration clearly states, "No one shall be subjected to torture or to cruel, inhuman or degrading treatment or punishment." Probably, this charter does not apply to the forces operating in Jammu & Kashmir state. It is rather imperative to point out here that while talking about the activities of the militants and the security forces, one cannot apply a similar yardstick to them. Militants took up gun but were never answerable to any one. On the contrary, the armed forces and the paramilitary troops are supposed to be bound by unflinching discipline, moral, ethical and legal obligations. Their reported violations of basic rights are not therefore acceptable under any circumstances.

There are also complaints pouring in regularly that Kashmiri youths who are out in the Indian states to earn their livelihood are subjected to victimisation by the police. They are physically manhandled all over. Even hotels in different cities are instructed to avoid providing accommodation to the Kashmiri visitors. It was on 13th of this month that three Kashmiris were taken into custody in Maharashtra for no obvious reasons. Several state regimes have publicly admitted that on occasions, forces in Kashmir overstep their brief and that the guilty shall be punished. One has yet to ascertain beyond doubt whether any erring soldier was ever awarded deserving punishment.

The present situation across the State is comparatively conducive to rub off black scars of this menace from the face of Kashmir. Firstly, all detunes jailed for their involvement in militancy or on suspicion, must be tried properly in a legal court to affirm or nullify their alleged crime. Only then, can their fate be decided in a democratic way. As a member of one working group constituted by the Honourable Prime Minister in 2007, those frustrated Kashmiri boys who had crossed over to Pakistan administrated Kashmir to receive training in use of arms, are now quite eager to return home, join their separated families and spend rest of their lives peacefully.

Their comeback should be facilitated both by the Central and the State governments. Constant police surveillance can be there to check their routine activities. Gradually, they will themselves turn to a normal life. There should be a strict ban imposed on the forces for their resorting to reckless use of force while dealing with the peaceful protesters. The declaration of zero tolerance assured by Prime Minister Dr Manmohan Singh before the Kashmiri people should be adhered to in letter and spirit. As was repeatedly demanded by the previous government headed by Mufti Mohammad Sayed, the Indian paramilitary forces, now largely the Central Reserve Police Force, be withdrawn from the cities and towns to be replaced by the State police.

This will undoubtedly reduce instances of human rights violations being committed all over the State. This popular demand has not met with any positive response. Needless to mention here that the imposition of the Armed Forces Special Powers Act in force in the State since 1990 does not empower or authorise the State authorities to initiate any inquiry against the forces including the army, the BSF, the CRPF and other paramilitary troops.

TRENDS IN SOUTH ASIA

Torture and extra-judicial killings are also common in other neighbouring South-Asian countries. In India, the definition of unlawful activity is vague and has been misused by the state and state authorities, especially in the case of the minority community as in the case of Gujarat and also in the case of Delhi University Arabic lecturer Syed Abdul Rahman Geelani. Arbitrary and unlawful deprivation of life by government forces (including deaths in custody and staged encounter killings) is still continuing in India. The highest incidences were in Uttar Pradesh, Andhra Pradesh, Bihar, Chhattisgarh, as well as states with ongoing conflict in States such as Jammu and Kashmir, Manipur, and Assam.

Security forces offered bounties for wanted militants. Police and prison officers also committed extra-judicial killings of criminals and suspected criminals in a number of states. Human rights groups alleged that security forces killed numerous captured non-Kashmiri militants from Pakistan or other countries, often after torturing them, and staged many encounters, summarily executing suspected militants and civilians believed to be assisting them. In Jammu and Kashmir, the State Human Rights Commission reportedly received 15 complaints relating to custodial deaths in 2003 and 27 complaints relating to disappearances.

Human rights organisations sought to clarify these cases by submitting numerous requests to Jammu and Kashmir authorities in recent years, but received inadequate and unsatisfactory responses. According to human rights activists, press reports, and anecdotal accounts, the bodies of persons detained by security forces in Jammu and Kashmir were often returned to relatives or otherwise discovered with multiple bullet wounds and/or marks of torture. In February 2004 in the Bandipora area of north Kashmir, five civilian porters were killed after security forces allegedly used them as human shields in a gunfight with militants and the incident led to widespread demonstrations and rioting.

Following the incident, Army Chief of Staff General N.C. Vij announced that the Army would no longer use civilian porters in combat operations. On March 31, 2004, State Finance Minister Muzaffar Beig and Northern Commander Lt. General Hari Prasad reported that those responsible for the incident had been punished, but gave no details. In June 2004, Gujarat police killed three men and a woman, alleged to have been on a mission to kill Gujarat Chief Minister Narendra Modi. The National Human Rights Commission (NHRC) asked the Director General of Police and Senior Superintendent of Police in Ahmedabad to investigate. Human Rights activists challenged police allegations that these persons were linked to this plot, but the case was never fully resolved. A Gujarat court later dismissed charges against 13 other persons implicated in this case due to lack of evidence.

The family members of those killed did not file petitions claiming the killings were extra judicial, and no action was taken against police involved in the killing. On July 11, 2004, Manorama Devi, an alleged member of the People's Liberation Army (PLA) in the north-eastern state of Manipur, died while in the custody of the Assam Rifles, a paramilitary unit in the state. Officials initially denied that Devi was killed, tortured, or raped, but the post mortem found that she died of multiple gunshot wounds, was bleeding from the vagina, and had a perforated liver and gall bladder, among other injuries, and forensic tests detected semen stains on her clothes. The case prompted demonstrations and riots, and led to a serious deterioration of the security situation in Manipur.

The National Commission for Women (NCW) publicised the case, and the Army ordered an investigation; however, by year's end, culpability for her death had not been established. The killing of civilians continued during operations in Jammu and Kashmir. Human rights activists stated that accurate numbers were not available due to limited access to the region. In 2003, the Home Ministry reported 28 civilians killed, between April and June, and Amnesty International (AI) alleged that over 340 were killed during the year. The Armed Forces Special Powers Act (AFSPA) and the Disturbed Areas Act remained in effect in Jammu and Kashmir, Nagaland, Manipur, Assam, and parts of Tripura, where active secessionist movements existed. The Disturbed Areas Act gives police extraordinary powers of arrest and detention, and the AFSPA provides search and arrest powers without warrants. Human rights groups alleged that security forces operated with virtual impunity in areas under the Act.

The Unlawful Activities Prevention (Amendment) Ordinance 2004 (UAPO), which was promulgated on September 21, 2004 has encompassed the provisions of POTA and has the inevitable problem of defining 'terrorism'. The amendments of the 1967 Act include several sections taken verbatim from POTA. As a result, the government retains the power it gained under POTA to designate organisations as 'unlawful' with only a limited pro forma judicial review. The list of 32 organisations banned under POTA has been included in the amended 1967 law. The amended 1967 Act also includes, with only a light modification, Section 21 of POTA, which created a new crime of supporting a terrorist organisation.

Furthermore, the government has refused to drop cases registered under POTA against more than 1,600 individuals, many of whom have been denied bail and have been languishing in jail for more than two years, for demanding equality, social justice and raising concerns on the political situation either by women, minority communities, *dalits, adivasis* (tribals) and opposition groups, especially in the states of Jharkhand, Gujarat, Uttar Pradesh and Tamil Nadu. The Indian Border Security Force (BSF) has also been instrumental in killing approximately 326 Bangladeshi citizens at the border areas during the last 5 years and 5 months (since January 2000 to May 2005).

In Pakistan, the Anti Terrorism Act (amended) 2001 provides the legal framework to deal with terrorism in all aspects. This Act contains detailed provisions for the suppression of terrorism. Along with this Act, the Frontier Crimes Regulations (FCRs) of 1901 is still in force in the Federally Administered Tribal Areas (FATA). Promulgated first by the British in 1872, the FCRs have been amended a number of times, mostly before independence, but their provisions remain cruel and inhuman and are wholly inconsistent with the norms of civil society. The FCRs, as they exist today, defy all principals of justice, fair play, human and civil rights. As the recent military operations in South Waziristan have shown, entire communities have been economically blockaded or forced out of their homes and hearths for the action of few foreign Taliban members whom some of their kinsmen chose to provide shelter to.

The military operation also caused the imprisonment of a number of allegedly innocent civilians, among them women and children, who belong to the families or tribes of the proclaimed offenders and fugitives wanted by the Pakistan government. In Nepal the use of force by the Nepali armed forces against innocent civilians and students, peacefully exercising their democratic rights to assembly, association and expression, has begun since the dissolution of Parliament and King Gyanendra's takeover of the executive power by dissolving the cabinet through royal proclamation on February 1, 2005; and forming a government under his chairmanship.

A large number of political activists, human rights activists, journalists and students have been arrested and allegedly tortured on the grounds that they either have links with the Maoist guerrillas or are simply opposed to the King

Gyanendra's regime. In Sri Lanka the peace process is yet to see any political solution and the Muslim internally displaced persons from the LTTE held north are yet to get back to their homes or to a permanent address.

Trends in the Rest of the World

The rise of xenophobia in the post cold war era has gained momentum after the 9/11 situation. This has added to the definition of 'terror' and 'terrorism' and the margin between the self-determination of the communities and nations as well as communities and individuals fighting to realise universal goal of human rights could often termed as 'terrorist' by their political opponents. In the global context racism, castes, religious hatred, increased militarisation and rampant state terror has given rise to torture.

The torture and killing in the detention centers of Abu Gareb and Guantanamo Bay are not the only examples. There are many more secret prisons in the different parts of the world to torture, to dehumanise and even to kill more victims, either because they fought against foreign occupation, expressed the intention to exercise their right to self determination or just because of their cultural or religious beliefs. It must be noted that the small states are also facing pressure and threats to deliver economic privileges to corporations and hegemonic states, which results in the increased external vulnerability.

South Asian countries are trying their best to attain economic development. All of them are showing good or reasonable success in this area. Nonetheless, all the south Asian countries have badly if not extremely bad - records in the area of human rights. Torture, has unfortunately remained common practice. Large countries like India have more atrocities than their smaller neighbours, but these do not get necessary media attention. Even though India is a large country with a big population, with various ethnic, caste and religious minorities, the number and focus of the human rights organisations there and their coverage is inadequate. There is also a tendency of not responding to and not reporting to the human rights violations i.e. torture of those areas or states where 'insurgency' exists.

In the post 9/11 scenario, Indian policy makers and the media projected Bangladesh, Nepal, Bhutan and Maldives as 'failed' and 'dysfunctional' states and argued that India should militarily intervene in those countries as and when required in order to ensure her national security. This situation has seriously jeopardised the human rights activities in the small countries of South Asia, since the reports of torture and other kinds of human rights violations in small countries, has been used by imperial and hegemonic powers for their own gains. In the aforesaid context we believe that strengthening the solidarity and translating the voices of the oppressed peoples and their organisations of South Asia into actions for justice, can only bring positive changes.

The September 11 terrorist attack against the United States and the subsequent opening of active hostilities between a U.S.-engineered "anti-terror coalition" and the Taliban regime of Afghanistan has again focused international attention on the South Asia region, the India/Pakistan relationship and the Kashmir dispute. Both India and Pakistan have joined the anti-terror coalition, and their participation will play a crucial role in the success or failure of the coalition's efforts to dismantle the Taliban regime and the Al Qaeda network it has sponsored. In an effort to address the concerns of Pakistan in this regard, Secretary of State Colin Powell stated on October 16, while in Islamabad, Pakistan, "We too believe that the Kashmir issue is central to the relationship and can be resolved if all parties engaged with a willingness to address their concerns in mutually acceptable ways."

The importance of the Kashmir dispute was earlier underscored by an October 1 car bomb attack outside the Jammu and Kashmir Assembly building in Srinagar by the Jaish-e-Mohammed group, which killed 38 people, most of who were innocent bystanders. In a letter addressed to President Bush, Indian Prime Minister Atal Bihari Vajpayee suggested that Pakistan lied when it stated that it no longer has any connection with Jaish-e-Mohammed, a group linked to Osama bin Ladin and Al Qaeda. India repeated its stance that Pakistan's purported support to such groups makes it an unreliable member of the anti-terror coalition. The United States, which has long attempted to remain aloof from the Kashmir dispute, is likely to be driven by these cataclysmic events to rethink its position on Kashmir.

India and Pakistan have made a number of bilateral attempts to address the dispute, which has dogged their relations since 1947, but without success. Many international observers felt that the May 1998 nuclear tests in India and Pakistan and growing concern about renewed India/Pakistan hostilities that could theoretically go nuclear, would compel the international community and the Indian and Pakistani governments to renew efforts to normalize India/Pakistan relations. In a 1999 bilateral effort to address this issue, Prime Minister Vajpayee accepted Prime Minister Sharif's invitation and traveled to Pakistan on February 20, on the inaugural run of the first passenger bus service between Delhi and Lahore since independence. The two leaders then hammered out the details of three documents designed to turn their countries toward greater cooperation. To sustain the process begun in Lahore, Prime Minister Sharif accepted Prime Minister Vajpayee's invitation for a return visit to India.

The two countries also agreed that their foreign ministers would meet periodically in addition to regular rounds of foreign secretary-level talks. The subsequent hostilities at Kargil torpedoed these efforts, which have not yet been revived. The events of September 11 and the war on terrorism have changed foreign policy parameters on a number of issues, including India/Pakistan relations and the Kashmir dispute. India and Pakistan could emerge from the war having worked together as allies to rid Afghanistan of the Taliban and Al Qaeda. This cooperation could well extend into the protracted reconstruction process that will, hopefully, rebuild Afghanistan.

Perhaps India and Pakistan will learn to look at their relationship in a new light. Pakistan has already come to an important realization about the danger of involvement with Islamic terrorism. Pakistan is likely to keep such groups at arms length in the future, purge its military and intelligence apparatus of fundamentalist sympathizers, close down the

Islamic extremists groups in the country and rethink its policy regarding covert action. Basic Proposals Kashmir remains the longest-running and most contentious unresolved issue between India and Pakistan.

The Kashmir issue has remained a thorn in the side of both countries since the partition of British India. There have been a number of proposals aimed at addressing the dispute. They can be divided into two general categories: those calling for the permanent division of Kashmir, usually along the current line of control, and those calling for the reunification of Kashmir, followed by its independence or permanent absorption into India or Pakistan. For example, a proposal put forward by the Kashmir Study group would reunite the divided state, while the Stimson Center and a proposal put forward by Jammu and Kashmir State Autonomy Committee would permanently divide it.

These absolutist approaches are too intimidating to both governments. A "middle way" may be required to get recalcitrant India and Pakistan to move off of square one. Rather than attempting to devise a proposal from scratch, it would be better to examine a peace proposal that has already brought a measure of peace to an area with a seemingly intractable dispute bearing many similarities to that of Kashmir. The Northern Ireland Peace settlement, already negotiated, meets a number of these criteria. It succeeded in jump-starting a stalled peace process, and provides a ready example of how a protracted and bitter internecine dispute can be set on the way to resolution through international mediation.

The J & K Government Initiative On April 13, 1999, the State Autonomy Committee of the government of Jammu and Kashmir released its report. It outlines how Kashmir's long-denied autonomy could be restored. In late April Kashmir Chief Minister Farooq Abdullah stated publicly that in his view the issue could be permanently resolved if the Indian government adopted this autonomy proposal and India and Pakistan agreed to convert the current line of control (LOC) into the international border. He further stated that Pakistan should renounce all claims to the territory encompassed by the Indian State of Jammu and Kashmir. In return, he hinted that India, in the interests of peace, might be convinced to drop all claims to Kashmiri territory now controlled by Pakistan.

The Stimson Proposal

The ideas proposed by the Stimson Center are far more modest and therefore more easily obtainable. Stimson advocates a "track II" approach, utilizing a group of prominent Indians and Pakistanis, including Kashmiris from both sides of the LOC. Although it would presumably include retired government diplomatic and military personnel, it would have no governmental association. The group would conduct a new study/discussion of the problem, and likely concur with Abdullah that the only viable solution is to make the LOC the international border.

The group would then urge the governments of India and Pakistan to open talks aimed at realizing this objective. The Stimson proposal, unlike that of the Kashmir Study Group, does not envision reuniting Kashmir. It also tracks closely with the already expressed wishes of Farooq and many both within and outside the Indian government. The Pakistan government has flatly rejected all such proposals in the past, sticking to its insistence that the Kashmir dispute be resolved through international mediation and an internationally supervised plebiscite. Farooq would like to see the governments of India and Pakistan open bilateral negotiations based on his government's proposal.

In 1999, when the Jammu and Kashmir autonomy proposal was first released, many dismissed it out of hand, arguing that it was highly unlikely that the distance between the Indian and Pakistani government positions could ever be sufficiently bridged to bring about meaningful talks. The war on terror and the formation of an anti-terrorist coalition could well prove to be the catalyst that could break this logjam. However, I would argue, the State Autonomy Committee report is not a sufficient basis upon which to base internationally mediated Kashmir talks.

Plusses and Minuses

The position of the Indian government regarding a negotiated settlement remains murky. The Bharitiya Janata Party (BJP) manifesto calls for the creation of a united India (Akhand Bharat) which incorporates all of Kashmir. The party has repeatedly stated that not only the area currently incorporated into Pakistan's "Azad Kashmir", but all of the Northern Areas as well, belong to India. Despite this, few outside the BJP seriously entertain any prospect of recovering "Azad Kashmir" and the Northern Areas and integrating them into the Indian Union. Pakistan, driven by its internal dynamic, and the emotional language of jihad which Islamic militant groups adopted to describe the fighting in Kashmir, would have considerable difficulty backtracking on its previous positions.

In addition, the Stimson Center has not made it clear how yet another "track II" group would exert sufficient influence over the governments of India and Pakistan to overcome the numerous obstacles and convince them to adopt its proposed outlook. Both governments have largely ignored Track II efforts in the past, and there is no indication they would treat a new one any differently. This said, there is no reason why India and Pakistan in a postwar scenario, should not sit down together for serious talks on the Kashmir dispute, either within the bilateral context of the ongoing secretary-level talks, some other bilateral forum, or with international mediation.

India has long insisted that the Kashmir dispute can only be settled within a bilateral context. Despite this oft-repeated insistence, India seems to be losing ground, and the dramatic events associated with the war on terrorism may compel India to look at Pakistan's repeated insistence on the need for some form of international mediation in a new light, and it may grow much closer to accepting international mediation. The Kashmir Study Group Proposal The Kashmir Study Group, a private coalition of leading academics dealing with the South Asia region, has released its own peace proposal for Kashmir.

The proposal recommends that:

- "A portion" of Jammu and Kashmir is reunited as a "sovereign entity". Guaranteed by India, Pakistan and "international bodies" with its own citizenship, passport, and legislature.
- India and Pakistan would be responsible for foreign relations and defense.
- Those areas of Jammu and Kashmir that join the new entity would be determined through an internationally supervised plebiscite.
- The new mini-state would be given free access to India and Pakistan.
- It would have a secular, democratic constitution.
- All Pakistani and Indian forces would be withdrawn and internal security provided by a Kashmiri police force.
- Displaced persons, including Kashmiri Pundits (Hindus), would be invited to return.

Problems

This proposal contains an underlying assumption that the Muslim majority areas of Azad Kashmir, and the Vale of Kashmir, would join the new entity. Jammu and Ladakh (Hindu and Buddhist) would opt to remain permanently in India, while the Northern Areas (Muslim, but not Kashmiri) would opt to remain permanently in Pakistan. The insistence on a secular Kashmir would not long survive under such an arrangement. Pakistan and the Muslim parties opting to join the state would insist that it be openly Islamic. Likewise, there is almost no prospect that Hindus, Buddhist, and Sikhs would play any role in the new mini-state. This would touch off a major relocation of these communities to India.

The Kashmiri Pundits would never return to an Islamic Kashmir and would demand resettlement within India. Many Indians would also likely object to this proposal, arguing that carving out the last remaining Muslim majority area is an admission of failure of the secular state, and places the Muslim community within India in an awkward, if not untenable position. Few in Pakistan would publicly support a proposal calling for Kashmiri independence, even if thinly disguised by an "association" with Pakistan.

The Northern Ireland Proposal

There are a number of striking parallels between the situation in Northern Ireland and that in Kashmir.

- Northern Ireland, like Kashmir, is part of a divided state, straddling two countries that claim it.
- In both instances, members of a religious community, which claims it has been denied basic civil rights, want to join with a neighboring country of the same religion.
- The minority religious community wants to maintain the status quo and remain part of the country in which they are a majority.
- Insurgents seek sanctuary in the neighboring country, where they are supported by co-religionists.
- Pro and anti-government paramilitaries battle each other.
- The "rebels" have a military wing and a political wing and maintain a polite fiction that they are not mutually supportive.
- There is implacable hatred between the various groups and communities, and between the "rebels" and the government.

For decades, the consensus was that the dispute in Northern Ireland would never be resolved. Despite the nay sayers, a settlement was adopted on April 10, 1998 following protracted negotiations involving all parties and mediated by former Senate Majority Leader George Mitchell. On May 22, 1998 voters in Northern Ireland and the Republic of Ireland approved the accord, and elections to a new Northern Ireland Assembly took place on June 25. Despite terrorist incidents by both republicans and loyalists, a cease fire remains in effect, British troops remain largely within their barracks, the borders have been opened, extremists of both sides hunted down and disarmed, and the Assembly and a Joint Legislative Council convened with the active involvement of the Irish Republic.

The basis of the Northern Ireland Peace Agreement was concessions by both the UK and the Republic of Ireland. The UK conceded that the Republic of Ireland should have a voice in Northern Ireland, and that the Irish people living in the Republic and Northern Ireland should not be kept apart. The Republic of Ireland conceded that it should renounce claims on Northern Ireland until such time as there is popular support from both Protestants and Catholics for reunification. Until that time, Ireland agreed that Northern Ireland would remain part of the UK. Both the UK and Ireland agreed that they would in no way interfere, should the people of Northern Ireland, both Catholic and Protestant, decide to permanently join either the UK or the Republic of Ireland.

This points the way for a resolution of the Kashmir dispute as well. Like the dispute over Northern Ireland, the Kashmir dispute will not be resolved until the countries involved in the dispute are willing to make serious concessions. India would have to concede that Pakistan should have a voice on what transpires in Kashmir, and that the Kashmiri people should not be kept apart by an international border. Pakistan would have to concede that the Hindu and Buddhist communities of Jammu and Kashmir are not convinced that their rights would be preserved should the state join Pakistan.

It should therefore renounce its claims on the current Indian State of Jammu and Kashmir until such time as there is a sufficient change in attitudes. Like Northern Ireland, Jammu and Kashmir would therefore remain within Indian jurisdiction, but with significant Pakistani involvement until such time as the people of the region permanently decide their fate. Both India and Pakistan would have to agree that they would in no way interfere, should the people of Jammu and Kashmir, Muslim, Hindu, Buddhist and Sikh; decide to permanently alter Kashmir's status. Applicable Clauses Because of the similarities in the two cases, a number of clauses in the Northern Ireland Peace Agreement can be adopted in the case of Kashmir, with little or no modification.

This would make the negotiation process much simpler, as the essential elements would already be laid out. Such clauses, taken verbatim from the Agreement, demonstrate how the Northern Ireland Peace Agreement could be directly applicable to the situation in Kashmir. I have taken individual clauses of the agreement and substituted the words India, and Pakistan, and Kashmir, for UK, Ireland, and Northern Ireland. When this is done, the similarity between the two disputes and the possible applicability of the already- negotiated Northern Ireland Peace Agreement becomes striking. I would argue that the governments of India and Pakistan in future negotiations to settle the dispute could potentially adopt sections of this agreement verbatim.

- Constitutional Issues- "Change in the status of Kashmir can only come about with the consent of a majority of its people. Both the governments of India and Pakistan have a binding obligation to bring about whatever the wish of the people is." All claims by India and Pakistan to "jurisdiction over all of Kashmir is to be repealed."
- Democratic Institutions- "The accord provides for an Assembly with executive and legislative powers. All Ministers must affirm the terms of a Pledge of Office, which includes a commitment to non-violence and exclusively peaceful and democratic means."
- North/South Institutions- "A North/South Ministerial Council will be established consisting of those with executive authority in Jammu and Kashmir and Azad Kashmir to consult, cooperate and act within the State of Kashmir on matters within their competence. Members of the Council remain accountable to the Parliaments of India and Pakistan. The Council will be supported by a permanent joint Secretariat."
- India/Pakistan Institutions- "The India/Pakistan Council will include representatives of the Indian and Pakistani governments, and the devolved administrations in Kashmir. It will promote consultation and cooperation on matters of mutual interest, such as transport and culture." And "will deal with bilateral issues between the two governments with a particular focus on matters relating to Kashmir."

- Rights, Safeguards, and Equality of Opportunity- "The incorporation of the Universal Declaration on Human Rights into Kashmir law will be completed. A new Kashmir Human Rights Commission will be established. The Pakistani and Indian governments will take comparable steps to strengthen human rights protection."

Decommissioning

"All parties are committed to work with the Decommissioning Commission for total disarmament of all paramilitary organizations within two years. The Indian government is committed to reducing the numbers and role of the security forces.

- Policing, Justice, and Prisoners- "Kashmir would establish an independent commission to make recommendations for future policing arrangements for the state by a set date. The Indian government would pledge to carry out a review of the Kashmir criminal justice system. Both India and Pakistan would "put in place mechanisms to provide for an accelerated program of prisoner releases with the intention of releasing all qualifying prisoners within two years."
- India and Pakistan's Post- Agreement Economic Strategy would include: an Investment Fund of an agreed amount "concentrating on capital investment in roads, education, housing and other infrastructure projects. An employment and Skills Fund to provide additional opportunities for Kashmir's long-term unemployed - an Enterprise Fund funding a new provision that every rupee invested in plant and machinery in Kashmir in the coming four years will be completely tax deductible."

Kashmir Specific Provisions

The Government of India, unlike that of the UK in the case of Northern Ireland, has long declared that the status of Kashmir is non negotiable, that there is no scope for multilateral talks or international mediation, and that a referendum/plebiscite is out of the question. For the Irish model to succeed, India may have to give ground on all these points. Pakistan has long claimed that international mediation is absolutely essential for a resolution of the dispute. If bilateral talks fail to progress, India would have to come around to the same position in order to get the process moving.

This does not imply that the U.S. should play this role. Any mutually agreed mediator, whether a nation state, the UN, or a personality such as Nelson Mandela, could play that role. While recognizing that an internationally administered referendum on the status of Kashmir is the ultimate goal of the process, it could be deferred for a set time period, for example 20 years. The insurgents and pro-government paramilitaries would sign a cease-fire to remain in effect throughout the period.

The cease-fire would be followed by a timetable for disarmament of all combatants. Both India and Pakistan would agree not to support insurgency and accept international inspection to verify the absence of training camps and infiltration. All parties would agree to use the "time out" period to negotiate the final status of Kashmir. During this period, the Indian State of Kashmir would remain autonomous within the Indian Union. Azad Kashmir would remain autonomous within Pakistan, and cooperation between the two entities on a variety of common interests would be vastly increased.

All options would be considered, including the possibility of joining with Pakistan or independence. India would agree to allow the All Parties Hurriyat Conference (APHC) to participate in the talks, the political process and the administration of the state. The APHC would agree to represent the disarmed militants and guarantee their continued good behavior. Both countries would open talks to set a schedule for withdrawal of their armed forces, first from the line of control, and then from all of Kashmir. The LOC would be reduced to little more than a district boundary, manned by a joint Kashmiri police force. It would be open to commerce and family visitation. All Kashmiris would be issued identity cards allowing them to travel anywhere in Kashmir at will.

Bibliography

Alston, Philip and Henry J. Steiner, *International Human Rights in Context: Law, Politics, Morals: Text and Materials*. Oxford: Claredon Press, 1996.

Alston, Philip, "The Commission on Human Rights," *The United Nations and Human Rights*. New York: Oxford University Press, 1992.

Bauer, Joanne R. and Daniel A. Bell, eds. *The East Asian Challenge for Human Rights* Cambridge, Cambridge University Press, 1999.

Bell, Daniel A. *East meets West. Human Rights and Democracy in East Asia*. Princeton, Princeton University Press, 2000.

Bell, Lynda S., Nathan, Andrew J., and Peleg, Ilan, eds. *Negotiating Culture and Human Rights*. New York: Columbia University Press, 2001.

Brownlie, Ian, ed., *Basic Instruments on Human Rights*. Oxford: Clarendon Press, 4th ed., 1995.

Buergenthal, Thomas, *International Human Rights in a Nutshell*. St. Paul, MN: West Publishing Co., 2nd ed., 1995.

Burgers, J. Herman and Hans Danelius, *The United Nations Convention Against Torture: A Handbook on the Convention Against Torture and Other Cruel, Inhumane or Degrading Treatment or Punishment*. Boston: M. Nijhoff, 1988.

Center for the Study of Human Rights, *Twenty-Five Human Rights Documents*. New York: Columbia University, 2nd ed., 1994.

Center for the Study of Human Rights, *Women and Human Rights: The Basic Documents.* New York: Columbia University, 1996.

de Bary, Wm. Theodore. *Asian Values and Human Rights. A Confucian Communitarian Perspective.* Cambridge: Harvard University Press, 1998.

Foot, Rosemary. *Rights beyond Borders. The Global Community and the Struggle over Human Rights in China.* Oxford: Oxford University Press, 2000.

Goodland, Robert. *Tribal Peoples and Economic Development: Human Ecologic Considerations.* Washington, D.C.: World Bank, 1982.

Gurr, Ted Robert. *Minorities at Risk: A Global View of Ethnopolitical Conflicts.* Washington, D.C.: The United States Institute of Peace, 1993.

Gurr, Ted Robert. *Peoples versus States: Minorities at Risk in the New Century.* Washington, D.C.: United States Institute of Peace, 2000.

Hamalengwa, M., C. Flinterman and E.V.O. Dankwa, *The International Law of Human Rights in Africa: Basic Documents and Annotated Bibliography.* Boston, MA: M. Nijhoff, 1988.

Hannum, Hurst, ed., *Guide to International Human Rights Practice.* Philadelphia, PA: University of Pennsylvania Press, 2nd ed., 1992.

Heinz, Wolfgang. Indigenous Populations, Ethnic Minorities, and Human Rights. Berlin: Quorum Verlag, 1988.

Henkin, Louis and John Lawrence Hargrove, *An Agenda for the Next Century.* American Society of International Law, 1994.

Hitchcock, Robert K. Indigenous Peoples, Multinational Corporations, and Human Rights. *Indigenous Affairs* 2/97:6-11, 1997(b)

International Women's Rights Actions Watch and the Commonwealth Secretariat, *Assessing the Status of Women: A*

Guide to Reporting Under the Convention on the Elimination of All Froms of Discrimination Against Women. Minneapolis, MN: International Women's Rights Actions Watch (IWRAW) and Commonwealth Secretariat, 2nd ed., 1996.

International Women's Tribune Centre, *Rights of Women: A Guide to the Most Important Treaties on Women's Human Rights.* New York: IWTC, 1998.

Jacobsen, Michael and Ole Bruun. *Human Rights and Asian Values: Contesting National Identities and Cultural Representations in Asia.* Richmond, Curzon: 2000.

Kent, Ann. *Between Freedom and Subsistence. China and Human Rights.* Hong Kong: Oxford University Press, 1993.

Kimlycka, Will, ed. *The Rights of Minority Cultures.* Oxford and New York: Oxford University Press 1995.

Maybury-Lewis, David (1997) Indigenous Peoples, Ethnic Groups, and the State. Boston: Allyn and Bacon.

Pritchard, Sarah, ed. *Indigenous Peoples, The United Nations and Human Rights.* London: Zed Books, 1998.

Sachs, Aaron. *Eco-Justice: Linking Human Rights and the Environment. WorldWatch Paper 127.* Washington, D.C.: WorldWatch Institute, 1995.

Sigler, Jay A. *Minority Rights: A Comparative Analysis.* Westport, Connecticut: Greenwood Press, 1983.

Stavenhagen, Rodolfo. *Ethnic Conflicts and the Nation-State.* New York, New York: Macmillan Press, 1996.

Thornberry, Patrick. *International Law and the Rights of Minorities.* Oxford: Clarendon Press, 1992.

Turner, Terrence and Carole Nagengast, eds. Universal Human Rights versus Cultural Relativity. Special Issue of *Journal of Anthropological Research* 53(3):267-381, 1997.

United Nations, *Human Rights: A Compilation of International Instruments,* vols. 1 (*Universal Instruments*) and 2 (*Regional Instruments*). New York and Geneva: United Nations, 1994.

Van Ness, Peter, ed. *Debating human rights. Critical essays from United States and* Asia. London: Routledge, 1999.

Weissbrodt, David and Penny Parker, *The United Nations Commission on Human Rights, Its Sub-Commission, and Related Procedures: An Orientation Manual*. Geneva: International Service for Human Rights, 1993.

World Bank. *Operational Directive on Indigenous Peoples*. Washington, D.C.: World Bank, 1991.

Young, Elspeth. *Third World in the First: Indigenous Peoples and Development. London*: Routledge, 1995.

Index